AN ILLUSTRATED HISTORY AND DIRECTORY OF

ELECTRIC
GUITARS

AN ILLUSTRATED HISTORY AND DIRECTORY OF
ELECTRIC GUITARS

FEATURES OVER 230 INSTRUMENTS SHOWN IN 360 PHOTOGRAPHS

TERRY BURROWS

southwater

This edition is published by Southwater,
an imprint of Anness Publishing Ltd,
108 Great Russell Street,
London WC1B 3NA;
info@anness.com

www.southwaterbooks.com;
www.annesspublishing.com;
twitter: @Anness_Books

If you like the images in this book and would like to investigate
using them for publishing, promotions or advertising, please visit
our website www.practicalpictures.com for more information.

A CIP catalogue record for this book is available from the British Library.

Publisher: Joanna Lorenz
Senior Editor: Felicity Forster
Designed and produced by Ivy Contract
Project Editors: Judith Chamberlain-Webber and Georgia Amson-Bradshaw
Art Director: Kevin Knight
Photographer: Laurie Evans
Designer: J C Lanaway
Production Controller: Stephanie Moe

Previously published as part of a larger volume,
The Complete Illustrated Book of the Electric Guitar

PUBLISHER'S NOTE
Although the advice and information in this book
are believed to be accurate and true at the time of going
to press, neither the authors nor the publisher can accept
any legal responsibility or liability for any errors or
omissions that may have been made nor for any inaccuracies
nor for any loss, harm or injury that comes about from
following instructions or advice in this book.

ACKNOWLEDGEMENTS
The publisher would like to thank the following for their kind permission to
reproduce photographs in this book. Abbreviations key: T = top, C = centre,
B = bottom, R = right, L = left. All photography by Laurie Evans except the
following. **Alamy:** Images of Africa Photobank 10BL, Chesh 11BR, Pictorial
Press Ltd 57TR. **Bcrich.com:** 124R. **Burns London LTD:** 63TR. **Terry
Burrows:** 86R, 122R, 124L, 134R, 150L. **Clarence L. Miller Family Local
History Room, Kalamazoo Public Library, Michigan:** 16BC. **Duesenberg
Guitars:** 150R. **Eko Music Group:** 93R. **EMP Museum, Seattle, WA:** 38L.
E.L.V.H. Inc: 132L. **Fender Ltd:** 6TR, 9C, 16BL, 16CR, 50L. **Fodera.com:**
139L. **Getty Images:** 6BL, 15TL, 22BL, 23TL, 24BL, 31CR, 55R, 83R, 121R,
133R, 155R; AFP 21CR; Archive Photos 13TC; FilmMagic 125R, 158R;
Kallista Images 93 Grid 2 Michael Ochs Archive 18BC, 19, 33R, 39R, 59R,
89R; Photodisc 93 Grid 2 RedFerns 8TC, 8MC, 8BC, 13TL, 13TR, 17TL,
18BL, 20BL, 21T, 23BR, 24BC, 25TR, 35R, 67R, 77R, 99R, 109R, 111R,
131R, 136R, 149R, 157R; Time & Life Pictures 85R; Visuals Unlimited 93
Grid 1, 93 Grid 3, WireImage 81R, 103R, 123R. **Gibson Guitar Corp:** 25B,
95C, 159L, 159C. **Grosh Guitars:** 151R. **iStock:** TZfoto 14BR. **Malcolm
Maxwell:** 26L, 99L, 131L, 147R, 149L. **Outline Press:** 8L, 9TR, 12R, 14CR,
28R, 30L, 30R, 31L, 32L, 32R, 33L, 34R, 36L, 37L, 37C, 37R, 38R, 39L, 40L,
41L, 43R, 46L, 46R, 47L, 49R, 50L, 50R, 51L, 51C, 52L, 52R, 53L, 53R, 54L,
54R, 56L, 56R, 57L, 63L, 64R, 66L, 69R, 69R, 70R, 71L, 75R, 77L, 78R, 82L,
82R, 84R, 85L, 87L, 87C, 92L, 93R, 97L, 97R, 98L, 98R, 100L, 100R, 101R,
102R, 104L, 105L, 106L, 106R, 107R, 110R, 111C, 112L, 112R, 113L, 114L,
114R, 115R, 116L, 116R, 118L, 118R, 119CL, 119CR, 120R, 121L, 125L,
126R, 127L, 128R, 130L, 132L, 133L, 135L, 135R, 136R, 138L, 138R, 139R,
140L, 140R, 141L, 141R, 142L, 143L, 143R, 144L, 144R, 145L, 145C, 146L,
146R, 147L, 148L, 148R, 152L, 152R, 153L, 153R, 154L, 154R, 155L.
**Redpath Chautauqua Collection, University of Iowa Libraries, Iowa
City:** 11TL. **Eugene Earle Collection, Southern Folklife Collection,
Louis Round Wilson Special Collections Library, University of North
Carolina, Chapel Hill:** 29CR. **Sotheby's:** 157L. **Starlabs.com:** 136L.
Township Guitars: 156R. **Vintaxe.com:** 91R.

With special thanks to the following for allowing us to photograph their guitars:
David Crozier at Old School Guitars Ltd; Harris Hire, Beckenham; Hutchins
Guitars, Lancing; Guy Mackenzie; National Music Museum, South Dakota; Chris
Trigg of Vintage and Rare LTD, 6 Denmark Street, London WC2H 8CX; and
Wunjo Guitars, Denmark Street, London.

FENDER®, STRATOCASTER®, STRAT®, TELECASTER®
and P BASS®, and the distinctive headstock designs commonly
found on these guitars are registered trademarks of Fender Musical
Instruments Corporation, and are used herein with express written
permission. All rights reserved.

PAGE 1: Fender Coronado II, 1966.
PAGE 2 (clockwise from left): Rickenbacker Electro Spanish, 1933;
     Eric Clapton; Charlie Christian; Elvis Costello.
PAGE 3: Paul Reed Smith Custom 22, 1985.
ABOVE: Gibson Les Paul Deluxe, 1968.

Contents

Introduction

The electric guitar is arguably the single most important musical instrument of the modern age. At the forefront of much popular musical innovation since the 1940s, it has taken centre stage across genres and decades, from 1950s rock 'n' roll through to present-day pop and indie. Evoking rebellion, youth and glamour, the electric guitar's popularity shows no sign of waning.

History

Acoustic guitars and their ancestors have existed for hundreds of years, but it was only in 1924 that Gibson engineer Lloyd Loar first attached an electric pickup to an instrument – a viola – translating the vibrations of the strings into an electrical signal which could be amplified. The first purpose-built electronic instrument wasn't produced for a further seven years – the Ro-Pat-In 'Frying Pan'. Over the next decade the amplified hollow-bodied guitar slowly grew in popularity, particularly among jazz guitarists who needed to be heard during ensemble playing. Then, in 1940, Lester William Polsfuss, or Les Paul, took the design of the electric guitar a step further, creating the first ever solidbody electric guitar: 'the Log'. By 1950 a young electronics hobbyist, Leo Fender, had designed and begun manufacturing the Fender Broadcaster, the first mass-produced solidbody guitar.

How a guitar works

In an acoustic guitar, sound is produced when the vibrations of the strings are amplified by air resonating in the hollow cavity of the body. On an electric guitar, the vibration of the strings is sensed by a magnetic pickup mounted on the body, and converted into an electric signal. This is passed through the guitar's circuitry to the amp, which converts the electrical signal back into vibrations, or soundwaves, at a volume that is loud enough for us to hear.

Many people learn to play guitar first on an acoustic instrument, due to budget considerations. As the basic tuning and the fingering on electric and acoustic guitars are the same, it doesn't matter whether you come to the electric guitar from the acoustic, or start on the electric as a complete beginner. However, certain styles of music are better suited to the electric guitar than the acoustic, and the greater sensitivity of an electric guitar, combined with the variety of sonic textures that can be created with electrical effects, means that electric guitarists can play around with a vast array of sounds.

The electric guitar phenomenon

More than any other instrument, the electric guitar defines the sound of rock music, a vastly diverse musical genre which in turn has influenced and characterized much of popular culture over the latter half of the 20th and the early 21st century. In the 1950s, the advent of rock 'n' roll in America coincided with the rise of the 'teenager'; a new conception of adolescence as a distinct, stormy, rebellious stage of life. Rock 'n' roll, a fusion of blues, country and jazz, was fast, fun, and easy to dance to. The electric guitar, with its versatility, and its inherent melodic and rhythmic potential, was perfectly suited to this groundbreaking new musical style.

Early electronic amplification of the guitar generated unintended but pleasing sonic side effects. Being low on output, the sound produced by early amps would often distort when played at full volume, giving a pleasant, 'warm' tone. Artists began deliberately recreating the distorted sound

RIGHT: *Les Paul, musician and creator of the first-ever solidbody electric guitar, and his wife Mary Ford demonstrate two Les Paul Gibson guitars in 1952.*

ABOVE: *A Custom Shop Fender Snake Head Telecaster – an exact reproduction of the prototype that Leo Fender would take around clubs for artists to try.*

RIGHT: *The electric guitar was so popluar during the 20th century that the available repertoire of music created for the instrument is now unimaginably vast. Aspiring players can learn music in a hugely diverse range of genres and styles.*

FAR RIGHT: *A large part of the appeal of the electric guitar in comparison with the acoustic guitar is the huge variety of addtional tones and musical effects that can be created, including vibrato produced by using a tremolo arm.*

by damaging their amplifiers. Eventually, in the early 1960s, the first purpose-built distortion effects circuits came to market. From that point on, the technology surrounding the electric guitar became increasingly important, and the effects available to players proliferated. Present-day guitarists have an astonishing level of electronically generated sonic possibility available to them, with the newest guitars featuring sophisticated onboard computer technology.

Back in the 1960s, wielding electric guitars and making use of the instrument's cutting-edge capabilities, The Beatles burst on to the international scene. The best-selling band in history, their hugely varied output paved the way for the rock-centered pop culture paradigm of the next two decades and beyond. At the centre of it all was the electric guitar.

At the same time, virtuoso guitarists such as Eric Clapton and Jimi Hendrix established a new iconography – the guitar hero. The influence of these solo players, as well as the Beatles-esque guitar groups, propelled the popularity of the guitar to pole position, with millions of aspiring players worldwide taking up the instrument.

The seminal musical styles of the early rock pioneers have generated endless mutations and variations in the decades since, through prog rock, punk, new wave, metal, grunge, Britpop, and all the derivations thereof. However, in spite of the wide array of generic innovation, the electric guitar has remained the central component of a great proportion of popular musical output, right up to the present day.

The electric guitar as a collectible item

Many electric guitars aren't simply valued for their practical use as musical instruments. Perhaps because of their physical beauty, or their historic and cultural significance, many guitars are highly collectible as objects in themselves. Sales of particularly rare models, or instruments that belonged to musical icons, will sell at auction for large sums of money. In 2005, a Stratocaster was sold at auction to raise funds for victims of the 2004 Tsunami signed by Bryan Adams, Eric Clapton, Jimmy Page, Mick Jagger, Keith Richards, Ronnie Wood, Brian May, Liam and Noel Gallagher, Jeff Beck, Pete Townshend, Ray Davies, David Gilmour, Tony Iommi, Mark Knopfler, Angus and Malcolm Young, Paul McCartney and Sting. It reached an incredible $2.8 million.

In this book

This book begins with a history section covering the evolution of the electric guitar, from the first-ever instruments to the cutting-edge models of today. Next, a directory section features all the famous makes, such as Gibson, Fender, Gretsch and Rickenbacker, and also includes curiosities, rare guitars and boutique brands. Each entry provides detailed information about the instrument's date, place of origin, the material it is made from, and any unusual features. The book contains over 230 historically significant instruments, and there are also panels describing electric guitar heroes and their styles of play.

Famous electric guitar players

The popularity of the electric guitar has been reinforced by iconic players of the 20th century.

Guitarists
- Charlie Christian – jazz
- Scotty Moore – rock 'n' roll
- Chet Atkins – country
- Hank Marvin – rock 'n' roll
- Jimi Hendrix – rock
- George Harrison – pop/rock
- Pete Townshend – rock
- Eric Clapton – blues/rock
- Jeff Beck – rock/fusion
- Brian May – rock
- Jimmy Page – heavy rock
- Slash – heavy rock
- Johnny Marr – indie/pop
- Yngwie Malmsteen – metal
- Steve Vai – heavy rock
- Joe Satriani – heavy rock

Bassists
- Paul McCartney – pop/rock
- James Jamerson – Motown
- Marcus Miller – jazz
- Sting – pop

BELOW: *Johnny Marr, guitarist with British indie band The Smiths, played a large part in reclaiming the guitar's role in pop music in the 1980s; his innovative use of multitrack recording to create a 'layered' texture has been much imitated.*

A thoroughly modern phenomenon, the electric guitar first appeared in the 1930s, but only really came of age in the '50s.

History of the electric guitar

Solidbody instruments – including Leo Fender's iconic Stratocaster – influenced the very nature of the music that would follow. Indeed, without the electric guitar, most of the popular music since the 1950s would simply not exist.

The principles of sound

We can only guess at the circumstances whereby ancient humans discovered the musical principles underlying all stringed instruments, but it is generally accepted by historians that the first instrument to use a string to create sound was the musical bow. Indeed, pictorial evidence of its existence has been found in cave paintings in France which date back at least 15,000 years.

String and bow

At its simplest, the musical bow was identical in construction to a hunting bow – it was a curved piece of wood with a string stretched tightly across that was tethered to each end. The string would have been made from animal intestines, usually those of a cow, sheep or goat. Although gut strings are also referred to as 'cat gut', there is no record of cats' intestines having ever been used for this purpose.

The basic principle by which the musical bow operates also applies to a guitar, or any other stringed instrument. The bow is played by plucking the string with one hand, or by striking it with a piece of wood or stone. If the other hand's fingers are placed at different points along the string – thus altering its length – different pitches can be achieved. Whenever any string is struck, the pitch of the note is determined by the frequency at which it vibrates. This is referred to as the note's fundamental. By shortening the length of the string, or by tightening it, hence increasing its tension, the frequency will be increased, so raising the pitch of the note. By lengthening the string, or by decreasing its tension, the frequency is reduced, thus lowering the pitch.

ABOVE: *A stringed bow played by a San Bushman in the Kalahari, Botswana. The wooden bow is placed between his mouth and his foot. By pushing against it, the tension of the string is altered, creating notes at different pitches.*

The soundbox

Any sound that you hear comes about as a result of the displacement of air. Since the string on a musical bow displaces only a tiny amount of air, the audible sound it creates is quite soft. What it lacks is a soundboard. When the string is connected to a soundboard, which has a larger surface area and thus displaces a greater volume of air, the sound produced is much louder. (You can hear this effect clearly by comparing the volume of a plucked elastic band when wrapped around two fingers with the sound it makes when one end is held on a wooden table.) The volume is further increased if the soundboard can be fixed on to a resonant cavity, such as the hollowbody soundbox of an acoustic guitar. The string sits atop the bridge on the soundboard – the top surface of the acoustic chamber – and when it is plucked, it causes the whole body to vibrate, disturbing the air inside the chamber.

Soundwaves

The frequency at which a string vibrates creates its pitch. In the sine waves shown here, the horizontal axis represents the frequency a string vibrates each second, measured in Hertz (Hz), and the vertical axis represents its amplitude – the gentler a string is plucked, the lower its amplitude. Western concert pitch is defined by the note middle A having a value of 440 Hz. So, if diagram A is 440Hz, the soundwave of B has twice the number of peaks and troughs, raising the pitch by an octave. C is an octave higher again.

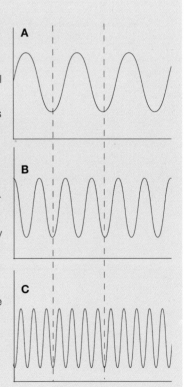

the sound. The vast majority of solidbody electric guitars built since 1950 have worked using either single or twin coils.

An alternative technology that is sometimes used in electric and electro-acoustic guitar construction is the piezoelectric pickup, which detects pressure variation caused by sound waves. Although these types of pickup have the benefit of not picking up any other magnetic fields, such as feedback or mains hum, they generate a very different sound to the more commonly used magnetic type.

Lloyd Loar and the first pickups

Although the principles of electromagnetism were well understood by the middle of the 19th century, it was not until the development of electrical amplification in the 1920s that the first experiments with pickups took place. A Gibson engineer and master luthier named Lloyd Loar is widely credited as the pioneer in this field, when he developed an electric pickup for a viola in 1924. In Loar's experiment, the strings passed vibrations through the bridge to the magnet and coil, which registered those vibrations and produced an electrical signal. These designs attempted to amplify the natural sound of the instrument, but produced a weak signal. It would be another seven years before the pivotal breakthrough in this field took place, with the invention of the 'Frying Pan' – the first true electric stringed instrument.

LEFT: *Before establishing his pioneering role in guitar history and experimenting with the first magnetic pickups, Lloyd Loar was a well-respected mandolin player who toured with his wife's concert company.*

A solidbody electric guitar on the other hand has no resonant cavity and so the sound it generates acoustically comes mostly from the strings themselves. For it to be heard, it must be amplified electronically. While it would be possible to position a microphone connected to an amplifier and speaker close to the strings, the results would be unsatisfactory. The quality of an acoustic guitar's tone comes from the design and construction of the instrument's body, not from the strings themselves. Consequently, the sound would be thin, and the problem of feedback from the microphone might also degrade it further.

The magnetic pickup

A far more effective approach is to use a magnetic pickup that is fitted directly beneath the strings. A magnetic pickup consists of a permanent magnet (or series of magnets) wrapped with a coil made up of several thousand turns of fine copper wire. The two ends of the coil are connected to the output socket on the body of the guitar, usually via very basic volume and tone circuitry. The output socket of the guitar connects via a cable to an amplifier and loudspeaker.

When the strings on the guitar are plucked, the vibration modulates the magnetic flux linking the coil, thus creating a magnetic disturbance, and inducing an alternating current through the coil of wire. This signal is carried to the amplifier, and is then made audible by the loudspeaker.

There are many different approaches to pickup design. The two main ones are: single-coil designs; and twin-coil humbuckers which reduce the undesirable electronic background noise picked up by single-coil types, but alter the nature of

BELOW: *The vibrations of the guitar's strings are read by the pickups as electromagnetic disturbances that are passed along the cable to the amplifier. Here, the signal is boosted and made audible through the loudspeaker.*

The first electric guitars

Experiments into electrically amplifying the vibrations of stringed instruments date back to the early part of the 20th century. Indeed, patents exist showing how early telephone transmitters had been adapted to fit inside violins and other stringed instruments as far back as 1910. However, it was not until the early 1930s that the first true electric guitars began to appear.

The 'Frying Pan'

Lloyd Loar may have experimented with pickup design during the 1920s, but the first significant breakthrough in the amplification of the electric guitar came in 1931 when Adolph Rickenbacker, Paul Barth and George Beauchamp joined forces to form the Ro-Pat-In (from Electro-Patent-Instruments) company.

Beauchamp – himself a well-known musician – had already played a pioneering role in the development of the National Resonator acoustic guitar, and had worked with Barth in an attempt to create an electrical amplification system. Their experiments came to fruition in 1931 with a pair of lap-steel Hawaiian guitars – the A22 and A25 models.

Commonly known as the 'Frying Pan' because of their shape, these instruments were powered by a pair of large horseshoe magnets with individual pole-pieces positioned beneath each of the six strings. These instruments, although not true Spanish guitars, were nonetheless the first electric instruments to go into production. The prototype models featured a body and neck made from a single piece of maple, but by the time the instruments went on sale to the public, they were being constructed from cast aluminium.

The Hawaiian connection

It may seem strange to think that the electric guitar effectively evolved from the electric Hawaiian lap steel. The reason for this is quite simple: during the 1920s there was a major vogue in the United States for Hawaiian music, and at the time there was considerably more popular interest in the lap steel than in the Spanish guitar. The A-25 Frying Pan was immediately popular – its first documented public use was in Wichita in 1931 when it was played by Gage Brewer as part of a duet with George Beauchamp's guitar. A year later the first recordings using an electric instrument were made; although there is scant historical evidence, they are thought to have featured well-known Hawaiian musician Andy Iona.

In 1933, Ro-Pat-In was renamed the Electro String Company, and the brand name Rickenbacker was applied to the Frying Pan. Aluminium turned out to be a problematic choice of material, however, as it reacted to changes in humidity and temperature, causing tuning difficulties. Consequently, strong Bakelite plastic was used instead. These models would remain in production until well into the 1950s.

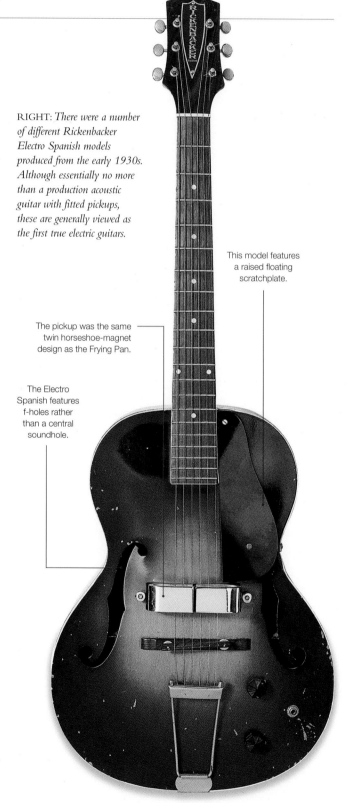

RIGHT: *There were a number of different Rickenbacker Electro Spanish models produced from the early 1930s. Although essentially no more than a production acoustic guitar with fitted pickups, these are generally viewed as the first true electric guitars.*

This model features a raised floating scratchplate.

The pickup was the same twin horseshoe-magnet design as the Frying Pan.

The Electro Spanish features f-holes rather than a central soundhole.

ABOVE: *Despite his brief professional life, Charlie Christian was the first influential electric guitarist.*

The electro Spanish

The specific time when the first true electric guitar emerged is, like many aspects of the instrument's history, a matter of conjecture. It seems that Ro-Pat-In included such an instrument in its 1932 catalogue, even if there is no evidence to support its existence at that time. We do know, however, that Rickenbacker himself had not been convinced that there was any commercial potential in electrifying the guitar. In 1935, however, the horseshoe circuitry from the Frying Pan was applied to a Spanish guitar shape. Within a year, a number of other well-established guitar manufacturers had applied magnetic pickups to acoustic guitars, among them the Gibson Guitar Corporation. Their first one, an electric Spanish-style model, the ES-150, was a substantially new instrument.

Because the ES-150 was not intended to be played as an acoustic instrument, Gibson's approach to its construction differed greatly from its usual way of making archtop guitars. The inside of the solid spruce top was not carved to follow the contours of the outside, which made it less well equipped to transfer the energy from the strings into the projection of sound, thus making it acoustically lower in volume. This also helped to reduce the problem of feedback (see 'Experimenting with solidbodies'). The electrics were simple: just a volume and tone control applied to a hexagon-shaped pickup.

The ES-150 became immediately popular among America's jazz orchestras. Although guitarist Eddie Durham is usually credited with making the first electric-guitar solo with the ES-150 (on Jimmie Lunceford's "Hittin' the Bottle"), in fact the player who would shape the immediate perception of the electric guitar was Charlie Christian, whose sublime playing, in an all-too-brief career (he died before his 26th birthday), alerted his contemporaries to the potential of this exciting new instrument.

The first amplifiers

Since the 1960s, players have debated the merits of various kinds of guitar amplification. When the first instruments appeared, however, no such choices existed. If you bought an electric guitar from a music store, it included everything you needed to make a sound: the Gibson ES-150 – so named because it was an electro-Spanish instrument with a retail price of $150 – came with an EH-150 amplifier and cable as part of the package. These first amplifiers were based largely on the circuitry found in a typical valve radio. They were small battery-operated units with a built-in loudspeaker, an output that was tiny by modern standards, and they had no means of altering either the volume or tone – any adjustment to the sound had to be made by using the controls on the guitar.

Leo Fender, selling only Hawaiian guitars and small amplifiers in 1946, created the first dedicated guitar amplifier to feature a volume control – the Fender Champion 600. A year later, Fender unveiled an upmarket model, the Dual Pro, which had two channels, each with its own volume control, and a single master tone control. It was not until 1952, with the Fender Bassman, that the kind of guitar amplifier with which we are now familiar came into being. As its name suggests, the amplifier was designed to work with Fender's new Precision bass guitar, the first mass-produced electric bass. However, its increased volume and sophisticated tone-shaping controls (separate treble, middle, bass and presence knobs) appealed to many guitar players, who chose it over other models designed specifically for their instrument.

RIGHT *First produced in 1958, the British-built Vox AC15 brought together a 15-watt amplifier with a single 305mm (12in) loudspeaker housed in a radio-style cabinet. This type of single-unit combination is still referred to as a 'combo'.*

Experimenting with solidbodies

During the 1940s, the amplified guitar slowly began to capture the imagination of jazz players in the United States. At this time, however, most of the early electric instruments were little more than standard acoustic models with a pickup fitted; it wasn't until the following decade that the electric guitar really evolved into an instrument in its own right.

Feedback

For most guitarists of the 1940s, the electrification of their instrument allowed them to be heard clearly. For the first time these musicians were able to compete as soloists with other loud acoustic instruments, such as horns. There was, however, an occupational hazard for the electric guitarist.

If the volume coming from the amplifier's speaker cabinet (or from the PA system) happened to be too loud, the guitar's acoustic chamber would resonate, causing the strings to vibrate of their own accord. This, in turn, created an unpleasant howling effect known as feedback. Some players had already begun to understand the nature of the problem; they noted that if they stuffed towelling or other material into the acoustic chamber through the soundhole(s) on the top of the body, the guitar was less likely to feed back. The key, it seemed, was to make the body of the guitar less prone to vibration by increasing its density.

Les Paul and the solidbody pioneers

Lester William Polsfuss (1915–2009), known professionally as Les Paul, was a country/jazz guitar player. An early convert to the electric guitar, he was all too aware of the feedback issue. Something of an inventor, Paul was determined to find a solution: if a vibrating body was the cause of the problem, then a redesign using materials less likely to vibrate was surely the answer. At this time, Paul was close friends with Epi Stathopoulo, the man behind the Epiphone guitar company, and during 1940 he was given access to his New York factory on Sundays when it was closed. Paul took a solid four-by-four piece of pine, attached a standard Gibson neck and a pair of his own home-built pickups, and (to make it look more conventional) he added the two halves of an Epiphone acoustic. The resulting instrument was dubbed 'The Log'. Les Paul thought that he would be able to interest other guitar makers in his invention, and he continued to refine his design. Guitar production in the United States was, however, severely disrupted during World War II, and it was not until 1946 that

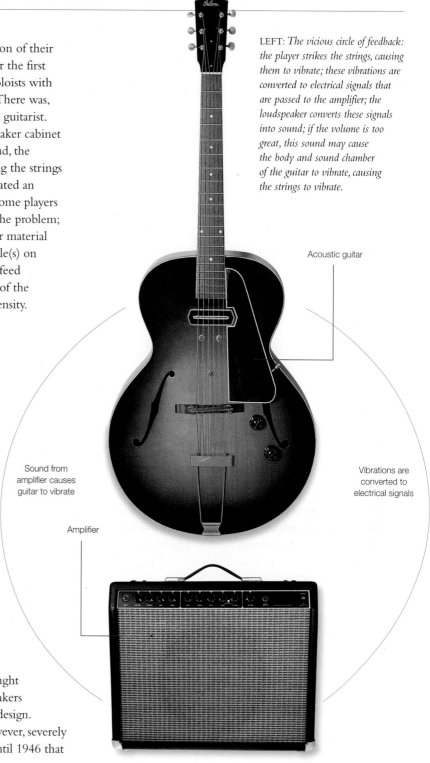

LEFT: *The vicious circle of feedback: the player strikes the strings, causing them to vibrate; these vibrations are converted to electrical signals that are passed to the amplifier; the loudspeaker converts these signals into sound; if the volume is too great, this sound may cause the body and sound chamber of the guitar to vibrate, causing the strings to vibrate.*

Acoustic guitar

Sound from amplifier causes guitar to vibrate

Vibrations are converted to electrical signals

Amplifier

ABOVE: *Les Paul pictured during the 1990s with his pioneering Log guitar, one of the precursors of the solidbody electric guitar.*

What affects the sound of an electric guitar?

Whenever you hear the sound of an electric guitar, a huge number of factors will have come together to create that specific tone – the materials, design, construction and electrics all contribute in unpredictable ways to make every guitar unique. It is also a subject of (often heated) debate among players and luthiers alike.

There is no doubt that different types of wood subtly affect the tone of an instrument. The specific choice is balanced against practical issues, such as weight and ease of working. Dense hardwoods, such as ash, alder, maple, mahogany, basswood and koa, have all been used widely for guitar bodies. Necks are most often made from maple, often with different woods used for the fingerboard.

One area of frequent disagreement concerns the way the neck is fitted to the body. On most electric guitars the neck is simply bolted on. In other cases, the neck is set in the form of a dovetail joint glued permanently into place. This is widely claimed to improve sustain, especially in the upper register. Less common is the neck-through-body approach, where the neck and central section of the body are carved from a single piece of wood. This is only usually found on prestige instruments, and is claimed to improve tone and sustain.

The most dramatic factor affecting the sound of an electric guitar, however, is the pickup itself. There are two basic types of pickup: single-coil and the twin-coil humbucker. Each creates a very different sound, even if fitted to the same guitar. There are numerous possible design variations that influence the sound, including the types of magnet and wire used and the number of windings. Furthermore, the position that a pickup is placed on the body, as well as the guitar's electrics – the tone and volume circuitry – will also have an effect on the guitar's overall sound.

Mahogany

Maple

Rosewood

Koa

ABOVE: *Tonewoods such as mahogany, maple and rosewood are all commonly used in the construction of guitars. Koa is a more exotic wood and, as a result, tends to be found on more exclusive instruments, often bass guitars.*

Paul demonstrated The Log to the heads of Gibson. As Paul would later recall, "They laughed at the guitar". By the end of the 1940s, Les Paul had become one of America's most successful musicians, releasing a string of hit records with his wife Mary Ford, and his invention frequently found use both on stage and in the studio. The Log's story was far from over.

Les Paul was not alone in his experiments. Similar research was known to have taken place at Rickenbacker and National, two Californian companies with a shared heritage. There is no documented evidence, however, of any specific instruments having emerged from this work. Also based in California, engineer/musician Paul Bigsby produced a solidbody electric guitar in collaboration with country picker Merle Travis. This instrument, built in 1948, is arguably the first *true* solidbody electric guitar. It didn't go into mass production, but very clearly had an impact on another Californian with an interest in the electric guitar – Leo Fender.

The great rivalry

During the early 1950s, a fierce new rivalry broke out in the guitar world. The story of Fender versus Gibson is a classic tale of old versus new, of a mighty corporation pitted against an upstart young competitor, and of craftsmanship pitted against the pragmatism of mass production. It was a rivalry that would remain in play for many generations.

Fender: production-line pioneers

In 1938, a young electronics enthusiast named Leo Fender set up a radio repair shop in his home town of Fullerton, California. By the end of World War II, having diversified and established a reputation for building PA systems for local musicians, he was quick to recognize the growing popularity of the amplified guitar. In 1949, Fender and one of his employees, George Fullerton, set out to create a solidbody electric guitar that could be mass-produced easily and cheaply, and so could be sold at a price that ordinary working musicians would find affordable.

His first prototype was a single-cutaway, single-pickup, solidbody instrument named the Esquire. Refining the design, a second pickup was added and, at the end of 1950, the first Fender Broadcasters came off the production line. These were the first mass-produced solidbody electric guitars. Fender salesmen reported that the new instrument was treated with a mixture of amusement and suspicion at trade shows. But musicians who tested the Broadcaster – mostly Western Swing players on the southern Californian music scene – responded favourably. The Fender Broadcaster, however, had a brief existence. Following a copyright infringement action initiated by the Gretsch Company in 1951, the Broadcaster was rechristened the Telecaster.

The return of 'the broomstick guy'

On the other side of the USA, a company named after its founder, Orville Gibson (1856–1918), had been responsible for many of the most important pre-war innovations affecting the guitar. These included the revolutionary acoustic body shapes, such as the arched tops, and the high-volume L-5, which had all but replaced the banjo in jazz bands. Then there was Lloyd Loar's pickup research and, of course, the ES-150 – undoubtedly the version that did the most to convince players that the electric guitar had a real future as a serious instrument.

Gibson had been caught on the hop by Fender's early success, but the company was nevertheless dismissive of an approach to making guitars that so contrasted with their own heritage of craftsmanship. Gibson's president Ted McCarty recalled that the attitude was "anyone with a band-saw and a router can make an electric guitar". Now the Fender factory at Fullerton was beginning to turn out large numbers of Telecasters. Furthermore, country player

LEFT: *Leo Fender's production-line approach to building guitars was viewed with scepticism by established luthiers such as Gibson.*

ABOVE: *The Snakehead Esquire: Fender and Fullerton's prototype of what would come to be known as the Telecaster was given a celebratory 60th-anniversary reissue in 2009 in a limited edition of 60, the body carved from 100-year-old pine.*

LEFT: *By the time Leo Fender started mass-producing electric guitars in 1950, the Gibson works, based at Kalamazoo, Michigan, had already been established for a half a century.*

The Les Paul reborn

The story of the Les Paul didn't end when production stopped. During the 1960s, a new generation of young blues-based rock guitarists discovered that the combination of a Les Paul and an overdriven valve amplifier produced a rich distortion ideally suited to this new music. As a result, original Les Paul models began to change hands for large sums of money – in particular those produced in the late 1950s, when the single-coil pickups had been replaced by Gibson-designed humbuckers. Noting this demand, Gibson once again began producing the Les Paul Standard model in 1968. It has remained in production ever since, and has established itself as one of the most important guitars of the past 60 years. It has since appeared in a huge array of popular variants.

These three classic instruments are without question the most famous electric guitars of all time. All three remain in production, and have been embraced by successive generations of musicians. Today the Fender and Gibson corporations remain the two giants of the US guitar world.

ABOVE: *Jimmy Page from Led Zeppelin is seen here performing live on stage at Earls Court in London in 1975, playing a Gibson Les Paul guitar with his typical flair and style.*

Jimmy Bryant, known as the "Fastest Guitar in the Country", was regularly seen brandishing a Tele on TV.

Gibson had spurned Les Paul when he showed them The Log in 1946. However, he was now one of America's best-known guitarists, and so he was recalled and invited to help with (and endorse) a new instrument. The result, the Gibson Les Paul, made its first appearance in 1952. A crafted instrument in the Gibson tradition built from mahogany and with a striking gold finish ("Rich means expensive" claimed Paul), the Les Paul nevertheless failed to capture the imagination of the public. By 1960 it had been withdrawn.

The iconic Stratocaster

Encouraged by the modest success of the Telecaster, Leo Fender sought to increase production with a new model. Aware that established competitors, such as Gibson and Gretsch, were producing more crafted instruments, he set about creating his own deluxe Fender. He cemented his early success by spending a lot of time listening to the views of his customers. Some Telecaster players were telling him that they wanted a more comfortably contoured body shape, better balance and wider tonal variety. Taking their views into account, in 1954 he unveiled the Fender Stratocaster. It was to become the most famous of all electric guitars.

The essential differences

Fender guitars have commonly used body woods such as ash and alder, and been fitted very simply with bolt-on necks; Gibson has tended to use mahogany bodies with the necks set and glued in place. With a number of notable exceptions, Fender guitars are usually fitted with single-coil pickups, creating a typically clean treble and bell-like tone capable of cutting through. Since the late 1950s, Gibson guitars have generally been fitted with twin-coil humbucking pickups, which reduce electromagnetic interference (mains hum, for example) and give a thick sound classically suited to rock.

ABOVE: *In production since 1954, the Fender Stratocaster is noted for its bright clean sounds and comfortable body shape; it remains widely used by rock, pop and blues musicians all over the world.*

ABOVE: *If you want to play rock, the Gibson ES355 1960 is a good choice, but it's also used for jazz and blues. This is an early version of the popular Gibson, which has a semi-hollow body, giving it a warm tone.*

The electric explosion

The electric guitar had established itself as a viable instrument in its own right during the 1940s, yet while it was commonly heard on popular recordings, it could never reasonably have been described as playing a central role in the music of that period. The decade that followed, however, saw the electric guitar enjoy a massive expansion in popularity, first in the United States and then across the globe.

Competitors emerge

Better known for its drums and percussion instruments, the Fred Gretsch Company of New York was one of the first major manufacturers to challenge the early success of the Fender Telecaster. The company had been sceptical about the simplicity of Fender's production-line approach to making guitars, but it changed course when the news broke that Gibson was bringing out the Les Paul model.

The Gretsch response was the twin-pickup Duo Jet, a partially solidbodied instrument that owed more than a little to the Les Paul design. Throughout the 1950s, Gretsch produced a succession of iconic instruments, such as the hollowbodied White Falcon, to give one example. More significant to the company at the time, however, were the Chet Atkins models. Designed in conjunction with country music's leading player, guitars such as the Country Gentleman were responsible for establishing Gretsch as a serious player in the guitar world.

BELOW: *Elvis Costello playing a Gretsch White Falcon, one of the most exotic – and expensive – production guitars of the 1950s.*

BELOW: *Keith Richards used a fuzz box in the introduction to that perenially enduring Rolling Stones' track "Satisfaction".*

Having created the first electric guitars in the early 1930s, the Rickenbacker name was already assured of its place in guitar history. The owner, however, had seen little commercial potential in electric guitars, and chose to concentrate on Hawaiian lap-steel instruments. Under new ownership from the early 1950s, Rickenbacker re-emerged with a number of important innovations, not least the straight-through neck.

In contrast to the other leading makers – Fender necks were simply bolted on and Gibsons were glued in place – the neck and central part of the body on Rickenbackers were cut from a single piece of wood, and the upper and lower wings were fixed on afterwards. This approach, although costly, was believed to be important with regard to the tone and sustain of the guitar. Rickenbacker became hugely successful in the 1960s following the patronage of John Lennon of The Beatles.

Europe and the Far East

The electric guitar was a wholly American development that gradually spread across the world with the advent of rock 'n' roll. Import tariffs in place at the time, however, made the US Gibsons, Fenders, Gretsches and Rickenbackers too expensive to export to foreign markets. In Europe, manufacturers such as Framus, Höfner and Hagström emerged to fill the void, but they mostly produced inferior models.

In the early 1960s, Burns in the UK arguably produced the first high-end rivals to the big American names, and the company's reputation was enhanced when its instruments were used by Britain's most popular pre-Beatles band, the Shadows.

Inevitably it was Japan that became master of cheap production-line electric guitars. During the early 1960s, a number of curious instruments were produced, strongly influenced by Mosrite, a lesser-known American brand. The reason for this was simple: while The Beatles were dominating the rest of the world, Japan's favourite band from the West was US surf-guitar instrumentalists The Ventures, who were, at that time, exclusive Mosrite users, and remain popular today.

ABOVE: *While the rest of the world was in thrall to The Beatles, Japanese teenagers favoured the twang of the US guitar-instrumental band The Ventures.*

One problem that many rock players found, however, was that they simply didn't sound the same as valves, especially when it came to achieving natural distortion. If you overdrive a valve amplifier, the sound is warm and sweet; if you overdrive transistors, the effect is abrasive and, for many, unpleasant. This dilemma led to a gradual movement back towards valve-based amplifiers – a rare example of new technology being rejected in favour of the old. While there are players who prefer the clinical sound of a solid-state amplifier – many jazz players, bass guitarists and keyboard players, for example – the general consensus is that valves play an important role in the classic electric-guitar sound. Transistorized guitar amplifiers do still exist, but they generally now appeal only to those on limited budgets.

Sound matters

Another important change took place during the 1960s. Many guitarists, especially those working in the rock and pop fields, began to place as much emphasis on the sound they produced as they did on their actual playing. The first electronically achieved effects had emerged by accident, for example by overdriving a valve amplifier to the point of distortion. However, from the middle of the 1960s, the technology surrounding the electric guitar took on an increasingly important role, opening up new ways for the guitarist to play, and creating new sounds that would otherwise have been impossible even to imagine.

Throughout the 1960s and the '70s, most of these developments took the form of stomp-box foot-pedal effects. These were small transistorized units that were inserted in the connection chain between the guitar and the amplifier. The first such device was a distorting transistor pre-amplifier known as a fuzz box. These were used to produce an alternative to valve overdrive, or to offer a more usable distortion to those with solid-state amps.

This effect can be heard on many classic rock tracks, one of the earliest being the Fuzz Tone FZ-1 used in 1965 by Keith Richards on the introduction to The Rolling Stones' "Satisfaction". Other effects that emerged over the decade included the wah-wah filter, phasing, flanging, echo, delay and octave-doubling. They all offered the guitarist a radically new sonic palate on which to draw, and had a huge impact on the music produced during the period.

Over time, the big Japanese factories began to concentrate on the production of copies of Telecasters, Stratocasters, Les Pauls and, occasionally, European brands such as Burns and Hagström. They were cheap, usually poorly made and difficult to play, and established a poor reputation for Far Eastern guitars that would take well into the 1980s to turn around.

Valves versus transistors

The 1960s saw a significant change in the sound technology relating to the guitar. At the start of the decade, the transistor, which had been invented in 1947 at AT&T's Bell Labs in the United States, had begun to make enormous inroads into everyday life. Thermionic valve technology, which had played a critical role in the evolution of radio broadcasting, television, radar, sound reproduction and telephone networks, was increasingly being rendered redundant by cheaper and more reliable solid-state transistor-based electronics.

Guitar amplification would succumb to the same pressures during the decade. On the surface, this was a wholly positive development. Valve amplifiers were bulky and heavy; valves behaved inconsistently and were delicate and hence prone to breakage or failure. Solid-state amplifiers were smaller, lighter, more reliable and a good deal cheaper to produce. Unsurprisingly, they were immediately popular. Indeed, throughout the 1970s the majority of guitar amplifiers produced were solid-state.

RIGHT: *The British-designed Vox wah-wah pedal first appeared in 1967. Rebranded by Vox's business partners in the USA as the Cry Baby, it was also famously used by Jimi Hendrix on many of his classic songs of the time.*

Altering the face of music

When the first electric guitars appeared in the 1930s, it is doubtful if even their pioneering inventors saw them as heralding a new era in music. They were, after all, a pragmatic response to a basic issue: despite alternative designs and the use of metal resonating units, acoustic guitars were simply not loud enough to be heard when played in a band with other instruments.

Early pioneers

Jazz, blues and country players were the first to embrace the new electric technology. Charlie Christian showed for the first time how important a role a soloing guitarist could take in a large ensemble. His work in the late 1930s redefined the role of the guitarist in jazz music, and set the benchmark from which other virtuoso players, such as Wes Montgomery, Jim Hall and Joe Pass, would develop.

Around the same time, Los Angeles-based musician T-Bone Walker became the first star of blues electric guitar. By the mid-1940s, Chicago was established as the home of electric blues, an emerging style that was perfected at the end of the decade by Muddy Waters. The contemporary blues scene was largely enjoyed by black audiences or white college students,

and so it lacked widespread national recognition. Despite this, it was a fertile period in this genre. Star performers included Waters, B. B. King, John Lee Hooker, Buddy Guy and Albert King, and their music and style of playing would become an important influence on the rock bands of the 1960s. Indeed, players like Eric Clapton and Peter Green, and bands like The Rolling Stones, cut their teeth playing covers of blues classics recorded two decades earlier.

Influential players

When Leo Fender launched the first solidbody electric guitars in 1950, almost all of his early customers were country players from the southern Californian music scene. Indeed, it was TV appearances by Jimmy Bryant, the self-styled 'Fastest Guitar in the Country', on *Hometown Jamboree* that gave the Telecaster its first important exposure. As Fender recalled, "Everybody wanted a guitar like Jimmy Bryant."

The decade also saw the emergence of one particular electric country musician whose impact was almost as profound as Charlie Christian's in jazz. Chet Atkins was a technical master whose influence placed the electric guitar at the centre of the Nashville sound that dominated country music until well into the 1980s.

During the 1960s, as technology evolved, a wide array of new sonic options became available to the guitarist. The first and most enduring of these came about by accident. Early valve amplifiers were typically low in output, and when played at full volume were prone to distortion. Some players – especially those using the twin-coil humbucking pickups first developed by Seth Lover at Gibson in 1955 – realized that overdriving these valves could produce a very pleasing sound.

LEFT: *As rock musicians began playing in larger venues, the Marshall stack offered the necessary boost in volume. Eric Clapton is seen here with his guitar connected to two powerful valve amplifiers, or heads, controlling stacks of four cabinets that house a total of 16 speakers.*

LEFT: *The Kinks illustrate the classic pop-group template, which is still widely in use: drums, electric bass, electric lead guitar and a vocalist who plays electric rhythm guitar.*

BELOW: *Contemporary Estonian composer Arvo Pärt made use of an electric guitar in his composition entitled* Miserere, *which successfully connected 20th-century minimalism with early sacred music.*

The distorted guitar sound has remained at the heart of most forms of rock music ever since. Indeed, without the distorted electric guitar the very notion of rock music, and its manifold metal offshoots, could simply never have existed. The first deliberate use of distortion on record is a matter of dispute; Link Wray's 1958 instrumental "Rumble" is certainly a candidate. Widely credited as the first heavy-rock track, The Kinks' "You Really Got Me" in 1964 uses a heavily distorted power-chord sequence. Interestingly, both sets of sounds were achieved as much by cutting strips into the loudspeaker as by distorting the valves.

From this period onwards, the technology surrounding the electric guitar took on an increasingly important role. It opened up new ways for the guitarist to play, and created new sounds that previously were quite unimaginable. The technology available to the contemporary electric guitarist is largely unrecognizable from the pioneers of the 1930s. Modern amplification, digital modelling and multiple effects units provide even the beginner with sonic options that these players could not even dream of. Indeed, the art of the modern guitarist is as much about choosing and manipulating a palette of sound as it is about playing chords and notes.

The electric guitar in classical music

Although primarily used in the pop, rock, jazz and country fields, the electric guitar has also featured in the world of classical music. In the 1950s, it was mostly employed by experimental composers. The electric guitar had a small role in Karlheinz Stockhausen's 1957 composition *Gruppen*,

which featured three orchestras playing at the same time, each with its own conductor. In 1966, Morton Feldman composed *The Possibility of a New Work for Electric Guitar*, its unusual registers creating an effect that makes the instrument difficult to recognize. During the same period, Francis Thorne was one of the first composers to make regular use of the electric guitar; his jazz-tinged *Sonar Plexus* (1968) and *Liebesrock* (1969) are both notable works.

Towards the end of the 20th century, there was a greater acceptance of the electric guitar as a bona fide musical instrument, worthy of serious consideration. In 1987, Steve Reich was commissioned to compose *Electric Counterpoint*. It incorporated repetitive motifs typical of Reich's work for performance by jazz guitarist Pat Metheny. Another significant classical work to feature the electric guitar is Arvo Pärt's 1992 liturgical composition *Miserere*.

A generation of composers has emerged recently who have grown up playing the electric guitar in bands. They have used this experience, and some of the sounds, in new symphonic works. Perhaps the best-known exponent of this is American Glenn Branca, who has produced pieces for large ensembles of up to 100 electric guitars.

The rise and fall of guitar groups

Rock 'n' roll music was unquestionably born in the USA, and by the late 1950s the small ensemble format, with the electric guitar at its heart, was well established. But by 1962, the US pop charts were filled with clean-cut, lightweight balladeers, and the electric guitar stepped back out of the limelight. The next critical phase in the instrument's narrative came from across the ocean, where the electric guitar was far from passé.

The British influence

Across the Atlantic, a new impetus emerged. Britain loved the rock 'n' roll sound, and visiting American stars, who had fallen out of favour in their homeland (and so were more inclined to tour overseas), were still very enthusiastically received there. Even Bill Haley, the chubby middle-aged singer of "Rock Around the Clock", had caused fans to riot on his first visit to British shores.

During the late 1950s, a generation of British rockers had tried to compete but, with a few notable exceptions, they were pale imitations of their US counterparts. It was the second generation of Britain's rockers, and the widespread popularity of the beat group, that played such an important part in the evolution of guitar-based music. Teenage musicians began to form their own small-ensemble groups, influenced by classic rock 'n' roll and, significantly, electronic blues music, which had enjoyed little mainstream exposure in the US - it had been played mainly by black musicians for black audiences. This small-band format was also popular with promoters. Bands tended to be small and self-contained, providing their own instruments and amplification, so they could play in smaller venues. Gigs were plentiful.

Beatlemania

Spearheading this 'Beat Revolution' was Liverpool four-piece The Beatles, whose unprecedented popularity in Britain with teenage girls during 1963 was, in itself, enough to convince a significant proportion of their male counterparts to take up the electric guitar. Striving to match demand, Britain's musical instrument market was quickly saturated by cheap electric guitars from Japan and Germany.

Few imagined this so-called Beatlemania would be repeated outside the shores of the UK. However, during 1964, the band's popularity in the USA paved the way for an invasion of other popular British beat groups, such as Gerry and the Pacemakers, The Animals and the Dave Clark Five. Previously, it had been rare for a non-US artist to achieve popularity; now almost half of the US top-ten entries for 1964 were by British electric guitar-based groups. Of course, the impact of The Beatles encouraged a similar response from young American men in trying to emulate them, and a plethora of American guitar bands appeared.

The Beatles' success also impacted other musical genres. In August 1964, while visiting the USA, the band spent time in the company of acoustic protest singer Bob Dylan. His influence heralded a significant shift in the band's songwriting, particularly in the case of John Lennon, whose lyrics began to take on a more serious tone. Dylan, in turn, horrified passionate folk fans at the 1965 Newport Folk Festival by performing on electric guitar as part of a band, rarely returning to his acoustic troubadour roots. Both of these musical shifts could be said to presage symbolically much of the music created during the next two decades.

LEFT: *The Beatles cast a giant shadow over the 1960s, redefining not only music but popular culture in general. More than four decades after the band's 1970 breakup, they continue to influence successive generations of musicians of popular music.*

the thriving punk, noise and metal underground scenes still revolved around distorted guitar sounds. Furthermore, in the mid-1990s the phenomenon known as Britpop saw an explosion of guitar bands playing '60s-tinged pop music. Manchester's Oasis, in particular, briefly enjoyed album sales to rival The Beatles, the band on which their sound was all too clearly modelled.

Fuelled by universal access to high-speed online links, the past decade has seen the music industry struggle vainly to retain control of the market. As user-maintained social-networking websites wield ever more communal power, listeners have unprecedented access to most of the music ever made. Now that the market is so fragmented, it is increasingly difficult for a company to hold the necessary sway to influence major commercial shifts in musical fashion.

Indeed, the global nature of the Internet has enabled even the tiniest of niche musical cults to thrive, making room, quite literally, for every possible genre to coexist and thrive. Given that most of the popular music produced since the 1950s has revolved around the electric guitar, there is little to suggest that this is likely to change greatly in the future.

The importance of the soloist

From the middle of the 1960s, rock music began dividing into recognizable sub-genres – a process that continues to this day. The birth of heavy rock, exemplified by such bands as Cream and the Jimi Hendrix Experience, was accompanied by the first generation of electric-guitar virtuosi, players capable of wielding a technique that was equal to any classically trained player. Although his active life was brief – he died at the age of 27 – Jimi Hendrix is still viewed with awe more than four decades after his death. His musical prowess and subsequent canonization into guitar lore epitomizes the figure of the 'Guitar Hero'.

The electric guitar soloist would also be central to the metal sound that first emerged at the end of the 1960s. Initially a British phenomenon popularized by bands such as Black Sabbath and Deep Purple, by the 1980s it enjoyed global popularity with an ever-expanding list of niche sub-genres, such as death metal, drone metal, prog metal and grindcore to name but a few. Although often very different in tone, they are nonetheless united by combining heavily distorted electric guitar sounds with solos played at extremely high speed.

A new type of sound

During the 1980s, the electric guitar took less of a starring role in many areas of popular music, as the electro sound emerged in the wake of swiftly advancing keyboard and drum-machine technology. When the vogue for digital sampling took hold, and electronic dance music reached the peak of its popularity during the 1990s, the guitar was further relegated in importance. This is not to suggest that the electric guitar had had its day. Away from the public mainstream,

ABOVE LEFT: *During his brief career, Jimi Hendrix redefined the art of electric-guitar playing. Here he is playing the Olympic White Stratocaster he famously used at the Woodstock Festival in 1969.*

BELOW: *R.E.M. became one of the world's most popular alternative rock bands in the 1980s. Their unique sound was driven by the unusual lyrics of Michael Stipe and the nimble guitar work of Peter Buck (shown below).*

The modern era

Since the earliest days, guitarists with a bent for experimentation have taken standard models and customized them to their own individual needs. In the early 1980s, this vogue became so pronounced that it gave rise to new breed of guitar. This was a souped-up instrument known as the superstrat, and the production lines of companies such as Kramer, Jackon and Charvel were devoted to them almost entirely.

Genesis of the superstrat

The popularity of the various forms of metal music in the early 1980s led some players to seek out instruments that seemed better suited to the music they were making. Guitar heroes of the period, such as Ritchie Blackmore, did use standard Stratocasters, but they were heavily customized. Blackmore installed overwound pickups and non-standard tone circuitry. He scalloped his fingerboard, so that his fingers didn't come into contact with the fretboard.

It was Eddie Van Halen, a guitarist who routinely customized his instruments, who created the first well-known Superstrat. He liked the basic Stratocaster design but disliked almost everything else about it. He took a Strat body, added a thin Charvel neck, and teamed this with a Gibson PAF humbucker to create what he called 'the Frankenstrat'.

Another important development at this time was the Floyd Rose locking tremolo system. Metal players wanted a tremolo arm that could produce extreme pitch bends without putting their guitar out of tune. Floyd Rose came up with a double-locking floating bridge with a clamp behind the nut locking the strings in place. It was hugely successful and was used on virtually every high-performance guitar of the period.

Fender itself was in no position to respond. The marque had lost some of its lustre because it was generally believed that the quality of its instruments had diminishe significantly. As a result, some independent workshops that had been kept busy souping up standard models began to produce their own high-powered guitars. One name that became prominent during this time was Grover Jackson, whose Soloist, with its straight-through neck and 24-fret fingerboard, was the first Superstrat to be produced in quantity. Jackson would go on to produce other fine metal-geared instruments, such as the sharply angular Randy Rhoads model.

Fender eventually did manage to produce a series of high-performance rock guitars, models such as the Katana and Performer. Gibson even produced the US-1 – the company's first Strat-shaped instrument. None, however, achieved any great popularity.

During the mid-1990s metal fell out of fashion and most of the niche Superstrat makers went out of business, or were acquired by larger concerns. However, the desire for customized guitars clearly still remained, as Fender proved with its successful artist signature series, which has mainly consisted of heavily modified Stratocasters.

FAR LEFT: *Rock legend Randy Rhoads was killed in an air crash in 1982, aged just 25. His eponymous Jackson guitar, commissioned shortly before his death, remains extremely popular among metal players.*

LEFT: *Ritchie Blackmore was one of the founders of the English heavy-rock pioneers Deep Purple, and later formed his own band, Rainbow. He frequently customized his instruments, and was one of the first players to scallop his fingerboard, scooping out the wood between the frets, allowing for tonal variation and increasing the ease and range of string bends.*

Onboard technology

Over the past 50 years there have been attempts to marry guitars with every new technological innovation. Yet from the guitar-organs of the 1960s through the MIDI guitar synths of the 1990s, nothing of any *lasting* value came from this cross-breeding. This situation may have changed since the emergence of a new generation of computer-driven instrument in the 21st century. Perhaps the best example is the Gibson Robot series of guitars, launched in 2007, which feature an onboard computer capable of controlling the machine heads. Its use in practice is simple: you choose how you want your guitar tuned, press a button, and the machine heads turn until the strings are correctly tuned. Furthermore, it maintains the tuning while you play. It remains to be seen if this technology is destined to make a lasting impression – it *is* extremely expensive – but what it offers over earlier innovations is a basic functionality that every guitarist wants: that is the ability to stay in tune.

Different materials

If you flick through the pages of any guitar magazine nowadays, you could be forgiven for thinking that the majority of the instruments on sale are based on models that first appeared before 1960. Yet while much of the guitar market *is* decidedly retro, there have always been pioneers who want to push back the boundaries. One particular area of interest has been the use of materials other than wood. We may recall that the Rickenbacker Frying Pan was built from bakelite. In the 1970s, Kramer built a range of guitars with aluminium necks intended to improve sustain. These were popular among bass players, who often have a greater willingness to experiment. A decade later, Steinberger built a briefly popular series of instruments constructed entirely

ABOVE: *Matt Bellamy of Muse, a musician with a keen interest in innovative guitar technology, is seen here playing the Parker Fly, one of the most radical electric-guitar designs since the 1990s.*

RIGHT: *When it first appeared in 2011, the Gibson Firebird X was the most technologically advanced production guitar on the market. Not only did it feature automated on-the-fly tuning and an assortment of digital effects, but it also had modelling software to produce a variety of different amplifier sounds.*

from a proprietary mix of graphite and carbon fibre. Immediately recognizable for having no headstock, the Steinbergers were fine instruments that ultimately failed once their unusual appearance became unfashionable. Arguably the most radical production guitar developed since the 1990s is the Parker Fly. Creator Ken Parker set out to build an instrument that was lower in mass than a regular guitar, but just as solid in strength. It consists of a wooden frame with an exoskeleton made from a powerful carbon fibre/epoxy composite; the neck also features a similar composite fingerboard. Also revolutionary, the Fly's electrics feature not only a pair of switchable humbuckers but also an internal battery-powered Fishman piezo pickup for an amplified acoustic sound. First produced in 1993, the Fly has continued to evolve and is now an established high-end electric guitar, favoured by players such as Matt Bellamy of Muse, and Joe Walsh of the Eagles.

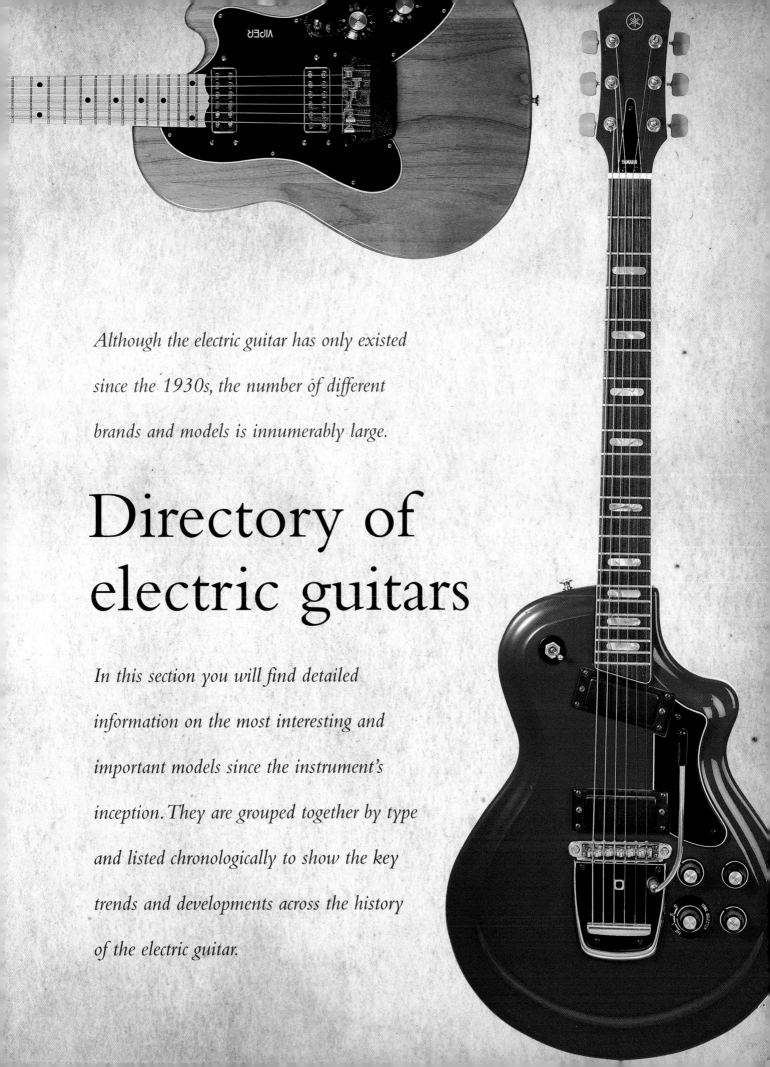

Although the electric guitar has only existed
since the 1930s, the number of different
brands and models is innumerably large.

Directory of
electric guitars

In this section you will find detailed
information on the most interesting and
important models since the instrument's
inception. They are grouped together by type
and listed chronologically to show the key
trends and developments across the history
of the electric guitar.

Electric lap steels

By the start of the 1930s, the guitar was still to achieve mainstream popular recognition. Curiously, for an instrument that would have such an impact on the music and popular culture of the 20th century, the first electric guitars were modelled on the small Hawaiian lap-steel instruments rather than the more familiar figure-of-eight shapes associated with the traditional Spanish guitar.

Ro-Pat-In 'Frying Pan', 1931

The Ro-Pat-In electric lap-steel model, known as the 'Frying Pan' because of its body shape, was the first commercially marketed electric-stringed instrument. George Beauchamp's prototype was created from maple, but by the time it went into production had been redesigned from cast aluminium. The Frying Pan was plugged into an amplifier via connections to a pair of terminals on the body. Two models were built, the A-25 and the shorter-scaled A-22.

The cast aluminium construction was sturdy but heavy.

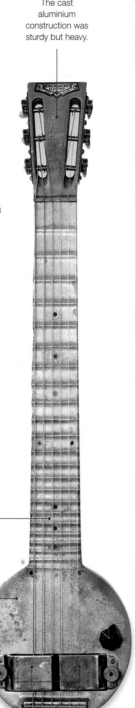

- **DATE** 1931

- **ORIGIN** Los Angeles, California, USA

- **WOOD**
  Prototype built from maple; cast aluminium used for production models.

- **UNUSUAL FEATURE**
  Pickup design featured a single coil of copper wire wrapped around a pair of horseshoe magnets.

The pitch on a lap-steel guitar is altered by moving a metal bar along the strings.

The first Frying Pans were built from aluminium; later they were made from Bakelite.

George Beauchamp's pickup was built from two 38mm (1½ in) horseshoe magnets.

Rickenbacker Model B Lap Steel, 1935

By 1935 Ro-Pat-In had adopted the name of one of its founders, Adolph Rickenbacker. The Model B, although still a lap steel, saw the body shape of the Frying Pan taking on the familiar contours of the Spanish guitar. Construction also evolved as the cast aluminium – heavy and with intonation overly affected by temperature – was replaced by Bakelite, a robust plastic used on domestic electrical products of the period.

- **DATE** 1935

- **ORIGIN** Los Angeles, California, USA

- **WOOD**
  Hollow-cavity Bakelite body, bolt-on/detachable neck with frets moulded into the fingerboard

- **UNUSUAL FEATURE**
  Rickenbacker's Bakelite lap steels were produced until the company was sold in 1953.

23 double frets are moulded into the neck/ fingerboard.

The body cavities are covered by five chrome plates.

The Model B also featured a vibrato arm.

Single-coil horseshoe-magnet pickups were used on of the all early Rickenbackers.

Gibson EH-150 Lap Steel, 1936

Along with Martin and Epiphone, by the middle of the 1930s Gibson had become established as one of the USA's most important guitar manufacturers. Responding to the success of Rickenbacker, Gibson's first electric instrument was also a lap steel, the 1935 aluminium-bodied E-150. Less than 100 of these were built during its 18 months in production. This was followed a year later by the EH-150, in essence a small maple-topped guitar, which was available until 1943.

- **DATE** 1936

- **ORIGIN** Kalamazoo, Michigan, USA

- **WOOD**
  Hollowbody construction (solid mahogany body was introduced briefly in 1942) with maple top and screw-on back.

- **UNUSUAL FEATURE**
  There was one single-coil steel-magnet blade pickup with single volume and tone controls.

The rosewood fingerboard has pearl inlays.

Fret markers are positioned over more than two octaves.

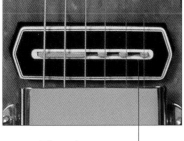

ABOVE: *The steel-magnet blade pickup is widely known as the Charlie Christian because of that guitar's close association with the pioneer of electric jazz guitar.*

Combined bridge and tailpiece is covered by a chrome plate.

The electrics on the EH-150 are identical to those used in Gibson's ES-150 – the first successful electric guitar.

Why Hawaii?

That the first commercially viable electric guitars were lap-steel instruments can be explained in part by the prevailing vogue in the USA during this period for Hawaiian music. The Panama Pacific Exhibition in San Francisco in 1915 is widely cited as having introduced Americans to the music of the island – indeed, so popular was the combination of ukulele and lap steel that within a year records of Hawaiian music had outsold all other genres. Not surprisingly, sales of ukuleles and lap-steel guitars gradually followed suit. The Spanish guitar at this time was something of a niche instrument, used mainly in folk and blues music, so it is hardly surprising that those experimenting with the first magnetic pickups would focus on instruments with the greatest sales potential. Additionally, construction of the lap-steel guitar was a simpler and cheaper process, requiring far less specialized skill than producing an acoustic instrument.

ABOVE: *Sol Hoopii (centre) and his trio were very important in the popularization of Hawaiian music in the USA. Seen here in the late 1920s playing a National Resonator, Hoopii took up the electric lap steel in 1935, quickly becoming one of the finest exponents of the instrument, even developing his own C$^{\sharp}$ minor tuning system.*

Early archtops

With the Frying Pan, the principles of the magnetic pickup were proven as a means of amplifying volume, so Rickenbacker applied this invention to the Spanish guitar – and other makers quickly followed. These, however, were not designed as electric guitars but were regular steel-string acoustics with pickups fitted that were usually sold as part of a set that included a small amplifier.

Rickenbacker Electro Spanish, 1933

Arguably the first true electric guitar, Rickenbacker made use of his business connections to the National company, for whom his partner Beauchamp had designed the first resonator guitars. In truth, it was little more than a standard-issue National Trojan with horseshoe-magnet pickups fitted. As guitars, they were extremely basic, made with cheap plywood bodies. Rickenbacker himself had little faith in the idea of the electric guitar and thereafter concentrated on electric lap steels until he sold the company.

- **DATE** 1933
- **ORIGIN** Los Angeles, California, USA
- **WOOD**
  Plywood body with maple veneer, maple neck, rosewood fingerboard.
- **UNUSUAL FEATURE**
  Initial model had limited electrics; separate volume and tone controls were added on later instruments.

Since the guitar was designed to take a central metal resonator unit, the f-holes had to be positioned on the upper bouts.

Volume and tone controls appeared on later models.

Trapeze tailpiece

Gibson ES-150, 1936

A significant instrument, the ES-150 was the first commercially successful electric guitar. Some of its popularity can be attributed to its pioneering use as a solo instrument by jazz guitarist Charlie Christian – although equally important was that the ES-150 was a fine instrument, reflecting its Gibson pedigree. Electric guitars had been viewed with suspicion by many musicians, but hearing such an instrument played by a virtuoso all but established the electric guitar as a serious musical proposition.

The inlays are pearl dots.

This guitar has a 527mm (24¾in) fingerboard scale.

- **DATE** 1936
- **ORIGIN** Kalamazoo, Michigan, USA
- **WOOD**
  Maple back and sides, spruce top, mahogany set neck, rosewood fingerboard.
- **UNUSUAL FEATURE**
  A single-coil steel-magnet blade pickup is in the neck position – replaced by P-90 in 1946.

The scratchplate is floating.

Note the twin f-holes.

Trapeze tailpiece

Gibson ES-125, 1938

With the ES-150 having established itself as the market leader among electric guitars, in 1938 Gibson introduced an entry-level electric, the ES-100. It was a basic, no-frills, small-bodied archtop with a single pickup and a sunburst finish, and it retailed for $49. In 1941 the ES-100 was renamed the ES-125. It featured an unbound rosewood fingerboard, a single-coil blade pickup in the neck position with a volume control and tone control. Production ended early in 1942, resuming after the end of World War II with a larger body and a P-90 pickup. It remained in production until 1970.

- **DATE** Launched in 1938 as ES-100; ES-125 from 1938

- **ORIGIN** Kalamazoo, Michigan, USA

- **WOOD**
  Maple top, mahogany sides, rosewood fingerboard.

- **UNUSUAL FEATURE**
  The Charlie Christian blade pickup was replaced by a P-90 in 1946.

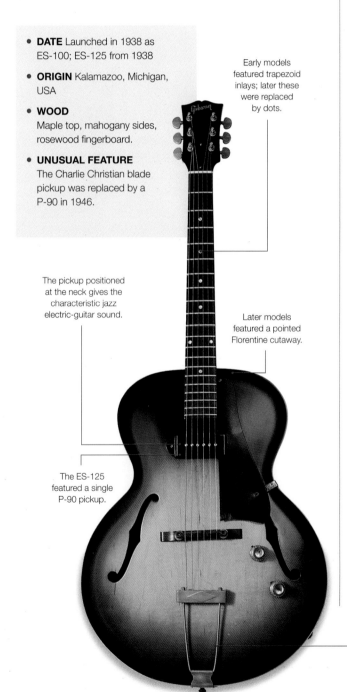

Early models featured trapezoid inlays; later these were replaced by dots.

The pickup positioned at the neck gives the characteristic jazz electric-guitar sound.

Later models featured a pointed Florentine cutaway.

The ES-125 featured a single P-90 pickup.

Trapeze tailpiece

Charlie Christian

A seminal figure in the history of jazz guitar, Charlie Christian (1916–42) enjoyed the briefest of careers before his sudden death at the age of 25. During the course of barely three years in the limelight, often with bandleader Benny Goodman, Christian combined his amplified Gibson ES-150 electric guitar with a virtuoso single-string technique that helped to bring the guitar out of the rhythm section and establish itself as an important solo instrument. In spite of a small body of recorded work, Christian was a major influence on the next generation of jazz players, including such famous names as Wes Montgomery, Barney Kessel, Herb Ellis and Jim Hall. His significance in paving the way for the modern electric guitar sound was also properly acknowledged in 1990 when he was inducted into the Rock and Roll Hall of Fame as an Early Influence.

ABOVE: *Charlie Christian playing his Gibson ES-150, in one of a small number of existing photographs of the first great electric soloist. Christian was to become an influence for successive generations of jazz guitarists.*

The luxury Gibsons

With the success of the ES-150, Gibson quickly became the brand of choice for the serious player. Throughout the 1940s, the company's only real competition came from Epiphone in New York. Indeed, during this time, the two companies enjoyed a rivalry only matched by that which later developed between Gibson and Fender during the 1950s.

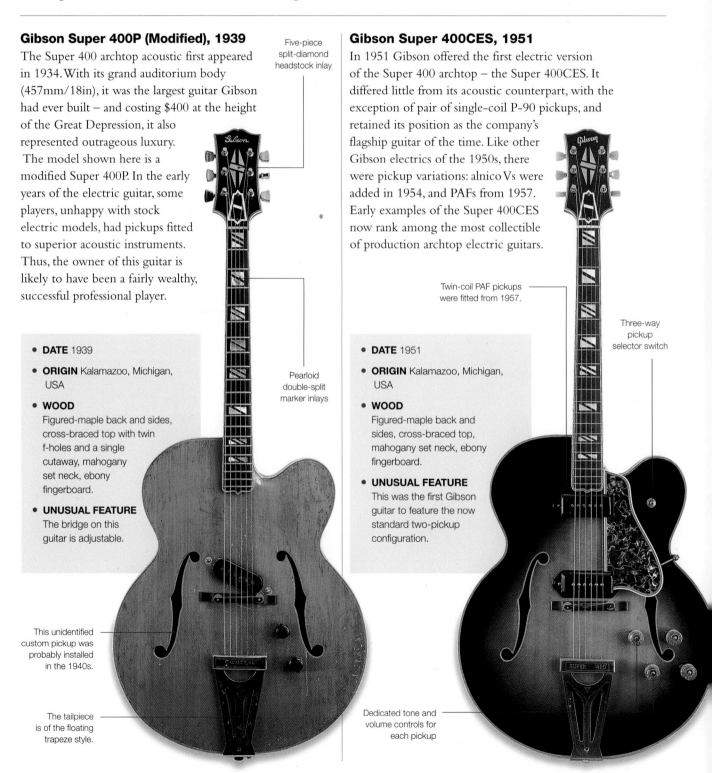

Gibson Super 400P (Modified), 1939

The Super 400 archtop acoustic first appeared in 1934. With its grand auditorium body (457mm/18in), it was the largest guitar Gibson had ever built – and costing $400 at the height of the Great Depression, it also represented outrageous luxury. The model shown here is a modified Super 400P. In the early years of the electric guitar, some players, unhappy with stock electric models, had pickups fitted to superior acoustic instruments. Thus, the owner of this guitar is likely to have been a fairly wealthy, successful professional player.

Five-piece split-diamond headstock inlay

- **DATE** 1939

- **ORIGIN** Kalamazoo, Michigan, USA

- **WOOD**
  Figured-maple back and sides, cross-braced top with twin f-holes and a single cutaway, mahogany set neck, ebony fingerboard.

- **UNUSUAL FEATURE**
  The bridge on this guitar is adjustable.

Pearloid double-split marker inlays

This unidentified custom pickup was probably installed in the 1940s.

The tailpiece is of the floating trapeze style.

Gibson Super 400CES, 1951

In 1951 Gibson offered the first electric version of the Super 400 archtop – the Super 400CES. It differed little from its acoustic counterpart, with the exception of pair of single-coil P-90 pickups, and retained its position as the company's flagship guitar of the time. Like other Gibson electrics of the 1950s, there were pickup variations: alnico Vs were added in 1954, and PAFs from 1957. Early examples of the Super 400CES now rank among the most collectible of production archtop electric guitars.

Twin-coil PAF pickups were fitted from 1957.

Three-way pickup selector switch

- **DATE** 1951

- **ORIGIN** Kalamazoo, Michigan, USA

- **WOOD**
  Figured-maple back and sides, cross-braced top, mahogany set neck, ebony fingerboard.

- **UNUSUAL FEATURE**
  This was the first Gibson guitar to feature the now standard two-pickup configuration.

Dedicated tone and volume controls for each pickup

Gibson L5-CES, 1951

Radical in size and construction, the 1922 Gibson L-5 had been the premier rhythm guitar of the Big Band era. Later, European jazz pioneer Django Reinhardt garnered attention when, in 1946, he played an electrified L-5 that had been modified with a DeArmond pickup. In 1949 Gibson offered an L-5 variant, the ES-5, and in 1951 the L5-CES, 31 models of which came off Gibson's Kalamazoo assembly line. Only it was only ever produced in small quantities, it nonetheless has remained since then in the Gibson catalogue.

- **DATE** 1951

- **ORIGIN** Kalamazoo, Michigan, USA

- **WOOD**
  Curly-maple back and sides, spruce top, maple neck, ebony fingerboard. Set maple neck.

- **UNUSUAL FEATURES**
  The hardware is gold-plated. Produced both with Venetian (curved) and Florentine (pointed) single cutaways.

'Bell' scratchplate cover

Block pearl marker inlays have been used.

Spruce top

Note the L-5 Varitone tailpiece.

The electric transformation

Charlie Christian is widely credited for his role in the popularization of the electric guitar in the jazz world between 1939 and his death in 1942. He was by no means alone, though. There is no clear agreement about who made the first recordings featuring an electric guitar, but one strong candidate is George Barnes, who cut the sides "Sweetheart Land" and "It's a Low-Down Dirty Shame" in Chicago on March 1, 1938. Around the same time, the better-known Eddie Durham, with the Kansas City Five, cut the first recorded solo using Gibson's popular ES-150. It was Durham who would introduce the instrument to Charlie Christian. However, it was blues music that first adopted the electric guitar *en masse*. Chicago musicians, including T-Bone Walker, Muddy Waters, Big Bill Broonzy and Tampa Red, and country-blues players, such as Memphis Minnie, created a whole new genre in the early 1940s: electric blues.

ABOVE: *Memphis Minnie was part of the first generation of blues artists to use the electric guitar – and one the few women during that time to be treated seriously as an instrumentalist. She is best remembered for the 1929 song "When the Levee Breaks", which she co-composed with her husband Kansas Joe McCoy, and was famously covered in 1971 by Led Zeppelin.*

Gibson ES-175 family

In 1949, Gibson launched the single-pickup ES-175 archtop electric guitar. Retailing at $175 (Gibson's ES numbers were often named after their original shop price), it represented good value for an instrument bearing the Gibson marque and proved to be extremely popular, especially with a new generation of jazz musicians in the 1950s, which remains the same today.

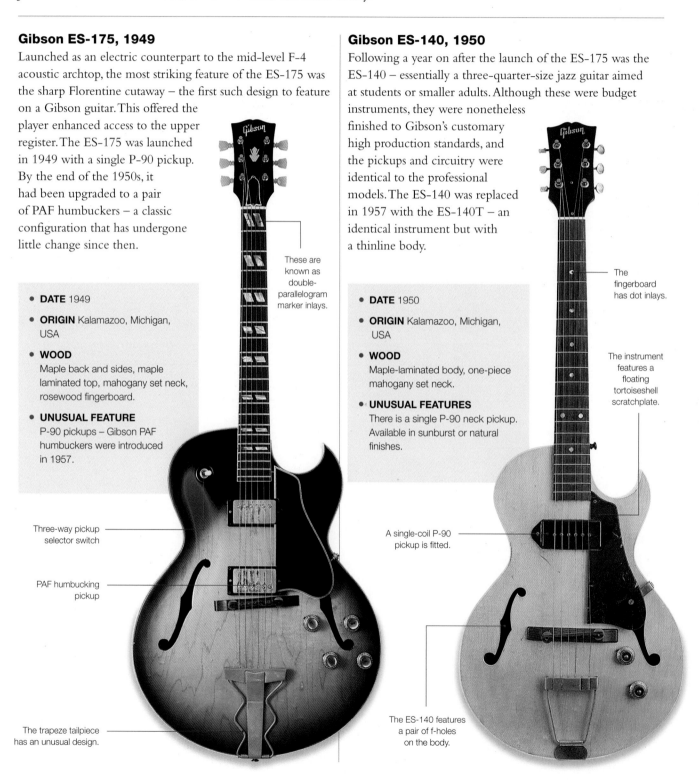

Gibson ES-175, 1949

Launched as an electric counterpart to the mid-level F-4 acoustic archtop, the most striking feature of the ES-175 was the sharp Florentine cutaway – the first such design to feature on a Gibson guitar. This offered the player enhanced access to the upper register. The ES-175 was launched in 1949 with a single P-90 pickup. By the end of the 1950s, it had been upgraded to a pair of PAF humbuckers – a classic configuration that has undergone little change since then.

- **DATE** 1949

- **ORIGIN** Kalamazoo, Michigan, USA

- **WOOD**
  Maple back and sides, maple laminated top, mahogany set neck, rosewood fingerboard.

- **UNUSUAL FEATURE**
  P-90 pickups – Gibson PAF humbuckers were introduced in 1957.

These are known as double-parallelogram marker inlays.

Three-way pickup selector switch

PAF humbucking pickup

The trapeze tailpiece has an unusual design.

Gibson ES-140, 1950

Following a year on after the launch of the ES-175 was the ES-140 – essentially a three-quarter-size jazz guitar aimed at students or smaller adults. Although these were budget instruments, they were nonetheless finished to Gibson's customary high production standards, and the pickups and circuitry were identical to the professional models. The ES-140 was replaced in 1957 with the ES-140T – an identical instrument but with a thinline body.

- **DATE** 1950

- **ORIGIN** Kalamazoo, Michigan, USA

- **WOOD**
  Maple-laminated body, one-piece mahogany set neck.

- **UNUSUAL FEATURES**
  There is a single P-90 neck pickup. Available in sunburst or natural finishes.

The fingerboard has dot inlays.

The instrument features a floating tortoiseshell scratchplate.

A single-coil P-90 pickup is fitted.

The ES-140 features a pair of f-holes on the body.

Gibson ES-295, 1952

In 1952, Gibson decided to capitalize on the success of the rather modest ES-175, and offered an unusual upmarket alternative. Although retailing at over one hundred dollars more, the ES-295 was essentially just the same instrument. Cosmetically, however, it was a very different affair, presented in a shimmering, luxurious gold-paint finish with an ornate floral-patterned back-painted scratchplate. Very unpopular, it is now remembered principally as a hollowbody counterpart to the legendary Les Paul solidbody.

- **DATE** 1952

- **ORIGIN** Kalamazoo, Michigan, USA

- **WOOD**
  Maple back and sides, gold-finished laminated top, mahogany set neck, rosewood fingerboard.

- **UNUSUAL FEATURE**
  The Tune-o-matic bridge with trapeze tailpiece is used on this model.

BELOW: *The ornate scratchplate of the ES-295 is decorated with a flower pattern painted on the reverse side of the clear plastic.*

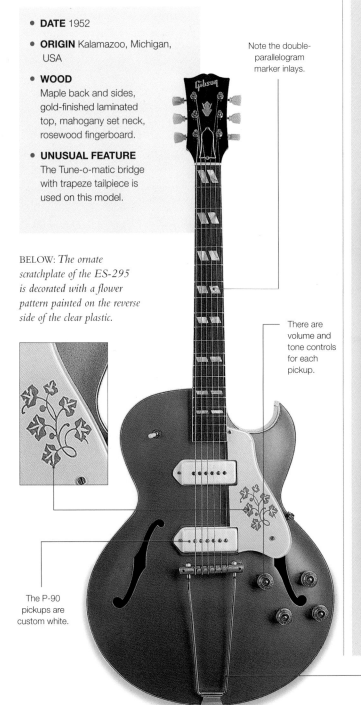

Note the double-parallelogram marker inlays.

There are volume and tone controls for each pickup.

The P-90 pickups are custom white.

The Gibson ES-175: the jazzer's choice

The ES-5 had been Gibson's flagship electric archtop, aimed squarely at the discerning jazz player. Yet it was the less expensive ES-175 that would ultimately establish itself as the most significant jazz guitar of them all. The first models featured one single-coil P-90 pickup in the neck position; a second alongside the bridge followed four years later. It was with the humbucker upgrade in 1957 that the smooth, warm tone, when played from the neck pickup, came to characterize perhaps the very essence of the classic jazz-guitar sound.

The list of ES-175 users reads like a who's who of jazz players, including Joe Pass, Pat Metheny, Kenny Burrell, Wes Montgomery, Pat Martino, Herb Ellis and Howard Roberts. Metheny achieves his own characteristic sound by using flatwound strings on his 1958 model, and playing off the neck pickup with the tone control rolled almost completely to the off position.

The ES-175 has also proved itself to be an unusually versatile instrument, its long association with Steve Howe of Yes being honoured by Gibson with his own signature model.

ABOVE: *Influenced by Django Reinhardt and saxophone legend Charlie Parker, Joe Pass was one of the finest exponents of solo jazz guitar. He played a Gibson ES-175 throughout most of his illustrious career.*

There is a long trapeze tailpiece.

Early Epiphone electrics

The Epiphone company was founded in 1928 by Greek émigré Epaminondas 'Epi' Stathopoulos. Although we tend now to think of the brand as Gibson's 'affordable' line, before the 1950s Epiphone and Gibson were competing for largely the same market, and between them supplying high-end instruments to a significant number of professional musicians.

Epiphone Zephyr, 1939

Produced between 1939 and 1958, the Zephyr is instantly recognizable from the bikini headstock logo. The Zephyr was a full-depth maple-bodied instrument, and was widely taken up as a first electric guitar by many US jazz musicians. Like most electric models of the period, the Zephyr was initially sold as part of a kit that included amplifier, lead and case. It retailed at $100, which, on its launch, represented a significant investment, since the USA was still recovering from the Great Depression.

- **DATE** 1939

- **ORIGIN** New York, USA

- **WOOD**
  Maple body, maple top, solid mahogany neck, rosewood fingerboard.

- **UNUSUAL FEATURE**
  The pickup is an Epiphone Master.

The distinctive metal bikini headstock badge

Epiphone Master pickup

The carousel knobs are on white Pyralin dial with position markers.

Trapeze tailpiece

Epiphone Zephyr Regent, 1950

The Regent monicker was applied as a suffix to many Epiphone models. It simply indicated that the guitar had a single cutaway. Introduced in 1950 as a variant to the popular Zephyr, the cutaway used was modelled on the Venetian curve of the Gibson ES-5/Super 400 – the need for access to the upper register reflecting the growing importance of the electric guitar as a soloing instrument. Both single- and twin-pickup versions were available, fitted either with Epiphone New Yorkers or DeArmonds.

- **DATE** 1950

- **ORIGIN** New York, USA

- **WOOD**
  Maple body, laminated maple top, solid mahogany neck, rosewood fingerboard.

- **UNUSUAL FEATURE**
  There are one- or two-pickup options.

Epiphone guitars were built with a three-a-side style headstock.

There are three Epiphone New York pickups.

Epiphone's revolutionary Frequensator tailpiece is shown here.

Epiphone Sheraton E212T, 1958

When Gibson took over the ailing Epiphone company in 1957, the first batch of new instruments drew strongly on contemporary Gibson models. The Sheraton was a double-cutaway thinline semi-solid guitar, and modelled very closely on the parent company's newly issued ES-335. It was, however, able to retain some important Epiphone characteristics, such as the fascinating Frequensator tailpiece, an innovation that created different string lengths (from nut to tailpiece) between bass and treble strings: the shorter top strings have a lower tension and are thus easier to bend and play single-note parts in the upper register.

- **DATE** 1958

- **ORIGIN** New York, USA

- **WOOD**
  Solid maple centre block with maple wings, mahogany set neck, rosewood fingerboard.

- **UNUSUAL FEATURES**
  This model has New York pickups and a Frequensator tailpiece.

ABOVE: *One of the distinguishing features of the Epiphone Sheraton was the Frequensator tailpiece. It was used to lengthen the bass strings to obtain a better response. It was later replaced by a fixed stop bar.*

On later models, the tortoiseshell scratchplate featured the company's stylized E logo.

Three-way pickup selector switch

Frequensator tailpiece

Epiphone and Gibson

ABOVE: *An Epiphone catalogue illustration from 1964. Epiphone remains one of the biggest-selling electric-guitar brands in the world. Its success, however, is now based on offering cut-price versions of classic Gibsons, rather than the high-end originals.*

The rivalry between Fender and Gibson is now legendary within the guitar world, drawing in both corporation and player alike. Yet before Fender's emergence on the scene in 1950, Gibson fought a similarly robust battle with Epiphone, both companies producing archtop guitars of the highest standard and competing for a share of the professional market.

The seeds of Epiphone's downfall were sown in 1944, when Epi Stathopoulos, the company's innovator and driving force, died from leukaemia. His brother Frixo took the reins, but the coming decade proved difficult, culminating in a crippling dispute with the workforce that resulted in closing the New York factory and moving to Pennsylvania.

In 1957, when Frixo Stathopoulos died, the company was unable to continue independently and was sold to its erstwhile rival Gibson. The Epiphone brand gradually evolved into Gibson's *de facto* diffusion name, offering cheaper, high-quality, Japanese-built versions of Gibson classics. Sales of the Epiphone brand now represent a critical part of Gibson's global business success.

The solidbody pioneers

Nobody can say with any certainty who invented the solidbody electric guitar. What is clear, however, is that during the early 1940s there were a number of experimentally minded individuals seriously looking into the problems of electrified acoustic guitars – including issues of feedback and sustain – and independently they were reaching similar conclusions.

Tutmarc Audiovox Bass, c.1937

Seattle-based musician and teacher Paul Tutmarc first experimented with the electrification of musical instruments in the early 1930s, developing, with his friend Arthur Stimpson, a wire-wound magnetic pickup that enabled a guitar to be played through a modified radio set. Tutmarc also worked on amplifying pianos and zithers. In 1935 he developed the first electronically amplified double bass, but his place in music history comes, two years later, from having built and marketed the first solidbody electric bass guitar – the AudioVox Model #736.

- **DATE** *c.*1937
- **ORIGIN** Seattle, Washington, USA
- **WOOD**
  Front/Back & Sides
  One-piece walnut body and neck with purpleheart 760mm (30in) fingerboard.
- **UNUSUAL FEATURE**
  The earliest example of an electric bass guitar.

The Audiovox has a short 16-fret fingerboard.

Single volume control

The bridge is completely non-adjustable.

Les Paul Log, c.1945

During the late 1930s, inventor and fledgeling country/jazz guitarist Les Paul experimented with his ideas for a new kind of instrument. He took the neck from a Gibson acoustic guitar and fitted it to a block of pine on which he mounted the bridge, tailpiece and a home-built pickup. To make it look more like a regular guitar, he chopped the wings off an Epiphone acoustic body and fitted them either side. The contraption became known as The Log, and featured on many of Les Paul's 1940s recordings.

The Gibson logo can still be seen on the headstock.

- **DATE** *c.*1945
- **ORIGIN** New York, USA
- **WOOD**
  Pine central body with maple cosmetic wings, Gibson mahogany neck with rosewood fingerboard.
- **UNUSUAL FEATURE**
  The hardware is home-made, including pickup, bridge, tailpiece and vibrato arm.

Pickup wired by Les Paul himself.

The bridge and tremolo arm were crudely crafted by the guitarist himself.

Bigsby Merle Travis, 1947

It was a shared love of motorcycles that brought engineer Paul Bigsby and celebrated country guitarist Merle Travis together, and in 1946 Travis brought Bigsby a Gibson vibrato unit for him to repair. It was then that he came up with his own revolutionary – and still widely used – vibrato system. A year later, Travis showed Bigsby a sketch he had drawn of a new type of guitar and asked him if he could build it. The resulting instrument can lay claim to be the first solidbody guitar.

- **DATE** 1947

- **ORIGIN** Downey, California, USA

- **WOOD**
  Maple body, straight-through neck, rosewood fingerboard.

- **UNUSUAL FEATURES**
  The guitar has a home-built single-coil pickup, bass and treble tone controls, and filter switches.

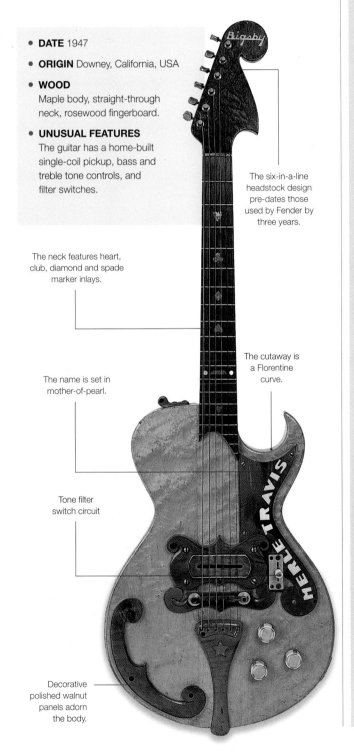

The six-in-a-line headstock design pre-dates those used by Fender by three years.

The neck features heart, club, diamond and spade marker inlays.

The name is set in mother-of-pearl.

The cutaway is a Florentine curve.

Tone filter switch circuit

Decorative polished walnut panels adorn the body.

Les Paul: musician, engineer and inventor

The name Les Paul is guaranteed immortality through the iconic Gibson electric guitar to which he gave his name – even if he played only a small part in its development. As a jobbing guitarist in the early 1940s, his dissatisfaction with the first wave of electro-Spanish guitars led him to experiment with alternative construction techniques – his Log was perhaps the first to show that by fixing neck, strings, bridge and pickup to a solid block of wood, feedback would be reduced and notes could be sustained for longer.

In 1946, Paul tried to sell his idea to Gibson, but the company was not interested at that time. Paul was also a pioneer of recording technology, one of the first to make successful use of sound-on-sound recording, a technique that enabled his famous recordings with his wife Mary Ford to feature multiple guitar and vocal parts.

ABOVE: *Les Paul was perhaps the first mainstream popular star of the electric guitar. His late 1940s hits – recorded with his wife, the singer Mary Ford – invariably featured multiple layers of guitar that he claimed were created by an electronic invention he called the Les Paulverizer. He later revealed that this was achieved by multitrack recording – a little-known technology at that time.*

The Fender production line

Leo Fender had been successful building lap steels and amplifiers when, in 1948, he and employee George Fullerton drew up plans for producing an affordable production-line electric guitar. The first prototypes for an instrument called the Esquire were built in 1949, and a year later history was made when the first of Fender's new guitars – by now renamed the Broadcaster – came out of the factory.

Fender Broadcaster, 1950

Leo Fender's first production-line endeavour made an inauspicious debut. Within months, he received notification from the Fred Gretsch Company that one of its trademarks had been violated – there was already a line of Gretsch drum kits named Broadkaster. Rather than engage in legal action, Fender agreed to back down. It was salesman Don Randall who came up with the idea of namechecking America's favourite new medium of entertainment – the television. Thus was born the legendary Fender Telecaster.

- **DATE** 1950
- **ORIGIN** Fullerton, California, USA
- **WOOD**
  Ash body, maple bolt-on neck, maple fingerboard.
- **UNUSUAL FEATURES**
  There are single-line Kluson tuners and a fixed three-saddle bridge with through-body string fixings.

Fender Telecaster, 1951

The key to Leo Fender's success was in the way he simplified the construction process. Companies such as Gibson and Epiphone employed highly skilled traditional luthiers; the Telecaster was simply a slab of solid ash with a maple neck bolted on – indeed, one Gibson executive jibed that "anybody with a buzzsaw" could build a Fender. Nevertheless, aided by television appearances in the hands of Jimmy Bryant – the 'Fastest Guitar in the Country' – the Telecaster began to capture the imagination of Californian country players.

- **DATE** 1951
- **ORIGIN** Fullerton, California, USA
- **WOOD**
  Ash (alder and poplar also used), maple bolt-on neck, maple or rosewood fingerboard.
- **UNUSUAL FEATURE**
  This basic model has remained in production since the early 1950s.

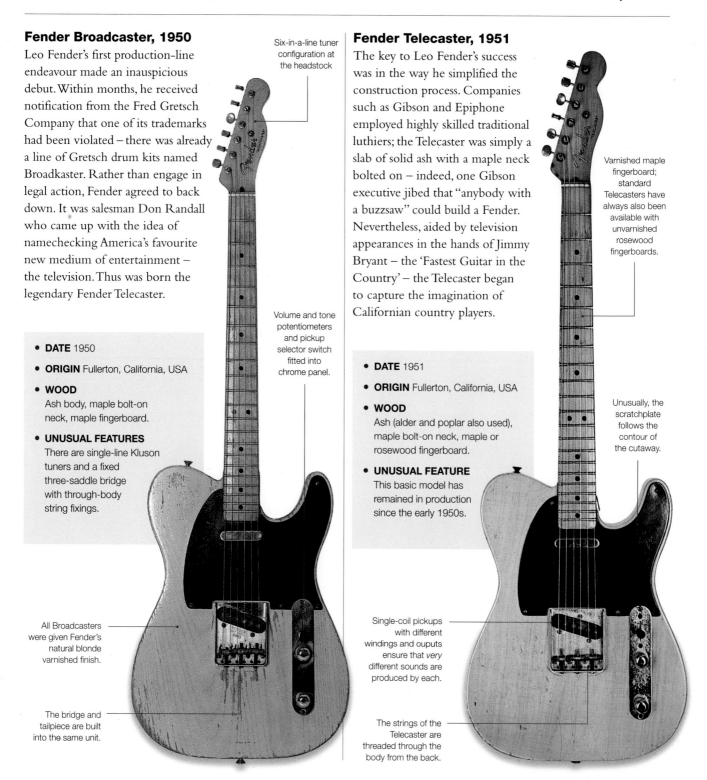

Six-in-a-line tuner configuration at the headstock

Volume and tone potentiometers and pickup selector switch fitted into chrome panel.

Varnished maple fingerboard; standard Telecasters have always also been available with unvarnished rosewood fingerboards.

Unusually, the scratchplate follows the contour of the cutaway.

All Broadcasters were given Fender's natural blonde varnished finish.

The bridge and tailpiece are built into the same unit.

Single-coil pickups with different windings and ouputs ensure that *very* different sounds are produced by each.

The strings of the Telecaster are threaded through the body from the back.

Fender Esquire, 1951

The Fender Esquire was a single-pickup instrument that evolved into the Broadcaster. Around 50 Esquires were built *before* the Broadcaster, but suffered from a number of design flaws – not least a lack of truss-rod support in the neck. The Esquire was made available as a production-line instrument in 1951. Even though it had just one pickup, the Esquire was built using the control plate from the Broadcaster, the pickup selector switch being wired to in-built tone-filter circuitry.

- **DATE** On the production line from 1951, but models bearing the name first produced in 1950
- **ORIGIN** Fullerton, California, USA
- **WOOD** Ash body (original prototypes built from pine), maple bolt-on neck, maple fingerboard.
- **UNUSUAL FEATURE** There is tone-filter switching.

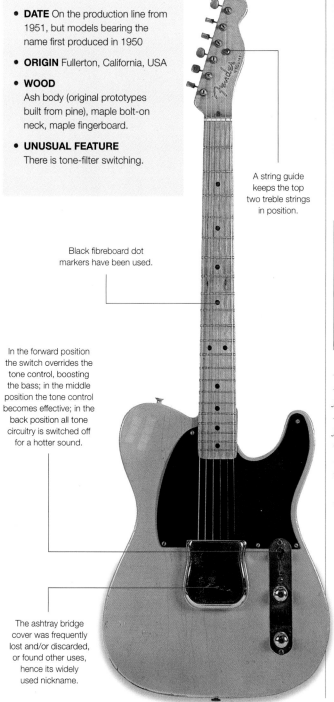

A string guide keeps the top two treble strings in position.

Black fibreboard dot markers have been used.

In the forward position the switch overrides the tone control, boosting the bass; in the middle position the tone control becomes effective; in the back position all tone circuitry is switched off for a hotter sound.

The ashtray bridge cover was frequently lost and/or discarded, or found other uses, hence its widely used nickname.

Fender Stratocaster, 1954

Although the Telecaster had taken off quickly, there was no denying that it was a very basic instrument, and Fender's feedback from players made it clear that some wanted a more sophisticated instrument. His response was the iconic Stratocaster – the most famous electric guitar ever made. Unlike its elder brother, the Strat's body was contoured for comfort, with a shape that worked just as well either standing or sitting. It also offered greater versatility in sound, with three pickups and a vibrato arm.

- **DATE** 1954
- **ORIGIN** Fullerton, California, USA
- **WOOD** Ash body (alder, poplar, basswood, mahogany and koa have also been used), maple bolt-on neck, maple or rosewood fingerboard.
- **UNUSUAL FEATURE** The bridge saddles are individually adjustable.

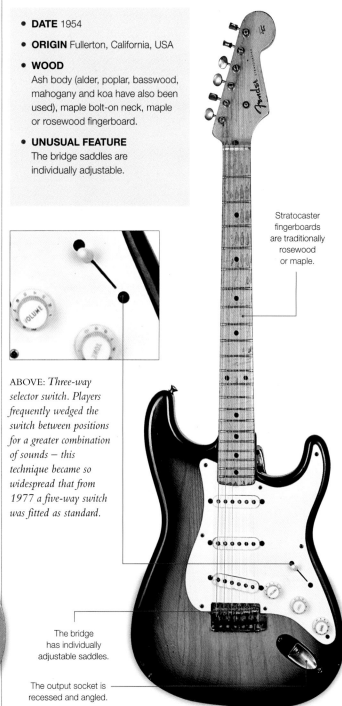

Stratocaster fingerboards are traditionally rosewood or maple.

ABOVE: *Three-way selector switch. Players frequently wedged the switch between positions for a greater combination of sounds – this technique became so widespread that from 1977 a five-way switch was fitted as standard.*

The bridge has individually adjustable saddles.

The output socket is recessed and angled.

Gibson Les Paul

In 1946, Les Paul had demonstrated his solidbody Log electric guitar to the management at Gibson. They had been unimpressed at the time, but five years later the success of Fender's solidbody electrics became a cause for concern. Les Paul – at the time a hugely popular celebrity musician – was offered the opportunity to put his name to Gibson's first solidbody electric instrument.

Gibson Les Paul Goldtop, 1952

Les Paul's role in the development of the guitar that took his name has always been a matter of dispute. President Ted McCarty always maintained that Paul was given a finished guitar for approval, and that his only real input had been the one-piece trapeze bridge and tailpiece. The first incarnation of what would one day become a legendary instrument appeared in a lurid gold finish and was launched alongside a semi-hollow counterpart, the ES-295.

- **DATE** 1952
- **ORIGIN** Kalamazoo, Michigan, USA
- **WOOD** Mahogany body, gold-painted maple top, mahogany set neck and rosewood fingerboard.
- **UNUSUAL FEATURES** The one-piece trapeze bridge has a wrap-over tailpiece, and there are two single-coil P-90 pickups.

Gibson Les Paul Custom, 1954

The Goldtop had not been the success Gibson had expected. Some thought that potential players had been put off by the garish look of the original, so in 1954 it was given a cosmetic overhaul. The result was the visually stunning Custom, dubbed Black Beauty. In 1957, the Custom underwent a major refinement, with the two single-coil pickups being replaced by three of Seth Lover's PAF humbuckers, thus creating the definitive version of the guitar.

- **DATE** 1954
- **ORIGIN** Kalamazoo, Michigan, USA
- **WOOD** Mahogany body, set maple neck and single-bound ebony fingerboard.
- **UNUSUAL FEATURES** Tune-o-matic bridge, and PAF pickups were fitted to the 1957 overhaul.

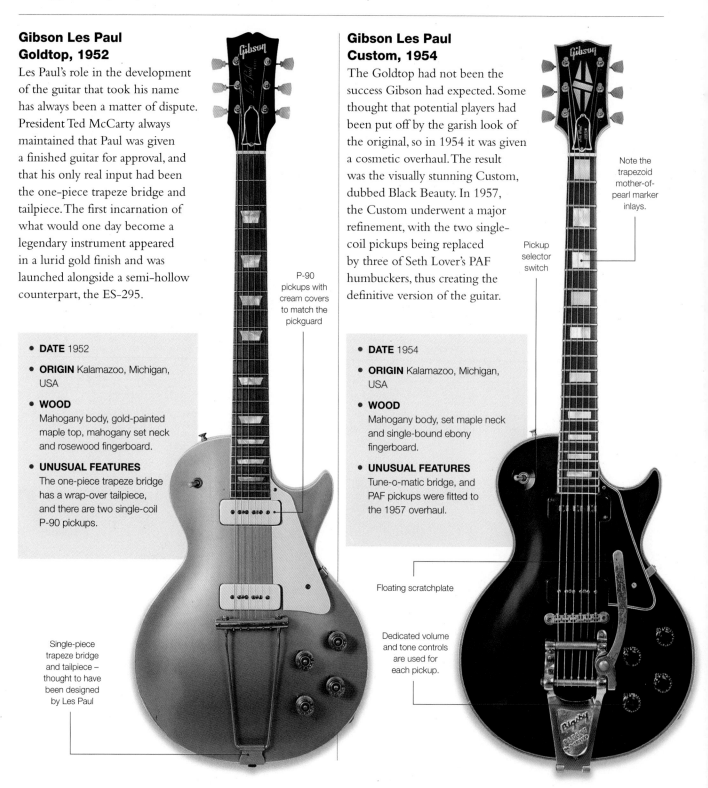

P-90 pickups with cream covers to match the pickguard

Single-piece trapeze bridge and tailpiece – thought to have been designed by Les Paul

Note the trapezoid mother-of-pearl marker inlays.

Pickup selector switch

Floating scratchplate

Dedicated volume and tone controls are used for each pickup.

Gibson Les Paul Junior, 1954

When Gibson launched the Les Paul Custom in 1954, it further extended the range with the Junior. As a basic instrument aimed at the beginner, it would prove to be a popular instrument, even among professionals. The earliest Junior was a single cutaway in the style of its elder brother, but in 1957 the body was given a dramatic overhaul. Paul Reed Smith would later use this new twin-cutaway shape as a template for his own hugely successful PRS brand.

- **DATE** 1954

- **ORIGIN** Kalamazoo, Michigan, USA

- **WOOD**
  Mahogany body, set mahogany neck, rosewood or ebony fingerboard.

- **UNUSUAL FEATURE**
  The body was significantly thinner than a standard Les Paul; body top was flat rather than arched.

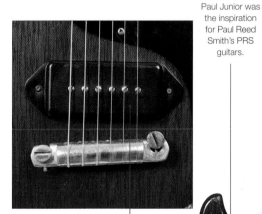

ABOVE: *The Gibson P-90 single-coil pickup was introduced in 1946 as a replacement for the Charlie Christian. It was used on most Gibson electrics until the PAF humbucker appeared in the late 1950s.*

The twin-cutaway Les Paul Junior was the inspiration for Paul Reed Smith's PRS guitars.

The twin-cutaway body was introduced in 1957.

A Gibson stud bridge/tailpiece unit is used here.

Gibson Les Paul TV, 1955

The Les Paul Junior appeared primarily in white, sunburst or cherry red finishes. In 1955, Gibson launched the TV, a new version of the Junior with a natural butterscotch finish. The guitar was a response to Gibson's concerns that white guitars would glare too much on early black-and-white television broadcasts, hence a new finish was created that was aimed at preventing this effect. Two years later, the TV was given the same twin cutaway body update as the Junior.

- **DATE** 1955

- **ORIGIN** Kalamazoo, Michigan, USA

- **WOOD**
  Mahogany body, set mahogany neck, rosewood fingerboard.

- **UNUSUAL FEATURE**
  A single cutaway was used from 1955 to 1957; a twin cutaway from 1957 to 1963.

The original Les Paul TV, like the Junior, featured a single-cutaway body.

Acrylic dot markers

P-90 pickups were replaced by humbucking PAFs from 1957.

The electric bass

Leo Fender had already kicked off a revolution in 1950 with the creation of the Fender Broadcaster – the first production-line solidbody electric guitar. His second great innovation came a year later when he used the same construction principles to produce the first electric bass guitar. By the end of the decade, it was well on the way to rendering the upright acoustic bass redundant in most forms of popular music.

Fender Precision, 1951

A counterpart to the six-string Telecaster, the Precision bass shared many of its design features. Its appeal was clear: it was smaller and easier for the jobbing musician to take to gigs, and the fretted fingerboard required less skill than an acoustic bass to play accurately, which saw many guitarists able to double up on bass. Jazz player Monk Montgomery was the first professional player to adopt the Precision when touring with the Lionel Hampton Orchestra.

- **DATE** 1951
- **ORIGIN** Fullerton, California, USA
- **WOOD**
  Ash body, maple bolt-on neck and rosewood fingerboard.
- **UNUSUAL FEATURES**
  The Precision was given a redesign in 1953, and has remained in production ever since. It also has a single split-P pickup.

Fender split-P pickup

Master volume and tone controls

Gibson EB-2, 1958

Previously well established as America's leading guitar manufacturer, Gibson struggled with the pace of change forced by Fender during the 1950s, spending much of the decade chasing each new innovation. Gibson responded to the Fender Precision with the unusual EB-1 violin bass, and the later EB-2, a semi-hollowbody instrument, was launched as a bass counterpart to the ES-355 six-string. It was widely used by beat groups during the 1960s.

- **DATE** 1958
- **ORIGIN** Kalamazoo, Michigan, USA
- **WOOD**
  Maple top, maple back and sides, one-piece mahogany set neck.
- **UNUSUAL FEATURE**
  Single pickup; the twin pickup version – the EB-2D – was launched in 1968.

The instrument features a 20-fret fingerboard.

Raised scratchplate

Note the f-holes.

The single-piece bridge unit includes a slotted tailstock.

Baritone bass filter switch alters the tone of the bass frequencies.

Silvertone 1444, 1959

US retailing giant Sears, Roebuck and Company used the brand name Silvertone. From the middle of the 1950s, Silvertone budget electric guitars and amplification offered many young US musicians their first opportunity to own such equipment. Sears did not produce their own instruments, however – those supplied by established US names such as Danelectro, National, Harmony and Kay were simply rebranded. The model here, produced by Danelectro and based on its U Series, was one of the cheapest basses on the market – retailing on launch at $79.99 – and it sold in the 1960s in large quantities.

- **DATE** 1959

- **ORIGIN** Neptune, New Jersey, USA

- **WOOD**
  Pine frame, Masonite top and back, vinyl tape edging, bolt-on maple neck and rosewood fingerboard.

- **UNUSUAL FEATURE**
  The Silvertone 'dolphin-nose' headstock shape.

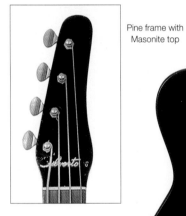

ABOVE: *Visually, the Silvertone models can be distinguished from their Danelectro counterparts by the headstock shape. Danelectros also have a characteristic contour like a Coke bottle.*

Vinyl tape edging

Pine frame with Masonite top

Who invented the bass guitar?

That Leo Fender was a great innovator is beyond all doubt. While he was responsible for the first mass-produced bass guitar, however, he certainly wasn't the first to come up with the idea. Indeed, Gibson's Lloyd Loar, who was known to have experimented with magnetic pickups during the 1920s, produced a prototype electric double bass. Perhaps the true father of the bass guitar, though, was Paul Tutmarc, a musician and inventor from Seattle, who began experimenting with a reduction in size of the double bass during the 1930s.

In 1935, he built an electronic upright bull fiddle, which he used primarily as a publicity device for his own Audiovox company. However, Tutmarc's place in history comes from the development of the Audiovox Model 736 Electronic Bass Fiddle. Launched in 1937, this solidbody fretted instrument, designed to be played in the horizontal position, was the first true electric bass guitar. That Tutmarc's invention was not a commercial success was probably related more to its unsuitability for the prevailing musical styles of the era rather than the quality of the instrument. Like the work of many other innovators, Tutmarc's invention was too far ahead of its time.

ABOVE: *Paul Tutmarc standing alongside his Audiovox Model 736, the first electric bass guitar.*

The Danelectro bridge unit is extremely basic. The string ends are secured in slots at the rear of a trapezoid metal block, and the saddle is simply a piece of rosewood. Overall height is governed by a screw on the metal block, and intonation is achieved by moving the saddle along the strings.

Gretsch solidbody electrics

The first electric guitar launched by Gretsch was the Electromatic Spanish, in 1939 – more than a half a century after German immigrant Friedrich Gretsch had settled in Brooklyn, New York, and created a successful music-retail business. During the 1950s, under the leadership of his son Fred Gretsch Jr, the company forged an international reputation for its drum kits and exquisitely designed electric guitars.

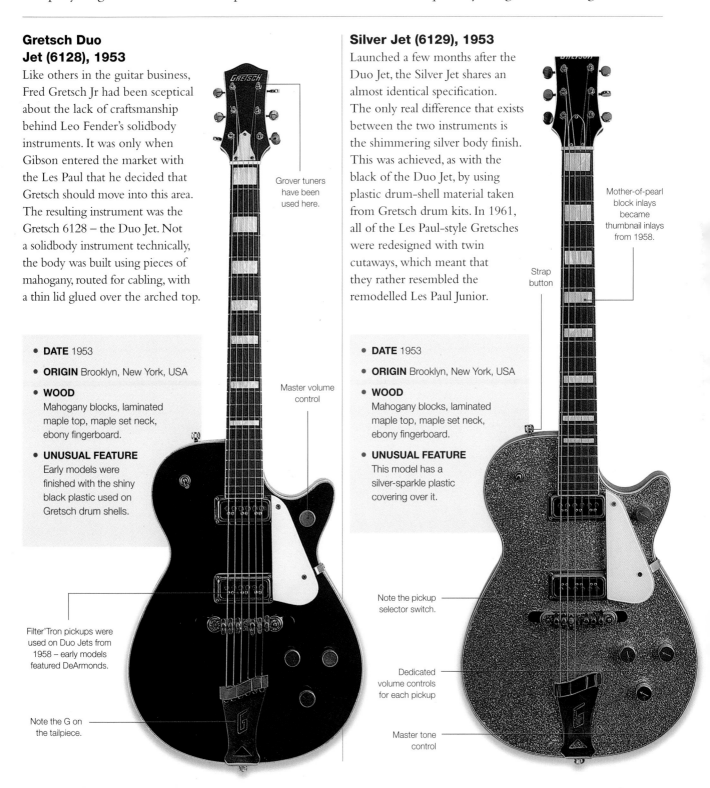

Gretsch Duo Jet (6128), 1953

Like others in the guitar business, Fred Gretsch Jr had been sceptical about the lack of craftsmanship behind Leo Fender's solidbody instruments. It was only when Gibson entered the market with the Les Paul that he decided that Gretsch should move into this area. The resulting instrument was the Gretsch 6128 – the Duo Jet. Not a solidbody instrument technically, the body was built using pieces of mahogany, routed for cabling, with a thin lid glued over the arched top.

Grover tuners have been used here.

Master volume control

- **DATE** 1953
- **ORIGIN** Brooklyn, New York, USA
- **WOOD**
  Mahogany blocks, laminated maple top, maple set neck, ebony fingerboard.
- **UNUSUAL FEATURE**
  Early models were finished with the shiny black plastic used on Gretsch drum shells.

Filter'Tron pickups were used on Duo Jets from 1958 – early models featured DeArmonds.

Note the G on the tailpiece.

Silver Jet (6129), 1953

Launched a few months after the Duo Jet, the Silver Jet shares an almost identical specification. The only real difference that exists between the two instruments is the shimmering silver body finish. This was achieved, as with the black of the Duo Jet, by using plastic drum-shell material taken from Gretsch drum kits. In 1961, all of the Les Paul-style Gretsches were redesigned with twin cutaways, which meant that they rather resembled the remodelled Les Paul Junior.

Mother-of-pearl block inlays became thumbnail inlays from 1958.

Strap button

- **DATE** 1953
- **ORIGIN** Brooklyn, New York, USA
- **WOOD**
  Mahogany blocks, laminated maple top, maple set neck, ebony fingerboard.
- **UNUSUAL FEATURE**
  This model has a silver-sparkle plastic covering over it.

Note the pickup selector switch.

Dedicated volume controls for each pickup

Master tone control

White Penguin (6134), 1955

The most desirable of Gretsch guitars, the White Penguin is the solidbody partner of the famous White Falcon. It is based broadly on the Duo Jet, but with a dramatic snow-white finish and opulent trimmings. The White Penguin's legendary status comes from the fact that nobody knows precisely how many of them were originally built – as few as 20, according to some experts – which explains why they can now reach $100,000 at auction.

ABOVE: *Long-term Gretsch employee Charles 'Duke' Kramer claimed the guitar was so named "because a penguin has a white front". The scratchplate also features a cartoon penguin.*

Grover Imperial tuners have been fitted on the headstock.

- **DATE** 1955
- **ORIGIN** Brooklyn, New York, USA
- **WOOD**
  Mahogany blocks, laminated maple top, maple set neck, ebony fingerboard.
- **UNUSUAL FEATURE**
  The gold-sparkle trim and gold-plated hardware.

A Melita Syncro-Sonic bridge has been used.

The arm-rest is gold-plated.

Gretsch G Cadillac tailpiece

Chet Atkins Solidbody (6121), 1955

The single most important figure in the popularization of Gretsch guitars was expert country-picker Chet Atkins. Long respected within the confines of the Nashville country-music scene, by the mid-1950s he was widely revered as one of the world's best guitarists. Gretsch put considerable efforts into courting Atkins before he finally agreed to put his name to two models: the 6121 Solidbody and the better-known 6120 Hollowbody.

- **DATE** 1955
- **ORIGIN** Brooklyn, New York, USA
- **WOOD**
  Mahogany body, maple top, maple set neck, ebony fingerboard.
- **UNUSUAL FEATURE**
  Early models had cowboy motifs, which Atkins disliked, so by 1958 these had been removed.

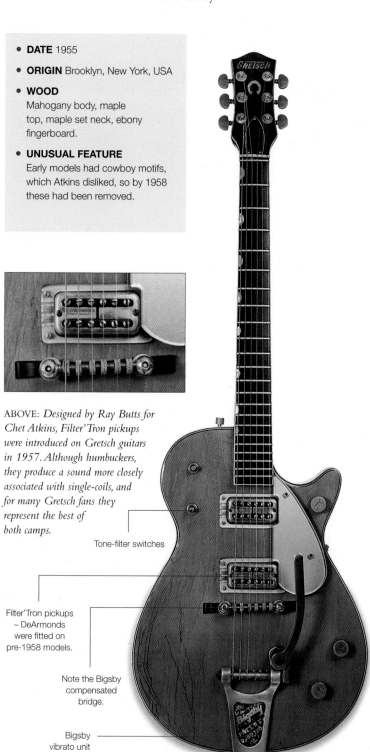

ABOVE: *Designed by Ray Butts for Chet Atkins, Filter'Tron pickups were introduced on Gretsch guitars in 1957. Although humbuckers, they produce a sound more closely associated with single-coils, and for many Gretsch fans they represent the best of both camps.*

Tone-filter switches

Filter'Tron pickups – DeArmonds were fitted on pre-1958 models.

Note the Bigsby compensated bridge.

Bigsby vibrato unit

Gretsch hollowbodies

The 1950s was a truly significant decade in the history of the guitar, most notably for the birth and rapid spread in popularity of solidbody electric instruments. Although the Gretsch company was quick to join this revolution, it is perhaps for its range of exquisite hollowbody models, launched during that same period, for which the brand is now most highly regarded.

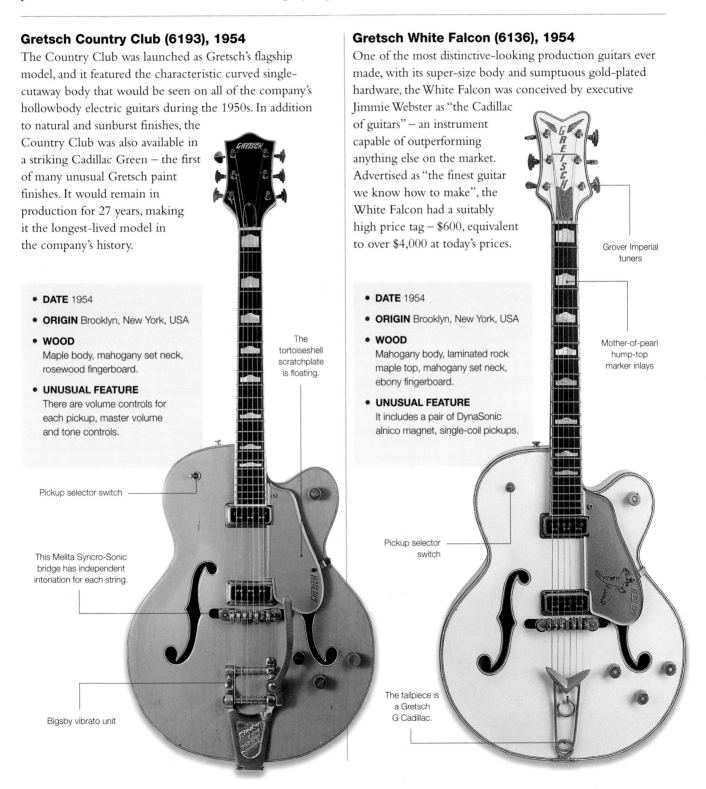

Gretsch Country Club (6193), 1954

The Country Club was launched as Gretsch's flagship model, and it featured the characteristic curved single-cutaway body that would be seen on all of the company's hollowbody electric guitars during the 1950s. In addition to natural and sunburst finishes, the Country Club was also available in a striking Cadillac Green – the first of many unusual Gretsch paint finishes. It would remain in production for 27 years, making it the longest-lived model in the company's history.

- **DATE** 1954

- **ORIGIN** Brooklyn, New York, USA

- **WOOD**
  Maple body, mahogany set neck, rosewood fingerboard.

- **UNUSUAL FEATURE**
  There are volume controls for each pickup, master volume and tone controls.

Pickup selector switch

The tortoiseshell scratchplate is floating.

This Melita Syncro-Sonic bridge has independent intonation for each string.

Bigsby vibrato unit

Gretsch White Falcon (6136), 1954

One of the most distinctive-looking production guitars ever made, with its super-size body and sumptuous gold-plated hardware, the White Falcon was conceived by executive Jimmie Webster as "the Cadillac of guitars" – an instrument capable of outperforming anything else on the market. Advertised as "the finest guitar we know how to make", the White Falcon had a suitably high price tag – $600, equivalent to over $4,000 at today's prices.

- **DATE** 1954

- **ORIGIN** Brooklyn, New York, USA

- **WOOD**
  Mahogany body, laminated rock maple top, mahogany set neck, ebony fingerboard.

- **UNUSUAL FEATURE**
  It includes a pair of DynaSonic alnico magnet, single-coil pickups.

Grover Imperial tuners

Mother-of-pearl hump-top marker inlays

Pickup selector switch

The tailpiece is a Gretsch G Cadillac.

Chet Atkins Country Gentleman (7670), 1957

The ideal endorsee, Chet Atkins was rarely photographed without one of his signature Gretsch guitars at hand during the 1950s. Although both solidbody and hollowbody Chet Atkins models had been successful, Atkins himself had not been entirely happy with the sound of the pickups, nor the corny cactus-and-cattle motifs. In 1957, he was given the opportunity to address these concerns with a new signature model. Widely used in the USA by country and rockabilly players, the Country Gentleman was exposed to a wider audience in the 1960s when, for a period, it became George Harrison's preferred guitar while performing with The Beatles.

- **DATE** 1957

- **ORIGIN** Brooklyn, New York, USA

- **WOOD**
  Mahogany body, mahogany set neck, ebony fingerboard.

- **UNUSUAL FEATURES**
  Filter'Tron humbucking pickups and a Bigsby vibrato unit are used.

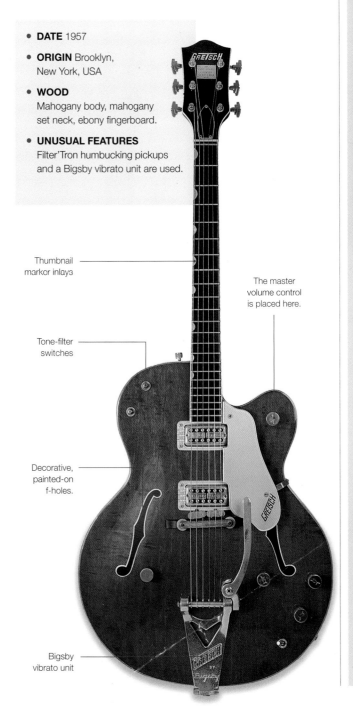

Thumbnail marker inlays

Tone-filter switches

The master volume control is placed here.

Decorative, painted-on f-holes.

Bigsby vibrato unit

Chet Atkins and Gretsch

ABOVE: *Chet Atkins was widely known in Nashville as the Country Gentleman.*

Having taken the decision to compete directly with the new electric guitar market leaders, executive Jimmie Webster knew that what Gretsch needed was its own Les Paul-type endorsement. In Chet Atkins he found a young, respected Nashville session player on his way to a global reputation as one of the instrument's all-time masters. Although the guitarist would take considerable persuading, the first two Chet Atkins models emerged in 1955. These instruments would become massively successful – establishing Gretsch to be taken seriously as a guitar manufacturer for the first time – and yet the perfectionist Atkins was unhappy with the thin tone of the DeArmond pickup.

His solution was to commission sound expert Ray Butts to come up with a humbucking pickup that could nonetheless retain the characteristic single-coil treble bite. The result was the Filter'Tron, which would soon become standard on all Gretsch guitars, and contribute to the enduring success of the 1957 Chet Atkins' Country Gentleman. Without Chet Atkins' endorsement, Gretsch guitars would almost certainly not have enjoyed the same profile or enduring reputation. He certainly saw it that way: "If Jimmie Webster were alive, he'd tell you that the most important thing he ever did was sign me... because they started selling the hell out of guitars!"

American hollowbodies

While Gibson, Epiphone and Gretsch may have been the most notable commercial names in the production of hollowbody electrics, there were a number of other outstanding American manufacturers in the market. John D'Angelico made some of the finest pre-war acoustic archtops, and his apprentice James D'Aquisto would later be described by George Gruhn as a "modern-day Stradivarius".

Guild Stuart X500, 1953

The Guild brand was founded in 1952 in Manhattan, mainly to produce high-end archtop jazz guitars, although much of its commercial success came in the 1960s by producing flat-top acoustics for the New York folk scene. The Guild Stuart X-500 was designed to compete with premium competitors, such as the Gibson L-5CES and Epiphone Zephyr Emperor Regent. It features a 432mm (17in) Venetian cutaway body and gold-plated hardware throughout. Humbucking pickups were added in 1963.

- **DATE** 1953

- **ORIGIN** Manhattan, New York, USA

- **WOOD**
  Maple back and sides, spruce top, ebony fingerboard. Set mahogany neck.

- **UNUSUAL FEATURE**
  The scratchplate style is influenced by D'Angelico.

D'Angelico electric, 1955

New York luthier John D'Angelico had little interest in mass production, his output peaking in 1939 when 30 guitars came out of his workshop. D'Angelico's guitars were clearly styled after the Gibson L-5, but since they were all custom-built, there is huge variation in individual specifications. Although primarily a maker of archtop acoustics, he did produce a number of electrics, of which this left-handed model is one example.

- **DATE** 1955

- **ORIGIN** New York, USA

- **WOOD**
  European maple back and sides, hand-carved spruce top, set maple neck, ebony fingerboard.

- **UNUSUAL FEATURE**
  This model is a rare left-handed D'Angelico.

Gold-plated Grover Rotomatic tuners

Bevelled Art-Deco stairstep scratchplate

From 1963, Guild produced its own humbuckers – as seen on the model shown here.

Compensated ebony bridge

This gold-plated tailpiece has been hand-engraved.

There are mother-of-pearl block inlays.

The basic body shape was inspired by the Gibson L-5.

Note the engraved D'Angelico tailpiece.

Harmony H71 Meteor, 1958

While not in the same league as D'Angelico or D'Aquisto, Harmony was notable as one of the biggest producers of acoustic and electric archtops. The marque dates back to 1892, but only became a major player after it was acquired by Sears Roebuck in 1916. In the 30 years following the end of World War II, Harmony is estimated to have mass-produced more than 10 million guitars. The thin hollowbody Meteor range first appeared in 1958 and, although reasonably priced, was the very top end of the department-store guitar market.

- **DATE** Launched with the H70 model in 1958

- **ORIGIN** Chicago, Illinois, USA

- **WOOD**
  Laminated maple body, spruce top, rosewood fretboard.

- **UNUSUAL FEATURES**
  Single- and twin-pickup versions were available, and trapeze tailpiece or Bigsby vibrato options.

The body is a blonde finish; the H70 was identical but with a sunburst finish.

Early models such as this featured Golden Tone pickups.

Each of the two pickups has dedicated volume and tone controls.

The pickup selector switch is fitted to the cutaway horn.

D'Aquisto electric, 1965

When John D'Angelico died in 1964, his former apprentice James D'Aquisto took over his workshop. Although his guitars show the clear influence of the D'Angelico tradition, D'Aquisto was soon established as one of America's most important luthiers, noted for his experimental approach to construction, bridge design and soundhole positioning. D'Aquisto died suddenly in 1995 – and his guitars can now fetch more than half a million dollars at auction.

- **DATE** 1965

- **ORIGIN** New York, USA

- **WOOD**
  European maple back and sides, maple top, set mahogany neck, ebony-covered headstock, ebony fingerboard.

- **UNUSUAL FEATURE**
  It has a pair of Guild gold-plated humbucking pickups.

Mother-of-pearl block inlays

Two-piece carved ebony bridge

ABOVE: *Even on his early models, D'Aquisto added his own touches to D'Angelico's style, using smooth-edged f-holes, unlike the more pointed versions of his predecessor.*

The new Rickenbacker

Adolph Rickenbacker had been one of the pioneers of the electric guitar in the 1930s, but had chosen to concentrate on lap steels instead of Spanish designs. In 1953, with his market in decline, Rickenbacker sold his company to Francis C. Hall, who had seen the commercial potential of the electric guitar while working as a distributor for Leo Fender, and who successfully relaunched the brand.

Combo 600, 1954

The first of the new-era Rickenbacker solidbody instruments emerged in 1954. The Combo 600 was a 21-fret, single-pickup instrument. Positioned by the bridge, the large horseshoe-magnet pickup was essentially the same design as that created by George Beauchamp in the 1930s. The Combo 600 was the first Rickenbacker to feature the now-famous pointed swoosh logo on the truss-rod cover, a design created by Francis C. Hall's wife.

- **DATE** 1954
- **ORIGIN** Santa Ana, California, USA
- **WOOD**
  Maple body, set maple neck, rosewood fingerboard.
- **UNUSUAL FEATURE**
  Filter switch for altering the guitar's EQ.

Combo 800, 1954

Launched alongside the Combo 600, the Combo 800 was essentially the same instrument but with a different pickup arrangement. The 800 featured the unpatented Rickenbacker Multiple-Unit, which had twin coils. When used in combination, these coils were, in effect, humbuckers; when used separately, one coil accentuated treble and one bass. A switch beneath the tailpiece controlled this operation. The new Rickenbacker line was designed mainly by Paul Barth, who was one of the original founders of the company.

- **DATE** 1954
- **ORIGIN** Santa Ana, California, USA
- **WOOD**
  Maple body, set maple neck, rosewood fingerboard.
- **UNUSUAL FEATURE**
  The multiple-unit twin-coil pickup, coil switch and tone switch are notable.

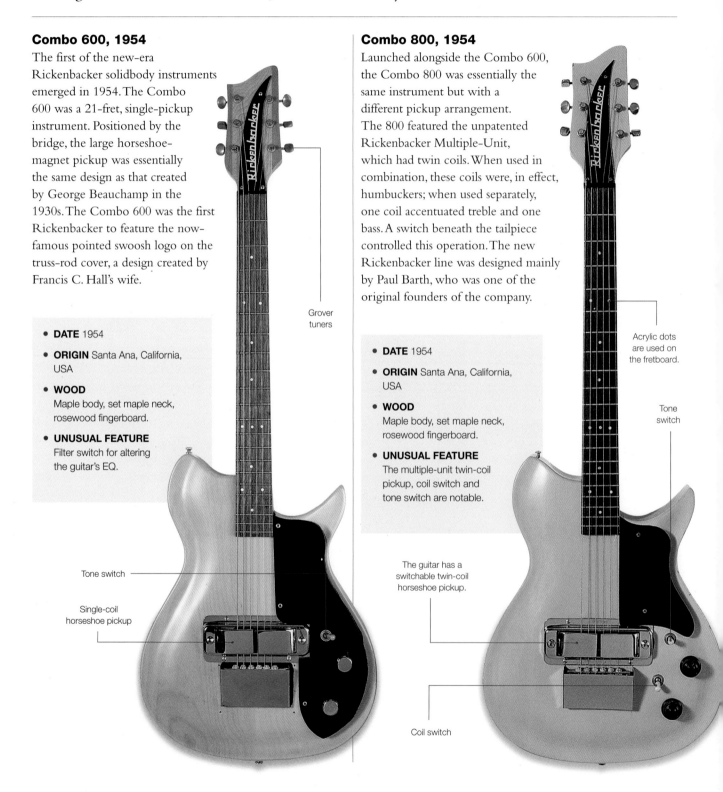

Grover tuners

Tone switch

Single-coil horseshoe pickup

Acrylic dots are used on the fretboard.

Tone switch

The guitar has a switchable twin-coil horseshoe pickup.

Coil switch

Combo 450, 1957

In 1956, Rickenbacker produced its first notable solidbody electric guitar, the single-pickup Combo 400, followed by the twin-pickup Combo 450. It was most significant, however, as the first Rickenbacker to use a straight-through neck construction, where the centre of the body and neck were cut from a single piece of wood, with treble and bass wings fixed on separately. Thought to improve tone and sustain, this technique became a standard feature of Rickenbackers thereafter.

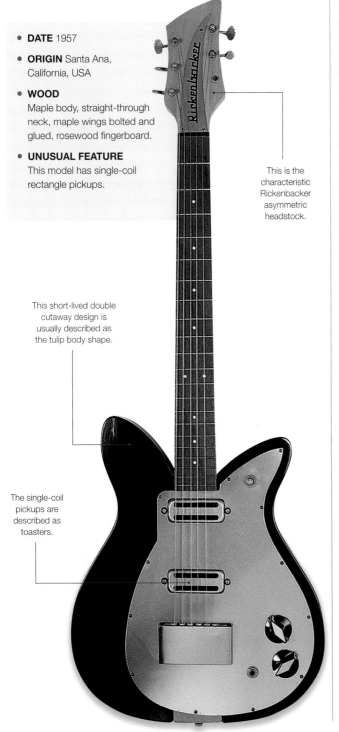

- **DATE** 1957
- **ORIGIN** Santa Ana, California, USA
- **WOOD** Maple body, straight-through neck, maple wings bolted and glued, rosewood fingerboard.
- **UNUSUAL FEATURE** This model has single-coil rectangle pickups.

This is the characteristic Rickenbacker asymmetric headstock.

This short-lived double cutaway design is usually described as the tulip body shape.

The single-coil pickups are described as toasters.

Model 1000, 1957

The double-cutaway tulip body shape enjoyed only a brief life, being replaced by the more famous cresting wave design in 1958. This range of instruments, however, saw the passing of the horseshoe pickup, in use in one form or another since the early 1930s. It was replaced by the smaller single-coil toaster design – so-called for its resemblance from above to a 1950s pop-up toaster. The Model 1000 was actually a three-quarter-size student model with an unusually short fingerboard of only 18 frets.

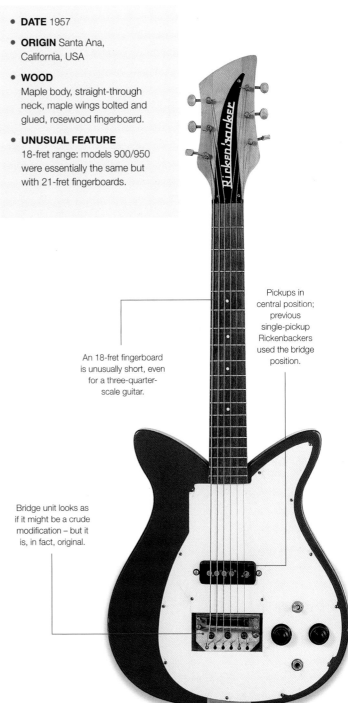

- **DATE** 1957
- **ORIGIN** Santa Ana, California, USA
- **WOOD** Maple body, straight-through neck, maple wings bolted and glued, rosewood fingerboard.
- **UNUSUAL FEATURE** 18-fret range: models 900/950 were essentially the same but with 21-fret fingerboards.

Pickups in central position; previous single-pickup Rickenbackers used the bridge position.

An 18-fret fingerboard is unusually short, even for a three-quarter-scale guitar.

Bridge unit looks as if it might be a crude modification – but it is, in fact, original.

Danelectro

Daniel Electrical Laboratories began life in 1947 in a New York loft. Founder Nathan Daniel was a talented engineer who established his company producing amplifiers for the Sears Roebuck retail catalogue. He built his first Danelectro guitars in 1954 with the aim of offering eye-catching designs, innovative construction techniques and, above all, an affordable price.

Danelectro U2, 1956

The Les Paul-inspired U range of guitars, launched in 1956, was the first to make use of Daniel's radical approach to guitar construction. Eschewing the traditional solid wood body, his Danelectro guitars comprised a frame built from cheap but strong poplar. It was covered top and bottom with Masonite – a material created from steam-compressed woodchips. The resulting instrument was light and could also be constructed at a greater speed than more conventional techniques allowed.

- **DATE** 1956
- **ORIGIN** Neptune, New Jersey, USA
- **WOOD**
  Poplar frame with bridge and neck blocks, covered with a layer of Masonite, maple bolt-on neck, rosewood fingerboard.
- **UNUSUAL FEATURE**
  The pickups are a lipstick-case design.

Danelectro Shorthorn, 1958

When Daniel dropped the U range in 1958, he replaced it with two new designs – the Shorthorn and the Longhorn, each identifiable by the depth of their twin cutaways. The Shorthorn was available with one, two or three pickups, as well as short-scale bass, and, most interestingly, as a double-neck guitar. Although Danelectros were budget instruments, they retained the affection of some of their early users: at the peak of his Led Zeppelin career, Jimmy Page would often use his Shorthorn in concert.

- **DATE** 1958
- **ORIGIN** Neptune, New Jersey, USA
- **WOOD**
  Poplar frame with bridge and neck blocks, covered with a layer of Masonite, maple bolt-on neck, rosewood fingerboard.
- **UNUSUAL FEATURE**
  This has concentric potentiometers.

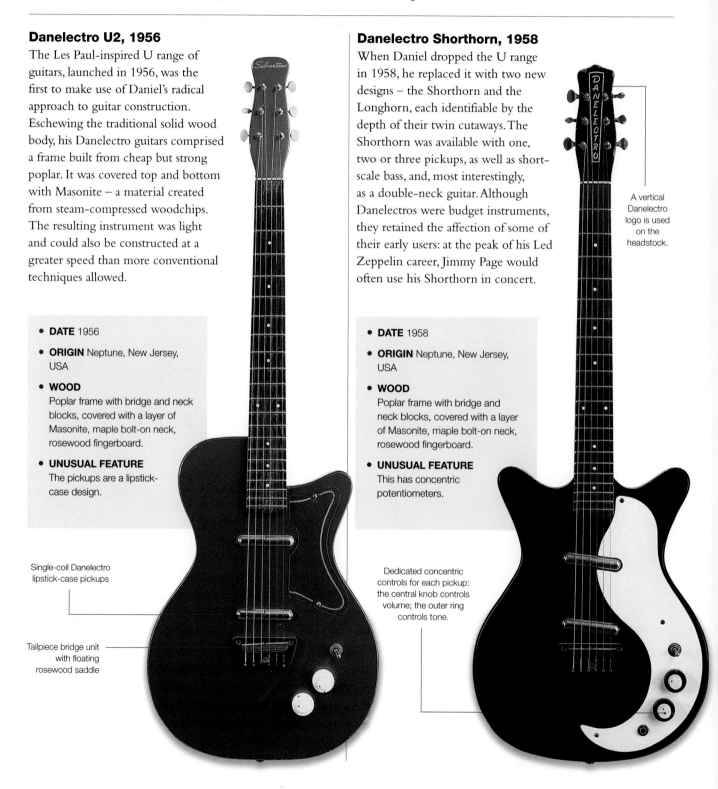

A vertical Danelectro logo is used on the headstock.

Single-coil Danelectro lipstick-case pickups

Tailpiece bridge unit with floating rosewood saddle

Dedicated concentric controls for each pickup: the central knob controls volume; the outer ring controls tone.

Danelectro Longhorn Bass, 1958

For over five decades since its launch in 1958, the Danelectro Longhorn has polarized players with its extreme appearance. Originally available as a four-string or six-string bass and as the curious Guitarlin – a six-string guitar with the pitch range of a mandolin – it was frequently heard on twangy rock 'n' roll guitar instrumentals of the period. The four-string bass, with its distinctive low-end thud, remains popular today, even as a modern-day reissue.

- **DATE** 1958

- **ORIGIN** Neptune, New Jersey, USA

- **WOOD**
  Poplar frame with bridge and neck blocks, covered with 15mm (⅝in) Masonite, maple bolt-on neck, rosewood fingerboard.

- **UNUSUAL FEATURE**
  Unusually deep cutaways and elongated horns.

This is known as a Coke-bottle headstock.

Λ two octave fingerboard is extremely unusual on a bass guitar.

'Chicken-head' knobs have been fitted to concentric potentiometers.

The Sears Roebuck effect

Silvertone has a special place in the affections of many American guitarists who, as teenagers, had a first taste of the electric guitar courtesy of the Sears Roebuck catalogue. These instruments were cheap, rudimentary and sold in massive quantities. Guitars and amplifiers were sourced by Sears from the likes of Danelectro, Harmony, Kay and National – and later from Japanese manufacturers such as Teisco. These guitars may have not have represented the last word in luthiery, but they were ideal for learning the basics. Age factors alone have now made some of these instruments quite desirable to collectors, or for young musicians seeking an authentic retro look.

ABOVE: *Beck Hansen is frequently seen in concert playing his vintage Silvertone 1448. Built by Danelectro in the early 1960s, it was sold by Sears Roebuck as part of the Amp-in-Case range. The package comprised a guitar, hard-shell case with small in-built amplifier and speaker, lead and how-to-play 7in record. It retailed for $67.95 – by contrast, during the same period, you could have expected to pay $450 for a brand new Gibson SG Custom.*

The Gibson Modernistic line

Although Gibson had produced some outstanding electric guitars, towards the end of the 1950s it looked increasingly as if it was Fender who had captured the imagination of the market. In an effort to redress the balance, Gibson President Ted McCarty set about personally designing a range of futuristic solidbody instruments aimed at shedding his company's conservative image.

Gibson Flying V, 1958

The first of McCarty's Modernistic guitars came off the production line in 1958. With its distinctive space-age looks, the Flying V was like nothing ever produced before. The prototypes for the Flying V had not been successful: the mahogany body resulted in a heavy, poorly balanced instrument, but the issued was resolved by using a lighter wood, korina. Blues star Albert King adopted the Flying V as his signature guitar, but few others followed. It was discontinued a year later.

- **DATE** 1958

- **ORIGIN** Kalamazoo, Michigan, USA

- **WOOD**
  Korina body, korina/mahogany set neck, rosewood or ebony fingerboard.

- **UNUSUAL FEATURES**
  Has a pair of Gibson PAF humbucking pickups and was successfully reissued in 1967.

Gibson Explorer, 1958

Originally dubbed the Futura, the Explorer was the second design in Gibson's Modernistic range. Its specification differed from the Flying V, although its body shape was just as radical. The first instruments were produced with an unusual split headstock, but this was quickly replaced by the better-known drooping hockey-stick style. However, it turned out to be a spectacular commercial failure; fewer than 50 original models are thought to have survived.

- **DATE** 1958

- **ORIGIN** Kalamazoo, Michigan, USA

- **WOOD**
  Korina body, korina/mahogany/maple set neck, rosewood or ebony fingerboard.

- **UNUSUAL FEATURE**
  It was successfully reissued in 1976.

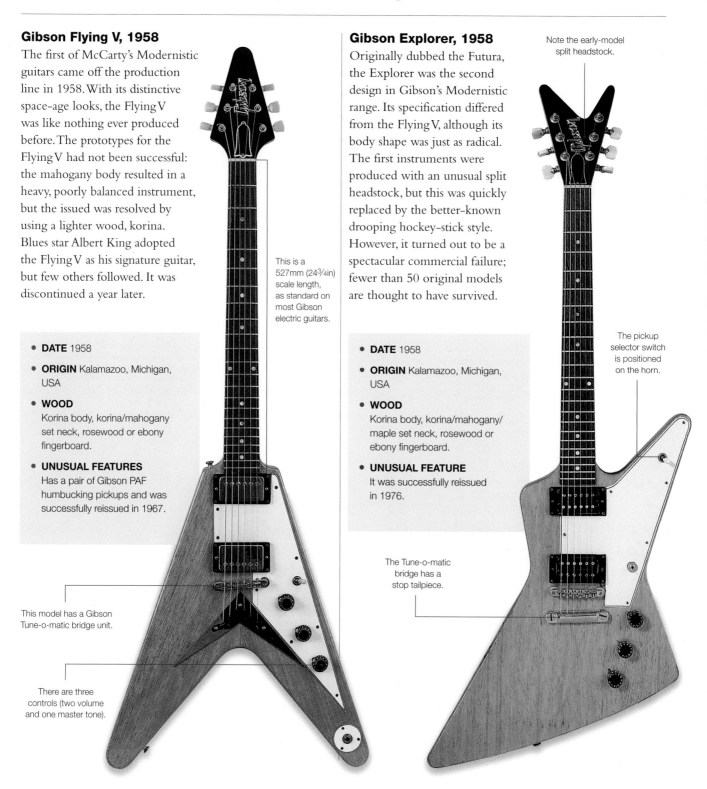

This is a 527mm (24¾in) scale length, as standard on most Gibson electric guitars.

This model has a Gibson Tune-o-matic bridge unit.

There are three controls (two volume and one master tone).

Note the early-model split headstock.

The pickup selector switch is positioned on the horn.

The Tune-o-matic bridge has a stop tailpiece.

Gibson Moderne, 1980

Ted McCarty's reinventions of the electric guitar concluded with the Moderne, which never actually made the production line in the 1950s. Possible prototypes have been described as the Holy Grail of collectible electric guitars, yet there is no proof that any instruments were ever built. Having successfully re-established the Flying V and Explorer years after their first, brief appearances, the Moderne finally debuted in 1980. It resembles a Flying V with a scooped-out treble bout and Gumby-style headstock, named after the animated character in a US television programme.

- **DATE** Designed in 1957 but first built in 1980.
- **ORIGIN** Kalamazoo, Michigan, USA
- **WOOD** Korina, mahogany or poplar body, mahogany set neck, rosewood or ebony fingerboard.
- **UNUSUAL FEATURE** Gibson models were built until 1983. Korean-built Epiphone Modernes were offered later.

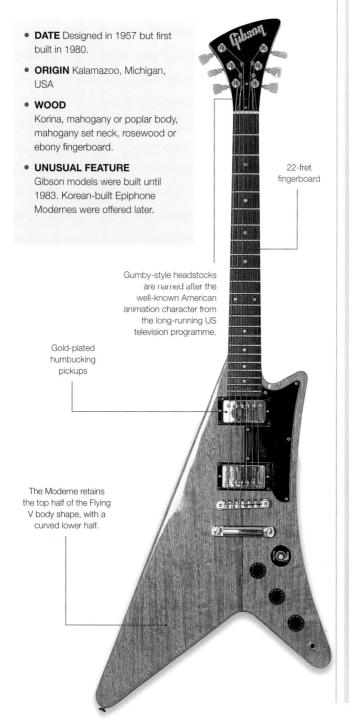

22-fret fingerboard

Gumby-style headstocks are named after the well-known American animation character from the long-running US television programme.

Gold-plated humbucking pickups

The Moderne retains the top half of the Flying V body shape, with a curved lower half.

The futuristic Gibsons

When asked in 2001 about the background to his Modernistic line, former Gibson president Ted McCarty gave a frank response: "Fender was talking about how Gibson was a bunch of old fuddie-duddies...I was a little peeved. So I said, 'Let's shake 'em up.' I wanted to come up with some guitar shapes that were different from anything else."

In 1957, US patents were granted for three new designs, and a year later the Flying V and Explorer models debuted at the annual NAMM trade show. Although they created a great deal of interest, they were dismal commercial failures. Mirroring the fate of the Les Paul, during the 1960s old Flying Vs began to increase rapidly in value until, in 1966, Gibson resumed production. Nowadays, however, vintage collectors regard these as among the most valuable of any Gibson production models.

ABOVE: *Albert King is considered to be one of the most influential electric blues guitarists of the 1950s. The only well-known musician to adopt a Flying V from the original launch, it became King's signature instrument throughout his career.*

Fender: the second generation

The late 1950s saw Fender – a company that barely existed ten years earlier – now dominating the electric guitar market with its Telecaster and Stratocaster models, and its revolutionary Precision bass guitar was increasingly usurping the traditional territory of the upright acoustic bass. Yet Leo Fender was still able to identify areas in which he felt his range required further development.

Fender Jazzmaster, 1958

First seen at the 1958, Fender's intended flagship model was aimed squarely at the jazz-and-blues musician. The most visually striking feature is the body's offset waist – the inward curves are not aligned as they had been on the Stratocaster. The aim was to make playing the guitar more comfortable sitting down – as favoured by jazz players. The soapbar pickups were also unusual for Fender, replicating the warmth of a Gibson humbucker without losing the clarity of a single coil.

- **DATE** 1958
- **ORIGIN** Fullerton, California, USA
- **WOOD**
  Alder or ash body (basswood on later models) maple bolt-on neck, rosewood or maple fingerboard.
- **UNUSUAL FEATURE**
  Non-standard Fender single-coil pickups' electrics are included in the rhythm-circuit tone-filter switch.

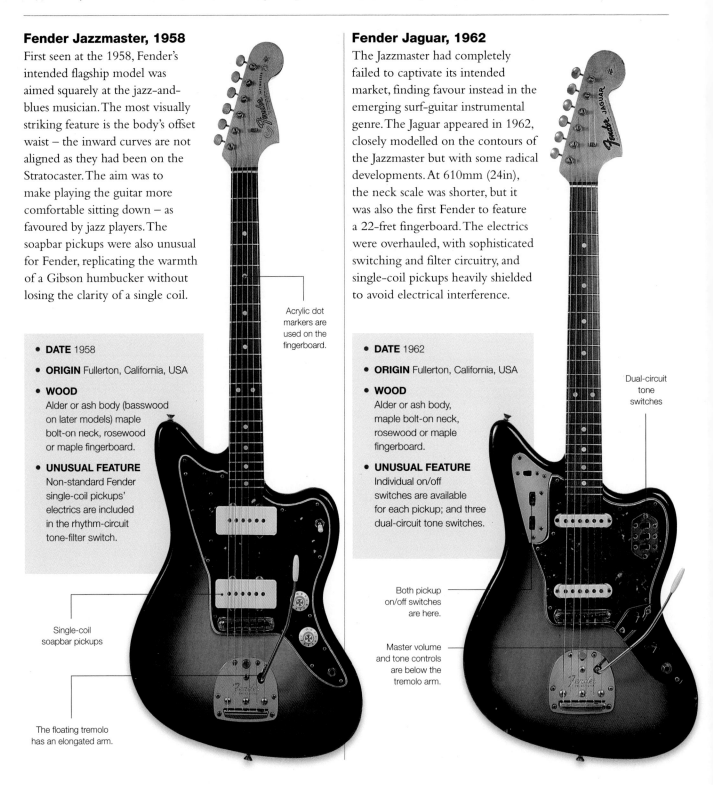

Acrylic dot markers are used on the fingerboard.

Single-coil soapbar pickups

The floating tremolo has an elongated arm.

Fender Jaguar, 1962

The Jazzmaster had completely failed to captivate its intended market, finding favour instead in the emerging surf-guitar instrumental genre. The Jaguar appeared in 1962, closely modelled on the contours of the Jazzmaster but with some radical developments. At 610mm (24in), the neck scale was shorter, but it was also the first Fender to feature a 22-fret fingerboard. The electrics were overhauled, with sophisticated switching and filter circuitry, and single-coil pickups heavily shielded to avoid electrical interference.

- **DATE** 1962
- **ORIGIN** Fullerton, California, USA
- **WOOD**
  Alder or ash body, maple bolt-on neck, rosewood or maple fingerboard.
- **UNUSUAL FEATURE**
  Individual on/off switches are available for each pickup; and three dual-circuit tone switches.

Dual-circuit tone switches

Both pickup on/off switches are here.

Master volume and tone controls are below the tremolo arm.

Fender Mustang, 1964

During the late 1950s, Fender had launched a number of basic models aimed at the novice player. With its small body, offset waist and three-quarter scale length, the new Mustang was ideal for small hands. Like Fender's other recent instruments, the Mustang also featured an unusual electronic arrangement for its time, notably in the way that each pickup can be switched on, off or out of phase. The Mustang achieved a degree of cult recognition during the 1990s through its use by such prominent alternative-rock bands as Sonic Youth.

- **DATE** 1964

- **ORIGIN** Fullerton, California, USA

- **WOOD**
  Poplar, alder, ash or basswood body, maplebolt-on neck, rosewood or maple fingerboard.

- **UNUSUAL FEATURE**
  The Dynamic Vibrato tailpiece was more sensitive than the existing standard Fender units.

ABOVE: *The highly regarded Dynamic Vibrato features an integral floating bridge. The strings are controlled by a tailpiece bar to which the tremolo arm is connected.*

Original Mustangs, like most Fender guitars, were available with rosewood or maple fingerboards.

Pickup on/off/ out-of-phase switch is featured here.

Surf sounds and guitar instrumentals

Originating in southern California at the start of the 1960s, the classic surf sound was pioneered by acts such as Dick Dale and Del-Tones. The music was usually instrumental and featured simple mid-tempo tunes played on an electric guitar with a reverb-drenched sound, often played with heavy use of a vibrato arm. The characteristic biting treble tone was typically derived from the single-coil pickups found on Fender guitars – the Stratocaster and Jaguar were particularly popular among surf musicians. There were many other guitar-instrumental bands during this time that produced a similar sound but were unconnected to Californian surf culture. The Ventures, for example, with their signature Mosrite guitars, proved to be curiously influential in Japan, where they were comparable in popularity with The Beatles throughout much of the decade. There was a strong resurgence of interest in this genre during the 1980s, and it has since remained a niche subculture with vibrant music scenes dotted around Europe and the USA.

ABOVE: *Dick Dale was one of the pioneers of the surf-instrumental sound. His impressively high-speed alternating pick style can be heard on hits such as "Let's Go Trippin" and "Misirlou", with its influential use of the Hilaz Kar, or double harmonic scale. The latter would find a new audience in the 1990s through its use in Quentin Tarantino's cult film* Pulp Fiction.

Jim Burns

From the end of the 1950s right up to the end of his life in 1998, Jim Burns played a pivotal role in the evolution of the electric guitar in Europe. Burns was always more of an innovator than a businessman, but even though his commercial ventures would regularly fail, during the first half of the 1960s his company, Ormston Burns London Ltd, managed to produce many classic, enduring designs.

Burns Vibra Artist, 1960

Cutting his teeth in the late 1950s with the short-lived Burns-Weill brand, Jim Burns' first solo venture was introduced with a range of three instruments, the flagship of which was the Vibra Artist. With its curious twin-cutaway body, a pair of asymmetric horns gave access to the upper register of a two-octave fingerboard that was unusual for its time. Early Burns models exhibit marked variations between models, the bodies often carved from counter tops recycled from bar and restaurant renovations.

- **DATE** 1960
- **ORIGIN** London, UK
- **WOOD**
  Mahogany body (although different materials were frequently used at the whim of their creator), maple set neck, rosewood fingerboard.
- **UNUSUAL FEATURE**
  Many variations between models in terms of materials and design.

Burns Bison, 1961

The Bison could be described as the first luxury solidbody electric guitar to be produced outside of the USA. Striking in its black finish and heavily curved horns, Burns commissioned new pickups from Goldring, then one of Britain's top hi-fi companies; when combined with the unique Rez-o-Matik circuitry, the guitar could produce a startling range of sounds. Absurdly expensive to manufacture, the Bison retailed at £157 – at a time when the average Briton earned just £10 a week.

- **DATE** 1961
- **ORIGIN** London, UK
- **WOOD**
  Sycamore body, maple set neck, ebony fingerboard (although quickly replaced by a cheaper simplified version).
- **UNUSUAL FEATURE**
  This model has four single-coil Ultra-Sonic pickups.

Fender-style six-in-a-line tuners

Two-octave, 24-fret fingerboard – one of the first of its type.

Three Burns Tri-Sonic pickups

Each pickup has its own set of volume and tone controls.

'Bat Wing' headstock – named after the shape of the curve.

A bolt-on neck was used on post-1963 models.

After 1963, the costly Ultra-Sonic pickups were replaced by three Rez-o-Matiks.

Rez-o-Tube vibrato. Original models featured a Burns Boomerang vibrato arm.

Burns Split Sonic, 1962

The Sonic had been the entry-level guitar of Burns' first range. It was a good basic instrument, affordable and popular among British lead guitarists. The Split Sonic first appeared in 1962 and was positioned in the range as an affordable alternative to the Bison. It only really differed from the original Sonic with the introduction of Burns' unique Split Sound pickup, which combined with on-board circuitry to enable the bass notes to be picked up at the neck pickup and the treble notes from the bridge.

- **DATE** 1962

- **ORIGIN** London, UK

- **WOOD**
  Mahogany body, maple bolt-on neck, rosewood fingerboard.

- **UNUSUAL FEATURE**
  A rotary pickup selector offered a choice of Treble (bridge pickup), Bass (neck pickup), Split Sound and Wild Dog – an out-of-phase effect with treble boost.

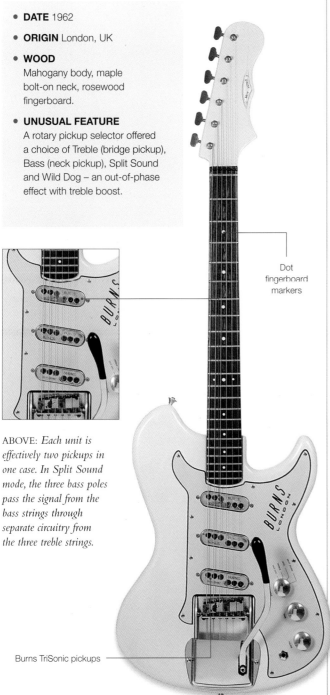

Dot fingerboard markers

ABOVE: *Each unit is effectively two pickups in one case. In Split Sound mode, the three bass poles pass the signal from the bass strings through separate circuitry from the three treble strings.*

Burns TriSonic pickups

Burns Hank Marvin, 1964

Britain's most popular band of the pre-Beatles era, the Shadows had carved out successful careers both backing pop singer Cliff Richard and creating instrumental guitar hits of their own. Famed for owning the first Fender Stratocaster in the UK, it was when guitarist Hank Marvin and colleague Bruce Welch began experiencing tuning problems with their Fender vibrato arms that they approached Jim Burns for a solution. His answer? The luxurious Burns Hank Marvin, one of the most collectible British guitars ever built.

- **DATE** 1964

- **ORIGIN** London, UK

- **WOOD**
  Honduras mahogany body, Canadian rock maple bolt-on neck, Indian rosewood fingerboard.

- **UNUSUAL FEATURE**
  The Rez-o-Tube vibrato unit was designed to avoid the tuning issues common on traditional systems.

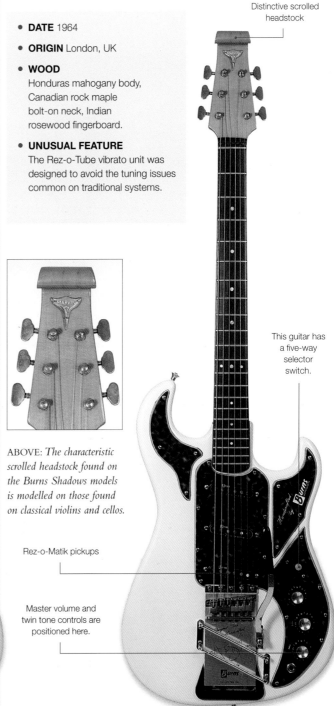

Distinctive scrolled headstock

This guitar has a five-way selector switch.

ABOVE: *The characteristic scrolled headstock found on the Burns Shadows models is modelled on those found on classical violins and cellos.*

Rez-o-Matik pickups

Master volume and twin tone controls are positioned here.

Britain in the 1960s

As the 1960s progressed, American guitars began to reach British shores in greater numbers. They were, however, very expensive. While Britain's first wave of electric guitar players were serviced by imports from Germany, Japan and the Netherlands, a number of local manufacturers began to emerge. Britain would never become a major force in the guitar world, but it produced some credible instruments nonetheless.

Broadway BW2, 1959

Rose-Morris of London began life as an importer of musical instruments. At the end of the 1950s, the company introduced its own Broadway brand, which it applied to guitars imported from Germany and the Netherlands, and, from 1960, a range built in the UK. The BW2 was a basic solidbody instrument with two pickups, and dedicated volume and tone controls for each. The electrics and pickups were supplied by Henry Weill of Burns-Weill. The guitar's most curious feature is the Palm tremolo panel. Imported from Framus in Germany, it was a crude vibrato mechanism that worked by pushing down on the strings between the tailpiece and bridge.

- **DATE** 1959
- **ORIGIN** London, UK
- **WOOD**
  Mahogany single cutaway body, maple bolt-on neck, rosewood fingerboard.
- **UNUSUAL FEATURE**
  The vibrato mechanism is a quirky German-built Framus palm tremolo panel.

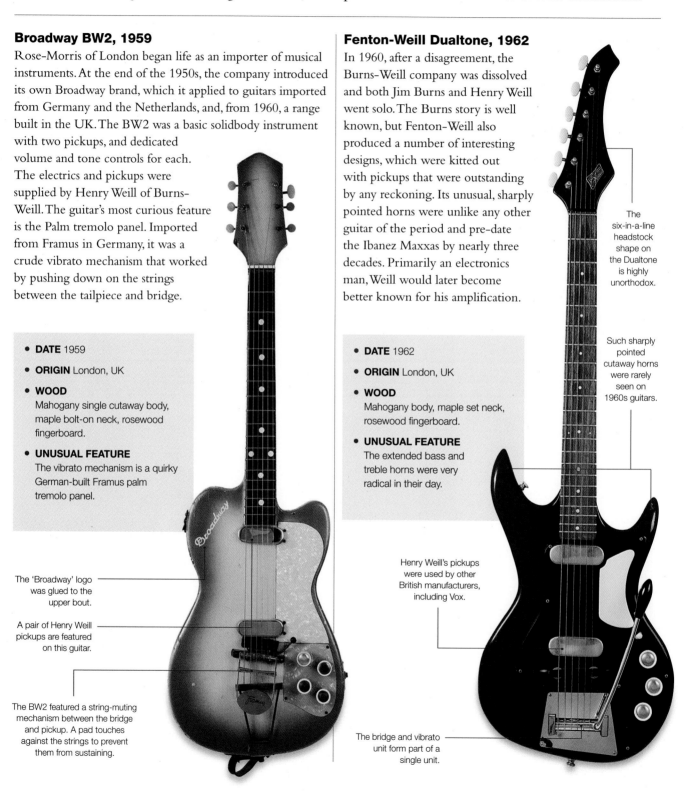

The 'Broadway' logo was glued to the upper bout.

A pair of Henry Weill pickups are featured on this guitar.

The BW2 featured a string-muting mechanism between the bridge and pickup. A pad touches against the strings to prevent them from sustaining.

Fenton-Weill Dualtone, 1962

In 1960, after a disagreement, the Burns-Weill company was dissolved and both Jim Burns and Henry Weill went solo. The Burns story is well known, but Fenton-Weill also produced a number of interesting designs, which were kitted out with pickups that were outstanding by any reckoning. Its unusual, sharply pointed horns were unlike any other guitar of the period and pre-date the Ibanez Maxxas by nearly three decades. Primarily an electronics man, Weill would later become better known for his amplification.

- **DATE** 1962
- **ORIGIN** London, UK
- **WOOD**
  Mahogany body, maple set neck, rosewood fingerboard.
- **UNUSUAL FEATURE**
  The extended bass and treble horns were very radical in their day.

The six-in-a-line headstock shape on the Dualtone is highly unorthodox.

Such sharply pointed cutaway horns were rarely seen on 1960s guitars.

Henry Weill's pickups were used by other British manufacturers, including Vox.

The bridge and vibrato unit form part of a single unit.

Vox Apache, 1961

Alongside Burns, the Vox name is perhaps the best-known British music brand of the 1960s, even if it is remembered more for its famous AC15 and AC30 amplifiers than guitars. The first Vox guitars were outsourced models built by Guyatone in Japan. In 1961, owner Tom Jennings decided that his guitars needed a unique look, and he began building the iconic Phantom teardrop-shaped instruments. The Apache, which featured in the Vox catalogue from 1961 to 1966, is a rare relative of the Phantom, and sports an asymmetric teardrop body and an unusual hooked headstock.

- **DATE** 1961

- **ORIGIN** Dartford, UK

- **WOOD**
  Pine body, maple bolt-on neck, beech or rosewood fingerboard.

- **UNUSUAL FEATURES**
  Asymmetric body and a hooked headstock.

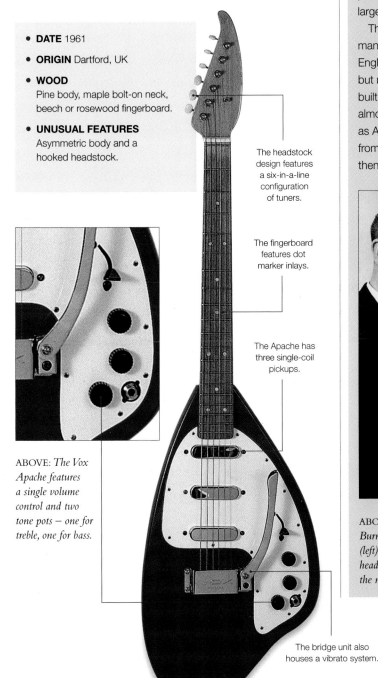

ABOVE: *The Vox Apache features a single volume control and two tone pots – one for treble, one for bass.*

The headstock design features a six-in-a-line configuration of tuners.

The fingerboard features dot marker inlays.

The Apache has three single-coil pickups.

The bridge unit also houses a vibrato system.

This take on the classic Vox 'teardrop' body shape features an unusual indentation at the bottom end.

The British scene

There have been relatively few major British guitar brands – at least those manufactured in the UK on any large scale. One name, of course, towers above all others: Jim Burns. Before making instruments bearing his own name, in the late 1950s he had been involved with the Supersound brand – arguably Britain's first production of electric guitars. His instruments gained an international reputation following his collaboration with Hank Marvin of the Shadows. He would continue to make guitars under his own brand or for Hayman, the predecessor or Shergold, which became Britain's last large-scale guitar maker in the late 1970s.

There was, however, a greater number of quasi-British manufacturers. Vox, for example, was an indisputably English company, building its own amplifiers and effects, but many of its best-known later models were actually built in Italy at the Eko and Crucianelli factories. Similarly, almost all of the cheap 'department store' models – such as Antoria, Jedson and Top Twenty – were in fact imported from the Teisco and Matsumoku factories in Japan, and then rebadged on arrival in the UK.

ABOVE: *Hank Marvin (right) takes delivery of the Burns guitar that bore his name. Jim Burns himself (left) points out the instrument's unusual scroll-top headstock. Original Burns Marvins are among the most collectible of British guitars.*

The birth of the SG

Throughout the 1950s, Gibson had persisted with the unpopular Les Paul range of solidbody electric guitars. Although its final incarnation, the Standard of 1958, is now recognized as one of the most desirable guitars of all, two years after this the company finally admitted defeat and ceased production, albeit temporarily. In its place, a new model was launched, the Solid Guitar – the Gibson SG.

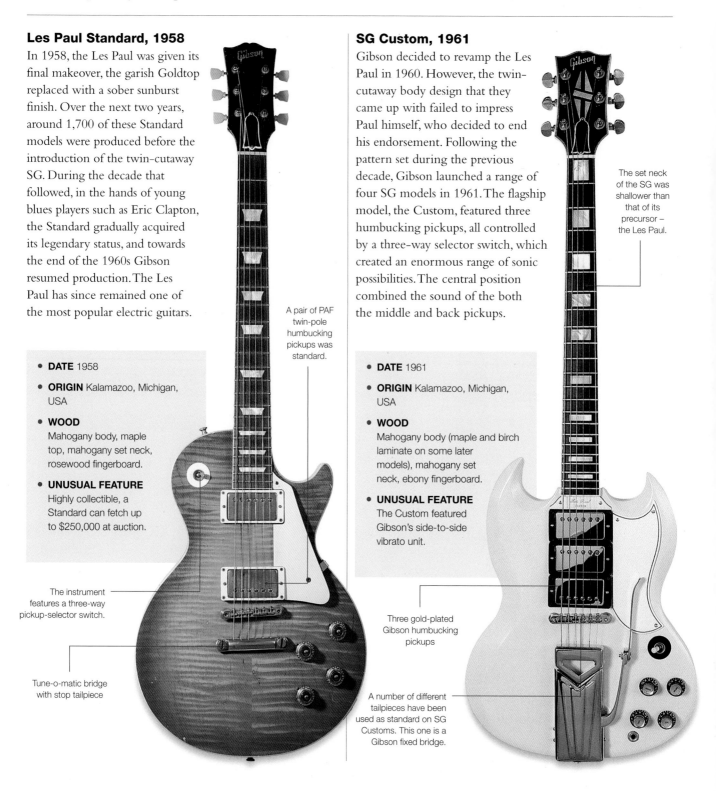

Les Paul Standard, 1958

In 1958, the Les Paul was given its final makeover, the garish Goldtop replaced with a sober sunburst finish. Over the next two years, around 1,700 of these Standard models were produced before the introduction of the twin-cutaway SG. During the decade that followed, in the hands of young blues players such as Eric Clapton, the Standard gradually acquired its legendary status, and towards the end of the 1960s Gibson resumed production. The Les Paul has since remained one of the most popular electric guitars.

- **DATE** 1958
- **ORIGIN** Kalamazoo, Michigan, USA
- **WOOD**
  Mahogany body, maple top, mahogany set neck, rosewood fingerboard.
- **UNUSUAL FEATURE**
  Highly collectible, a Standard can fetch up to $250,000 at auction.

The instrument features a three-way pickup-selector switch.

A pair of PAF twin-pole humbucking pickups was standard.

Tune-o-matic bridge with stop tailpiece

SG Custom, 1961

Gibson decided to revamp the Les Paul in 1960. However, the twin-cutaway body design that they came up with failed to impress Paul himself, who decided to end his endorsement. Following the pattern set during the previous decade, Gibson launched a range of four SG models in 1961. The flagship model, the Custom, featured three humbucking pickups, all controlled by a three-way selector switch, which created an enormous range of sonic possibilities. The central position combined the sound of the both the middle and back pickups.

- **DATE** 1961
- **ORIGIN** Kalamazoo, Michigan, USA
- **WOOD**
  Mahogany body (maple and birch laminate on some later models), mahogany set neck, ebony fingerboard.
- **UNUSUAL FEATURE**
  The Custom featured Gibson's side-to-side vibrato unit.

The set neck of the SG was shallower than that of its precursor – the Les Paul.

Three gold-plated Gibson humbucking pickups

A number of different tailpieces have been used as standard on SG Customs. This one is a Gibson fixed bridge.

SG Special, 1961

Introduced at the same time as the Custom, the Special shared much of the same hardware as its luxury relative. The significant difference is in the pickups – the Special is fitted with a pair of high-output, single-coil P-90s. By this time most Gibsons were fitted with humbuckers, but the continued popularity of the single-coil Fenders, with their characteristic treble bite, suggested there was room for a Gibson counterpart. Rock luminaries such as Black Sabbath's Tony Iommi and The Who's Pete Townshend clearly agreed.

- **DATE** 1961
- **ORIGIN** Kalamazoo, Michigan, USA
- **WOOD** Mahogany body (maple and birch laminate on some later models), mahogany set neck, rosewood fingerboard.
- **UNUSUAL FEATURE** A wraparound stairstep tailpiece was fitted on early models.

The fingerboard inlay markers are pearled dots.

The Gibson P-90 pickup had been introduced in 1946 as a replacement for the hexagonal Charlie Christian model. However, by the end of the 1950s, almost all of Gibson's electric guitars featured humbucking pickups.

The twin-pickup SG models featured similar electrics to the earlier Les Pauls, with dedicated volume and tone controls for each pickup.

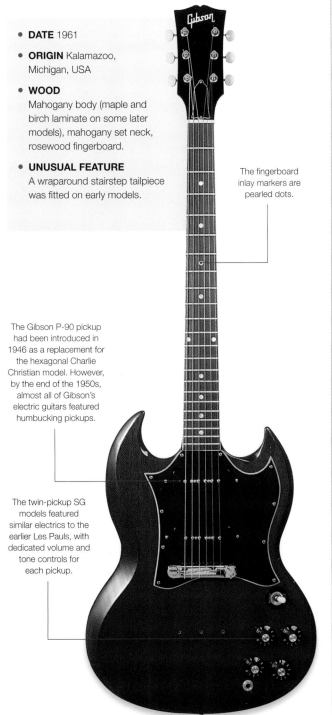

SG Standard, 1961

Although superficially similar to the original Les Pauls, a significant difference lay in the curvature of the body. If you take a side-on look at a Les Paul you will see that the body has a straight edge; the SG – taking its cue from Fender's Stratocaster – had a scalloped contour, intended to make the instrument more comfortable, with no sharp corners pressed against the body. The Standard is the original SG. Very briefly replaced in 1971 with the Standard Deluxe, it remains Gibson's biggest-selling electric guitar.

- **DATE** 1961
- **ORIGIN** Kalamazoo, Michigan, USA
- **WOOD** Mahogany body (maple and birch laminate on some later models), mahogany set neck, rosewood fingerboard.
- **UNUSUAL FEATURES** The fingerboard has pearloid trapezoid inlays and the headstock has a crown inlay.

Pearloid trapezoid fingerboard inlays

ABOVE: *Gibson marketed a number of Vibrola vibrato systems. The type shown here is a Lyre Vibrola, with its long tailpiece and characteristic engraved image.*

Gibson ES thinlines

One of the factors that drove the development of the solidbody electric guitar was the elimination of feedback that often occurred in an electric instrument with an acoustic chamber. Some players, however, felt these solidbodies lacked the warmth and tone of their hollowbody counterparts. Launched in 1958, Gibson's thinline ES range sought to find a middle ground.

ES-335, 1958

In its way, the Gibson ES-335 was a landmark in guitar design. Its body could be described as being neither hollow nor solid. A solid maple block runs through the centre of the body, but with hollow wings attached either side, each with its own f-hole to the chamber beneath. The 335 became an instant bestseller, finding homes in all genres of music, from jazz musicians such as John McLaughlin to the likes of rock legend Eddie Van Halen.

The ES-335 was also known as the ES-335TD: the T denotes a thinline body, and the D indicates a double-pickup guitar.

- **DATE** 1958
- **ORIGIN** Kalamazoo, Michigan, USA
- **WOOD**
  Maple centre-block, maple top back and sides, mahogany set neck, rosewood fingerboard.
- **UNUSUAL FEATURE**
  Options offered either a Gibson or Bigsby vibrato tailpiece (as shown here).

This finish is widely described as 'blond'.

ES-355, 1958

Two months after the successful launch of the ES-335, Gibson came up with its luxury counterpart, the ES-355. The principal difference was the opulent gold-plated hardware, which made the instrument considerably more costly. A year later, a new version appeared, the ES-355TDSV, which provided stereo sound as well as Gibson's Varitone filter control. Blues legend B. B. King became so fond of his 355 that he even gave it a name – Lucille.

Cherry Red is one of Gibson's classic finishes, and one of the most commonly found on ES thinlines.

- **DATE** 1958
- **ORIGIN** Kalamazoo, Michigan, USA
- **WOOD**
  Maple centre block, maple ply top, mahogany set neck, rosewood fingerboard.
- **UNUSUAL FEATURE**
  The gold-plated hardware gives it a luxurious appearance.

Original ES-355s without a vibrato arm – be it a Gibson Vibrola (shown here) or Bigsby – are both rare and collectible.

ES-345, 1959

Gibson frequently offered its customers a range of options on its instruments. Launched in 1959, the ES-345 was a souped-up version of the 335. As a guitar, it was virtually identical, except for tiny cosmetic details such as the split-parallelogram fingerboard inlays (with no first-fret marker), and the small crown headstock design. The principal difference between the two was the introduction of stereo outputs and Gibson's six-way Varitone filter circuitry. The 345 remained a part of the Gibson production range until 1981.

- **DATE** 1959

- **ORIGIN** Kalamazoo, Michigan, USA

- **WOOD**
  Maple centre block, maple ply top, mahogany set neck, rosewood fingerboard.

- **UNUSUAL FEATURE**
  The ES-345 marked the first appearance of Gibson's Varitone filter control circuitry.

ABOVE: *The Varitone control is a six-way notched rotary potentiometer. From 1 up to 6, the higher the setting the greater the filtering out of low frequencies. B. B. King favoured setting 2 on his 355.*

Like all new Gibson electrics launched at the end of the 1950s, the ES-345 features PAF humbucking pickups.

The two pickups are controlled by dedicated volume and tone pots.

B. B. King

Without doubt one of the most important blues guitarists of all time, B. B. King (b. 1925) established himself both as a player and singer from the late 1940s, with genre classics such as "Every Day I Have the Blues" and "Sweet Little Angel". His 1964 album *Live at the Regal* is rated by many critics as among the greatest-ever concert recordings.

King's extensive use of string bending, both as an interpretive playing technique and an alternative vibrato effect, has influenced successive generations of blues and rock guitarists, among them Jimi Hendrix, Eric Clapton, Buddy Guy and Robert Cray. Well into his ninth decade, and yet still an active performer at the time of writing, King is thought to have played over 15,000 concerts during his lifetime.

ABOVE: *Master bluesman B. B. King with his ever-present companion, Lucille – a black ES-355. King even named an album in 'her' honour in 1968. In 1982, Gibson launched the B. B. King Lucille models. At King's request, the f-holes were removed to reduce feedback. In the past, King had forced towels through the holes of his own 335s to achieve the same effect.*

Gibson Firebirds

With the dismal failure of Gibson's Modernistic guitars in 1958, company president Ted McCarty tried a different approach, this time hiring car designer Ray Dietrich, who was noted for his work on Chryslers and Lincolns in the 1950s. The result was the Firebird, a luxury instrument with an unorthodox body shape that was quickly destined to undergo a drastic redesign.

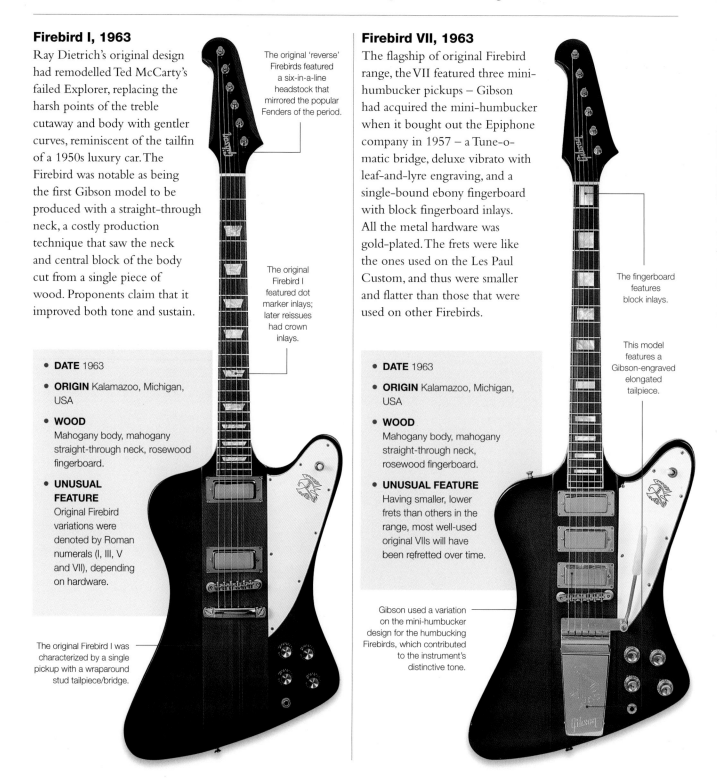

Firebird I, 1963

Ray Dietrich's original design had remodelled Ted McCarty's failed Explorer, replacing the harsh points of the treble cutaway and body with gentler curves, reminiscent of the tailfin of a 1950s luxury car. The Firebird was notable as being the first Gibson model to be produced with a straight-through neck, a costly production technique that saw the neck and central block of the body cut from a single piece of wood. Proponents claim that it improved both tone and sustain.

- **DATE** 1963

- **ORIGIN** Kalamazoo, Michigan, USA

- **WOOD**
  Mahogany body, mahogany straight-through neck, rosewood fingerboard.

- **UNUSUAL FEATURE**
  Original Firebird variations were denoted by Roman numerals (I, III, V and VII), depending on hardware.

The original 'reverse' Firebirds featured a six-in-a-line headstock that mirrored the popular Fenders of the period.

The original Firebird I featured dot marker inlays; later reissues had crown inlays.

The original Firebird I was characterized by a single pickup with a wraparound stud tailpiece/bridge.

Firebird VII, 1963

The flagship of original Firebird range, the VII featured three mini-humbucker pickups – Gibson had acquired the mini-humbucker when it bought out the Epiphone company in 1957 – a Tune-o-matic bridge, deluxe vibrato with leaf-and-lyre engraving, and a single-bound ebony fingerboard with block fingerboard inlays. All the metal hardware was gold-plated. The frets were like the ones used on the Les Paul Custom, and thus were smaller and flatter than those that were used on other Firebirds.

- **DATE** 1963

- **ORIGIN** Kalamazoo, Michigan, USA

- **WOOD**
  Mahogany body, mahogany straight-through neck, rosewood fingerboard.

- **UNUSUAL FEATURE**
  Having smaller, lower frets than others in the range, most well-used original VIIs will have been refretted over time.

The fingerboard features block inlays.

This model features a Gibson-engraved elongated tailpiece.

Gibson used a variation on the mini-humbucker design for the humbucking Firebirds, which contributed to the instrument's distinctive tone.

Firebird I 'Non-reverse', 1965

Although fine instruments, the original Firebirds did not meet sales expectations. Also, some suggested that the body shape might have breached Fender's design patents on the Jazzmaster – if you compare the body shapes you can see that the Firebird mirrors the Fender guitar. So in 1965, Gibson remodelled the guitar on more conventional lines, with the bass horn extending further than the treble. By reversing the 'reversed' body shape of the original design, the new Firebirds became known as 'non-reverse' models.

- **DATE** 1965
- **ORIGIN** Kalamazoo, Michigan, USA
- **WOOD**
  Mahogany body, mahogany set neck, rosewood or ebony fingerboard.
- **UNUSUAL FEATURE**
  The instrument features a stud tailpiece with plastic-tipped vibrato arm.

The 'non-reverse' models featured Fender-style headstocks.

ABOVE: *Apart from a brief period in 1963, all Firebirds featured the characteristic phoenix emblem engraving on the scratchplate.*

Twin pickup models were wired up with dedicated tone and volume controls.

The finish on this model is known as 'Classic White'.

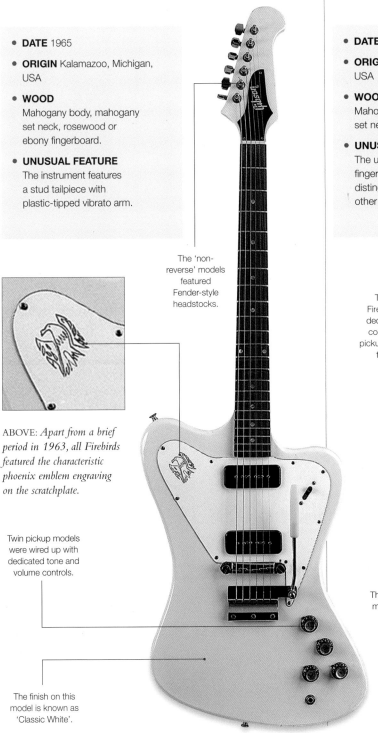

Firebird III 'Non-reverse', 1965

Like their predecessors, the new Firebirds were available in a variety of configurations. However, an alternative numbering system was introduced: I and III models now respectively featured two and three single-pole P-90 pickups, while the V and VII models were kitted out with either two or three humbuckers. No 'non-reverse' single-pickup models were produced. Although popular with many blues and rock players, after several years of poor sales, the Firebird was finally discontinued in 1969.

- **DATE** 1965
- **ORIGIN** Kalamazoo, Michigan, USA
- **WOOD**
  Mahogany body, mahogany set neck, rosewood fingerboard.
- **UNUSUAL FEATURE**
  The unbound rosewood fingerboard with dot inlays distinguish the III from other models.

Three-pickup Firebirds featured dedicated volume controls for each pickup, with a master tone control.

The pickups are activated using a three-way selector switch.

The finish on this model is known as 'Vintage Sunburst'.

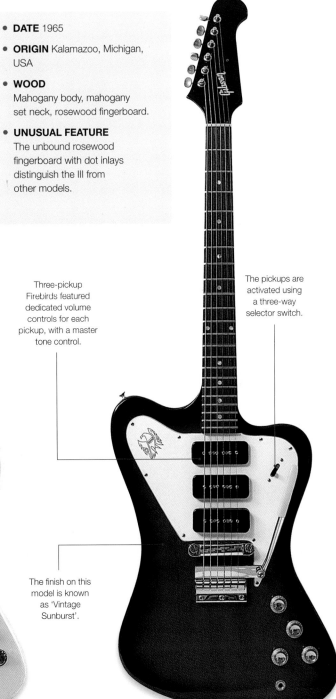

Player-endorsed Gibson models

Celebrity-endorsed electric guitars are nowadays commonplace, with often seemingly limited-edition instruments marketed to music fans at a premium price. The artist-endorsed models Gibson produced from the 1950s were, however, often a collaborative effort between player and manufacturer, born more of a desire to produce a special instrument than to sell slight variants on existing models.

Byrdland, 1955

The large-bodied L-5 archtop acoustic of 1922 was a significant instrument in guitar history, as its size helped with issues of volume. In 1951, an electric cutaway version was launched – the L-5CES. Based on the suggestions of country-jazz players Hank Garland and Billy Byrd, who found it overly bulky, Gibson produced an exquisite thinline version, the Byrdland, with gold-plated hardware. The players also specified a short-scale neck, enabling the fingering of unusual stretched chord voicings.

- **DATE** 1955

- **ORIGIN** Kalamazoo, Michigan, USA

- **WOOD**
  Maple back and sides, spruce top, maple set neck, ebony fingerboard.

- **UNUSUAL FEATURE**
  The Byrdland has a 597mm (23½in) short-scale neck, 32mm (1¼in) shorter than the Gibson standard.

Johnny Smith, 1961

Well-respected and versatile as a player, Johnny Smith is now largely remembered for the instruments he endorsed. Having been approached by Gibson's Ted McCarty, Smith's specification was for a fully acoustic archtop guitar with a single rounded cutaway as well as a floating mini-humbucker positioned close to the neck. The instrument that emerged was an opulent L-5CES variant that retailed at a princely $795 on its 1961 launch – at the time, Gibson's most expensive guitar.

- **DATE** 1961

- **ORIGIN** Kalamazoo, Michigan, USA

- **WOOD**
  Maple back and sides, spruce top, set five-piece maple neck, ebony fingerboard.

- **UNUSUAL FEATURE**
  The electrics are built beneath the floating scratchplate on which the controls are mounted.

The tuners, like the rest of the hardware, are gold-plated.

The Byrdland is fitted with Alnico V single-coil pickups.

The engraved triple-loop tubular tailpiece is unique to the Byrdland.

Split-diamond headstock inlay

The volume control is fitted into the floating scratchplate.

L-5-style tailpiece

Barney Kessel, 1961

One of the most popular US jazz guitarists during the 1950s was Barney Kessel, and his signature model was launched alongside the Jimmy Smith. It resembles a thinline version of the ES-175, but with a double Florentine cutaway – although its body dimensions also reveal its L-5 connections. Two models were available: the Regular, which retailed at $399 and found some success in the jazz world, and the rarer and more luxurious Custom, which fared less well, most players preferring the similarly priced Byrdland.

- **DATE** 1961

- **ORIGIN** Kalamazoo, Michigan, USA

- **WOOD**
  Laminated maple back and sides, laminated spruce top, one-piece mahogany neck, rosewood fingerboard.

- **UNUSUAL FEATURE**
  The Kessel features two Florentine cutaways.

ABOVE: *The inlays on the Barney Kessel Custom model, shown here, are unusual for a Gibson guitar. The headstock shows an array of musical notes.*

The fingerboard markers are the same bow-tie design found in the Gibson banjo.

In the style of the SG solidbody, the double cutaway features Florentine curves.

The Barney Kessel was a thinline model.

Trini Lopez, 1964

The first major Latino pop star, singer and guitarist Trini Lopez topped the charts across the world in 1963, with his version of the folk song "If I Had a Hammer". Gibson launched the Trini Lopez in 1964 to much hype, but, in truth, it was a cosmetically modified ES-335 with the f-holes replaced by unusual elongated diamond slits. The headstock also differed, the three-a-side design of the 335 replaced by the same six-in-a-row style that Gibson would use again a year later on the revamped Firebird.

- **DATE** 1964

- **ORIGIN** Kalamazoo, Michigan, USA

- **WOOD**
  Maple centre block, maple ply top, mahogany set neck, rosewood fingerboard.

- **UNUSUAL FEATURE**
  The use of the diamond-slit soundholes and the six-in-a-row machine-head configuration gives this guitar a unique look.

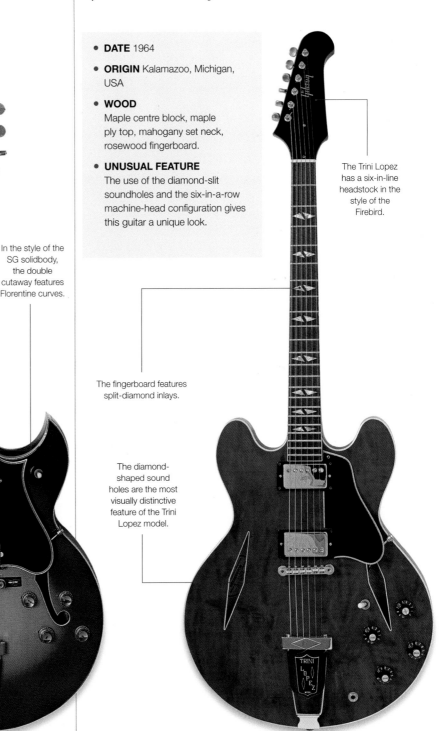

The Trini Lopez has a six-in-line headstock in the style of the Firebird.

The fingerboard features split-diamond inlays.

The diamond-shaped sound holes are the most visually distinctive feature of the Trini Lopez model.

Bass guitars in the 1960s

Apart from in the jazz world, by the time of the early 1960s beat boom, the acoustic upright double bass was all but dead in popular music. The Fender Precision, which had kick-started that revolution in 1951, was still the dominant bass instrument, but, as the decade moved on, other makers such as Gibson, Gretsch and, in particular, Rickenbacker, began to emerge as serious competitors.

Fender Jazz, 1960

Introduced in 1960, the offset-waisted Jazz was the bass counterpart to Fender's flagship guitar of the time, the Jazzmaster. As the name suggested, it was aimed squarely at acoustic-playing jazz bassists, suggesting they lay to rest their monsters and go electric. To this end, Fender offered a narrow neck width, ideal for the necessarily nimble-fingered jazzer, and twin single-coil pickups with two pole pieces per string, providing a cleaner treble sound at the bass end. The Jazz remains one of the most significant bass guitars ever built.

- **DATE** 1960

- **ORIGIN** Fullerton, California, USA

- **WOOD**
  Ash (sometimes alder) body, bolt-on maple neck, rosewood or maple fingerboard.

- **UNUSUAL FEATURE**
  The twin pole pieces on the pickups create a clean sound.

A circular string guide on the headstock keeps the D and G strings in place.

The twin-pickup Jazz had no selector switch built into the circuitry. The two larger knobs control the volume on each of the J pickups.

The Jazz is unusual in that there is no neck pickup – the second pickup is positioned at the centre of the body.

The smaller knob alongside the jack socket is a master tone control.

Gibson EB-3, 1961

Just as the 1958 semi-hollow EB-2 had been a bass counterpart to the ES-335, the EB-3 emerged in 1961 as part of the SG range. Gibson basses were, and have remained, rather unorthodox instruments. With its 762mm (30in) scale length, it was a full 102mm (4in) shorter than the Fenders, which in itself created a different sound in the lower register. It also featured a curious pickup configuration, with a large humbucker in the neck position and a mini-humbucker alongside the bridge.

- **DATE** 1961

- **ORIGIN** Kalamazoo, Michigan, USA

- **WOOD**
  Mahogany body, mahogany set neck, rosewood fingerboard.

- **UNUSUAL FEATURE**
  It has a basic bridge unit with limited adjustability.

Pearloid dot fingerboard inlay markers have been used.

The strings are held in place by positioning the ball-end in a slot; there are no individually adjustable saddles, although the one-piece saddle can be moved as a whole. Two large screws at either side enable the player to adjust the overall height of the bridge.

Rickenbacker 4001S, 1961

With its cresting-wave body shape and matching headstock, the 1957 Rickenbacker 4000 was a spectacular design that captured the imagination of players turning to the bass guitar. In 1961, in an effort to keep one step ahead of rival Fender – which had just introduced the Jazz – Rickenbacker created a deluxe model, the 4001. Equipped with two pickups – a large horseshoe for the bridge and toaster for the neck – the 4001 was also wired for the optional Rick-O-Sound twin-audio output. This would become a standard feature from 1971.

- **DATE** 1961
- **ORIGIN** Santa Ana, California, USA
- **WOOD**
  Maple body, straight-through neck, rosewood fingerboard.
- **UNUSUAL FEATURE**
  The Rick-O-Sound wiring allows a stereo cable to channel the sound from each pickup through its own input.

Unusually, the two-a-side tuners on the headstock are asymmetrically aligned.

The 4001 has both horseshoe and toaster pickups.

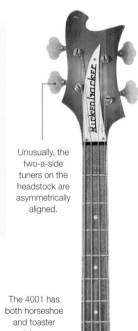

ABOVE: *The Rickenbacker 4001 features an unusually well-engineered bridge. With a combination bridge and tailpiece, each saddle is fully adjustable for both intonation and height. The 4001 is one of the few bass guitars to have challenged the ubiquity of Fender's big two – the Telecaster and the Stratocaster.*

Gretsch 6073, 1967

In general, Gretsch is not celebrated for its basses, and the 6073 is probably its best-known model, primarily through its use by Peter Tork on the popular 1960s TV show *The Monkees* – indeed, it was widely marketed as the 'Monkees Bass'. A hollowbody, short-scale instrument (737mm/29in), the 6073 was modelled on the successful Chet Atkins Tennessean and equipped with a pair of Super'Tron humbuckers. Gretsch also produced the similar single-pickup 6071. Both remained in production until 1972.

- **DATE** 1967
- **ORIGIN** Brooklyn, New York, USA
- **WOOD**
  Single-cut mahogany body with comfort padding on the back, maple straight-through neck, rosewood fingerboard.
- **UNUSUAL FEATURE**
  The instrument has a muting mechanism that helps to replicate the thud of an acoustic bass.

The 6073 is noteworthy as one of a small number of Gretsch models with an in-a-line tuner configuration.

The fingerboard has dot marker inlays.

There are thumb and finger rests above and below the strings; few bass players have found them useful, and they are now rarely seen.

There is a master volume on the cutaway horn.

Epiphone: after the Gibson takeover

The 1960s was a transitional decade for the Epiphone brand. Having previously been one of the giants of the guitar world, it was now merely part of the Gibson empire – once its bitter rival. Although the instruments were still able to retain some their former character, there were clear indications of the brand's future – Gibson's eventual intention to treat Epiphone as a diffusion line.

Casino, 1958

One of the first new models to appear after the Gibson takeover, the Casino was essentially an Epiphone-branded version of the Gibson ES-330. A thinline, hollowbodied, twin-pickup, twin-cutaway instrument, the Casino was able to overshadow its high-end counterpart by virtue of one fact – its association with John Lennon and The Beatles. Indeed, all three guitar-playing members of the band owned Casinos. In 2010, a 1965 Elitist model appeared, an exact replica of Lennon's own guitar, with its scratchplate removed, as Lennon had done.

- **DATE** 1958

- **ORIGIN** Kalamazoo, Michigan, USA

- **WOOD**
  Solid maple centre block with maple wings, mahogany set neck, rosewood fingerboard.

- **UNUSUAL FEATURE**
  Modelled on the Gibson ES-330.

Broadway, 1958

As an archtop acoustic guitar, Epiphone first introduced the Broadway in 1931, giving it a single cutaway two decades later. The electric archtop was launched in 1958. Like other models that spanned the Gibson takeover, the Broadway was initially built using existing stock from the Epiphone factory. Thus, the 1958 model shown here is equipped with a Frequensator tailpiece and New York pickups; from 1961, when old stocks were exhausted, Gibson mini-humbuckers and a Tune-o-matic bridge and end stop were installed.

- **DATE** 1958

- **ORIGIN** Kalamazoo, Michigan, USA

- **WOOD**
  Maple back and sides, spruce top, maple set neck, rosewood fingerboard.

- **UNUSUAL FEATURE**
  The unusual tailpiece was used when stocks ran out.

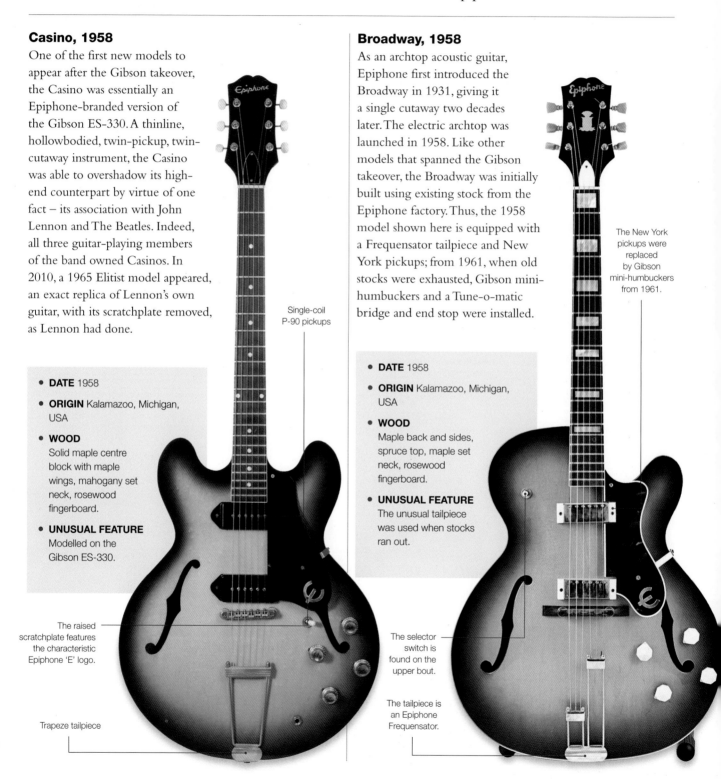

Single-coil P-90 pickups

The New York pickups were replaced by Gibson mini-humbuckers from 1961.

The raised scratchplate features the characteristic Epiphone 'E' logo.

Trapeze tailpiece

The selector switch is found on the upper bout.

The tailpiece is an Epiphone Frequensator.

Coronet, 1958

The Epiphone Coronet was designed as cheaper entry-level alternative to the Les Paul Junior – although, with its thicker body, many rate it as a far better instrument. To put that into perspective, however, the Coronet retailed at around $120, which was still more than double the price of a starter model from the Sears catalogue. The first Coronets featured a single Epiphone New York pickup; from 1960, P-90s were fitted. They were built in the USA until 1970, after which time the production of all Epiphones moved to Japan.

- **DATE** 1958
- **ORIGIN** Kalamazoo, Michigan, USA
- **WOOD** Mahogany body, mahogany set neck, rosewood fingerboard.
- **UNUSUAL FEATURE** The cutaways meet the neck at a 90-degree angle, giving a straight line across the top of the body.

Crestwood, 1958

The flagship of the Epiphone solidbody range, the Crestwood was pitched as a Les Paul alternative, but it was, in its own right, one of the finest models of the period – by the early 1960s, Crestwoods were being produced using the same woods and hardware as Gibson SGs. They were launched in 1958 with the characteristic symmetrical batwing cutaways, but a year later, renamed the Crestwood Custom, these were altered, with the treble horn made smaller. The Crestwood remained in production at Kalamazoo until 1970, resuming later in Japan.

- **DATE** 1958
- **ORIGIN** Kalamazoo, Michigan, USA
- **WOOD** Mahogany body, mahogany set neck, rosewood fingerboard.
- **UNUSUAL FEATURE** The model shown here has characteristic white 'New York' volume and tone knobs.

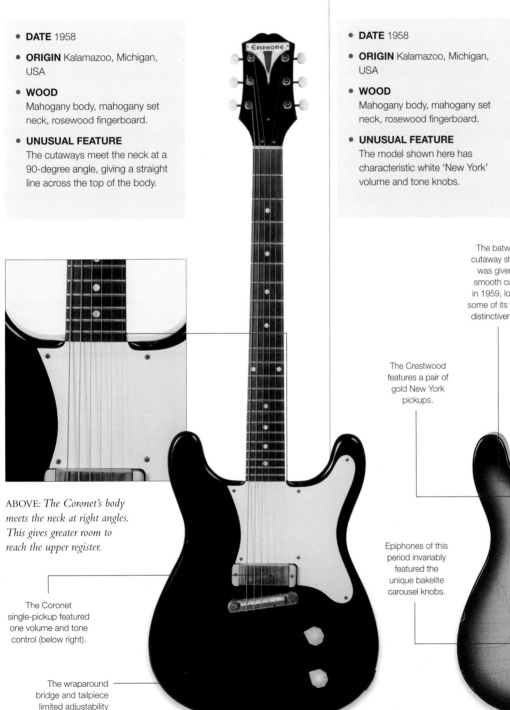

ABOVE: *The Coronet's body meets the neck at right angles. This gives greater room to reach the upper register.*

The Coronet single-pickup featured one volume and tone control (below right).

The wraparound bridge and tailpiece limited adjustability to overall height.

The batwing cutaway shape was given a smooth curve in 1959, losing some of its visual distinctiveness.

The Crestwood features a pair of gold New York pickups.

Epiphones of this period invariably featured the unique bakelite carousel knobs.

Rickenbacker in the 1960s

Throughout the 1950s, new owner Francis H. Hall skilfully managed the company's growth, establishing Rickenbacker as one of a handful of leading names in the American electric-guitar market. However, in 1964, the unexpected cultural tide that spread across the Atlantic from the UK – Beatlemania – suddenly made Rickenbacker guitars among the most immediately recognizable in the world.

325, 1958

Introduced as part of the 1958 Capri series, the Rickenbacker 325 was a semi-hollow, three-quarter scale-length model with three pickups. In 1960, while The Beatles were learning their trade in the clubs of Hamburg, John Lennon saw his first Rickenbacker. Clearly taken with the 325, he was rarely seen playing anything else during the Beatlemania period, and ended up owning four of them. Rickenbacker has since issued many limited-edition tribute models, such as the 325C58 Hamburg and the 325JL.

- **DATE** 1958
- **ORIGIN** Santa Ana, California, USA
- **WOOD** Maple semi-hollowbody, maple set neck, rosewood fingerboard.
- **UNUSUAL FEATURE** The short 527mm (20¾in) scale length is 102mm (4in) shorter than a standard Rickenbacker.

360, 1958

A part of the Rickenbacker 300 Series launched in 1958, the 360 is arguably the company's best-known instrument, both in its six- and twelve-string forms. It incorporates many standard Rickenbacker features, including a three-ply maple and walnut neck, shallow headstock and a thick rosewood fingerboard. The body features the characteristic crescent moon cutaway shape, rounded top edge, and the famous stylized R of the trapeze tailpiece.

- **DATE** 1958
- **ORIGIN** Santa Ana, California, USA
- **WOOD** Maple carved body, three-ply maple/walnut set neck, rosewood fingerboard.
- **UNUSUAL FEATURE** The pearloid-triangle fingerboard marker inlays.

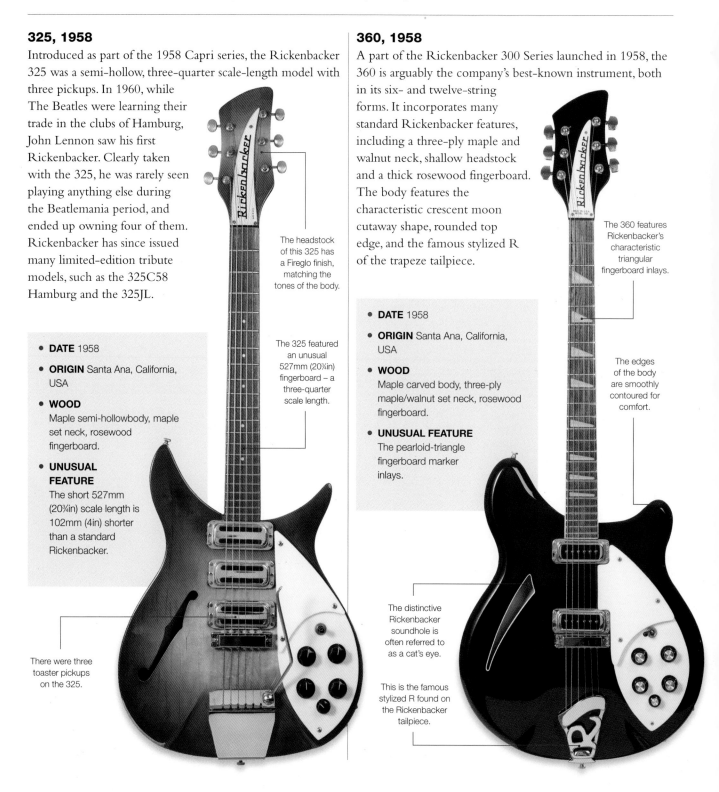

The headstock of this 325 has a Fireglo finish, matching the tones of the body.

The 325 featured an unusual 527mm (20¾in) fingerboard – a three-quarter scale length.

There were three toaster pickups on the 325.

The 360 features Rickenbacker's characteristic triangular fingerboard inlays.

The edges of the body are smoothly contoured for comfort.

The distinctive Rickenbacker soundhole is often referred to as a cat's eye.

This is the famous stylized R found on the Rickenbacker tailpiece.

460, 1961

The Rickenbacker range, while featuring a relatively small number of core models or body shapes, comprised many with minor variations. One such example, the cresting wave 460 introduced in 1961, is nothing more than a slightly more luxurious version of the earlier 450. The enhancements are few but nonetheless signify a deluxe instrument, with body binding and the simple dot inlays of the 450 replaced by pearloid triangle markers. The model shown here is from the first year of production; in 1962 the anodized metal scratchplate was replaced by plastic.

- **DATE** 1961
- **ORIGIN** Santa Ana, California, USA
- **WOOD**
  Maple body, maple straight-through neck, rosewood fingerboard.
- **UNUSUAL FEATURE**
  The anodized metal scratchplate on early models.

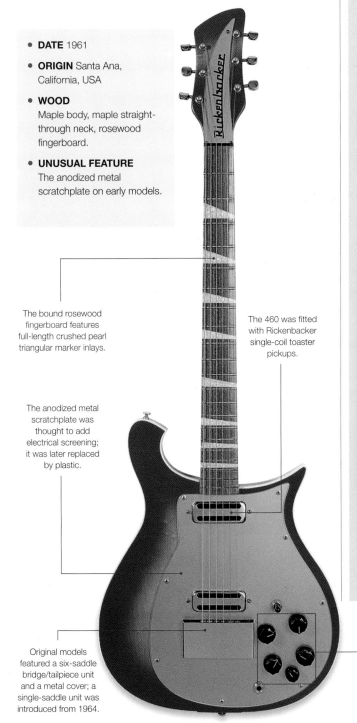

The bound rosewood fingerboard features full-length crushed pearl triangular marker inlays.

The anodized metal scratchplate was thought to add electrical screening; it was later replaced by plastic.

The 460 was fitted with Rickenbacker single-coil toaster pickups.

Original models featured a six-saddle bridge/tailpiece unit and a metal cover; a single-saddle unit was introduced from 1964.

The electrics comprise two pairs of volume and tone controls and one pickup balance.

Rickenbacker and The Beatles

In the UK, 1963 was the year of The Beatles, the first wave of what was to become known as Beatlemania. Although the band were largely unheard of in the USA at this time, European distributors began to send over press clippings of them, often featuring John Lennon and George Harrison playing Rickenbackers. Beatlemania repeated itself a year later in the USA, the band cementing its reputation with a celebrated performance on the *Johnny Carson Show*, with John Lennon singing at the front of the band and playing his Rickenbacker 325. After that evening, Rickenbacker was unable to produce enough guitars to satisfy demand, with the company's head office at Santa Ana receiving fan mail from all over the world.

The story continued in February 1964, when George Harrison was given one of the prototypes of Rickenbacker's new electric 12-string. He proceeded to use it heavily on the band's next album, *A Hard Day's Night*, including the famous opening chord chimes of the title track. The Beatles were, in the eyes of the public, a Rickenbacker band.

ABOVE: *The Beatles remain the most culturally significant pop group in history and, although they disbanded in 1970, their music continues to reach successive generations. Rickenbacker had previously been a well-respected name in the guitar world, but the marque's association with The Beatles suddenly made it one of the most desirable brands in the world.*

Japan in the 1960s

Having led the world in building cheap copies of American classics, Japan began to produce guitars with unique character as the 1960s progressed. They may have still been strongly inspired by Fenders, Gibsons and – perhaps surprisingly – models from Europe by makers such as Burns and Hagström, but this was the first generation of instruments from the Far East that hinted at future triumphs.

Teisco SS4L, 1962

Founded in 1946, this company was known under a variety of names before eventually settling on the Tokyo Electric Instrument and Sound Company – Teisco. Ubiquitous for starter instruments in the 1960s and '70s, its guitars were exported and badged up as Jedson, Kent, Top Twenty, Kay, and many other names. The SS4L first appeared in 1962, and features a huge selection of rocker switches with which to select various pickup configurations, along with rotary dials for controlling volume and tone.

- **DATE** 1962

- **ORIGIN** Tokyo, Japan

- **WOOD**
  Laminated with assorted hardwoods body, maple bolt-on neck, rosewood fingerboard.

- **UNUSUAL FEATURE**
  The metal scratchplate and control panel give it a unique appearance.

Yamaha SG5A Flying Samurai, 1966

Founded in 1887 as the Nippon Gakki Company, Yamaha was a latecomer to the guitar market, not producing its first electric until 1966. The Flying Samurai took the basic Mosrite formula of the extended treble horn and re-contoured the body to give it a uniquely oriental line. An original feature was the narrow headstock, which resembled a katana sword. The SG5A was extremely popular in Japan, and it was something of a coup for Yamaha when Japan's top player 'Terry' Terauchi began playing one in preference to his old Mosrite.

- **DATE** 1966

- **ORIGIN** Hamamatsu, Japan

- **WOOD**
  Alder body, maple bolt-on neck, rosewood fingerboard.

- **UNUSUAL FEATURE**
  The two bridge pickups are housed in a single unit, but can be used as a single humbucker or switched for use as two independent single coils.

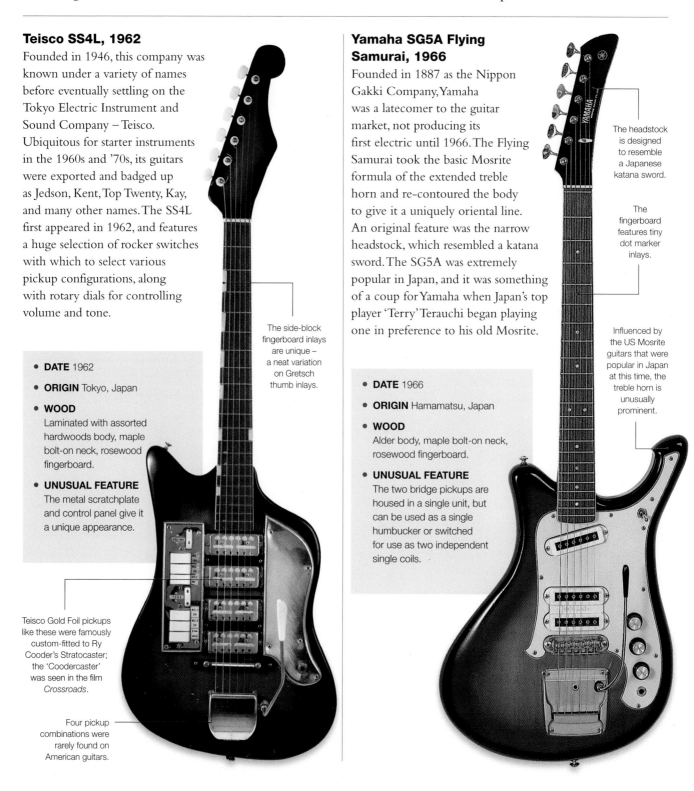

The side-block fingerboard inlays are unique – a neat variation on Gretsch thumb inlays.

Teisco Gold Foil pickups like these were famously custom-fitted to Ry Cooder's Stratocaster; the 'Coodercaster' was seen in the film *Crossroads*.

Four pickup combinations were rarely found on American guitars.

The headstock is designed to resemble a Japanese katana sword.

The fingerboard features tiny dot marker inlays.

Influenced by the US Mosrite guitars that were popular in Japan at this time, the treble horn is unusually prominent.

Teisco Del Rey, *c.1968*

The name Jack Westheimer may not be widely known outside of the guitar industry, but he played a key role in fuelling the guitar boom by bringing affordable instruments into the USA. In 1964, he began importing good-quality Japanese guitars from the Teisco factory under the Teisco Del Rey brand. The Del Reys produced towards the end of the decade were generally more flamboyant in design, with colourful finishes and ornately decorated scratchplates. They continued to appear until around 1973, when the brand ceased production.

- **DATE** *c.*1968

- **ORIGIN** Tokyo, Japan

- **WOOD**
  Laminated with assorted hardwoods body, bolt-on neck, rosewood fingerboard.

- **UNUSUAL FEATURE**
  The highly decorative scratchplate is key to the overall look.

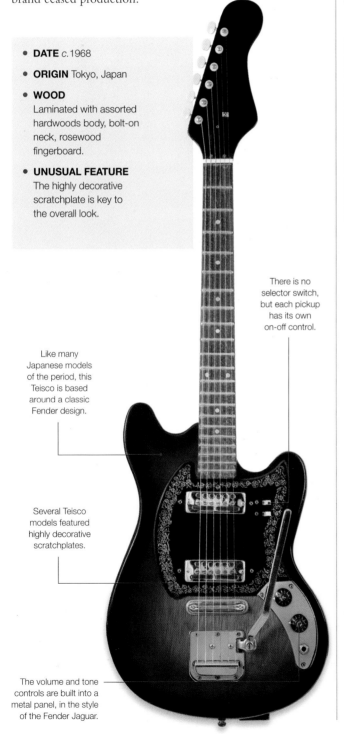

Like many Japanese models of the period, this Teisco is based around a classic Fender design.

Several Teisco models featured highly decorative scratchplates.

There is no selector switch, but each pickup has its own on-off control.

The volume and tone controls are built into a metal panel, in the style of the Fender Jaguar.

Heit Deluxe, *c.1968*

One of the more obscure American import brands, the Heit name was owned by G&H Imports of Lodi, New Jersey, which imported guitars largely from the Teisco factory, and later from Kawai. Many of the models it sold were inspired by the American Mosrite guitars that had made such an impact in Japan following the enormous success of surf band The Ventures. The Heit Deluxe shown here dates from around 1968, and displays a Stratocaster-style body with a rather elegant and distinctive rear cutaway.

- **DATE** *c.*1968

- **ORIGIN** Tokyo, Japan

- **WOOD**
  Laminated with assorted hardwoods body, maple bolt-on neck, rosewood fingerboard.

- **UNUSUAL FEATURE**
  The rear body cutaway gives it a distinctive and elegant look.

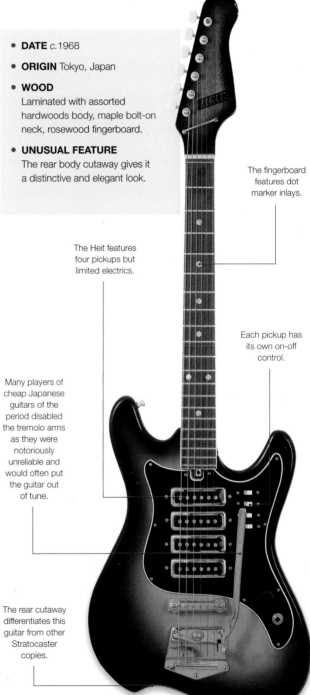

The fingerboard features dot marker inlays.

The Heit features four pickups but limited electrics.

Each pickup has its own on-off control.

Many players of cheap Japanese guitars of the period disabled the tremolo arms as they were notoriously unreliable and would often put the guitar out of tune.

The rear cutaway differentiates this guitar from other Stratocaster copies.

Northern Europe in the 1960s

As the 1960s progressed, so did electric guitar production outside of the USA. Jim Burns had shown in London that it was possible to produce viable, if often costly, alternatives to the Fenders, Gibsons, Gretsches and Rickenbackers that were by now being exported from across the Atlantic. Similarly, throughout other parts of Europe, guitar makers were slowly moving away from the world of cheap imitations of US models.

Hagström Futurama Coronado Automatic, 1963

Originally a Swedish accordian manufacturer, Hagström had established itself as one of Europe's large producers of electric guitars by the end of the 1950s – and the company's roots are evident in the guitars' distinctive accordion-like pearloid celluloid body finishes. In 1963, London-based distributor Selmer ordered 200 high-quality instruments for exclusive sale in the UK. These were the Futurama Coronados, the styling of which strongly resembles the Fender Jaguar. Selmer sold a number of guitars under the Futurama brand, mostly inferior models built in Czechoslovakia.

- **DATE** 1963
- **ORIGIN** Älvdalen, Sweden
- **WOOD**
  Birch body, maple 'King's' set neck, man-made 'high-speed' acrylic fingerboard.
- **UNUSUAL FEATURE**
  The instrument features an acrylic fingerboard and stainless-steel frets.

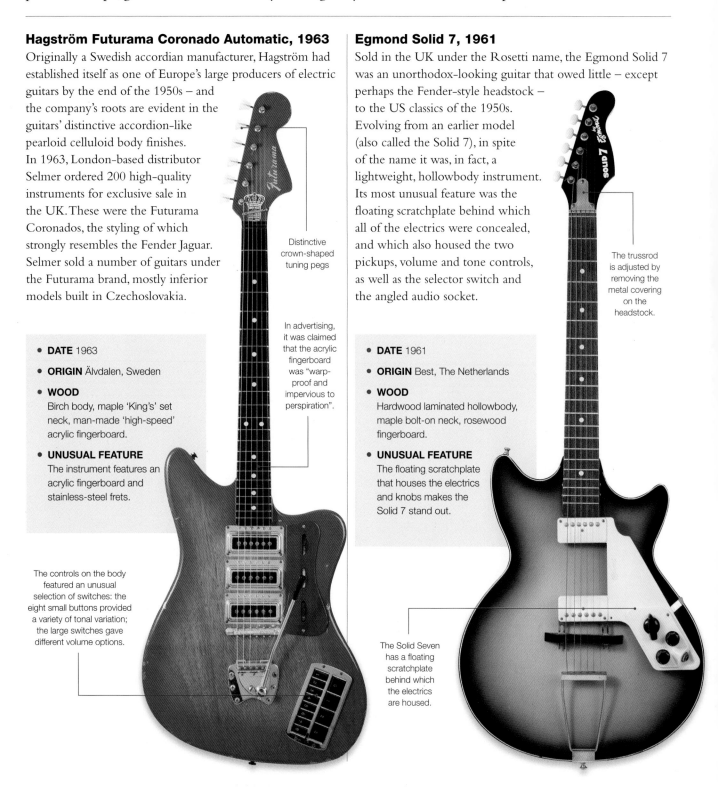

Distinctive crown-shaped tuning pegs

In advertising, it was claimed that the acrylic fingerboard was "warp-proof and impervious to perspiration".

The controls on the body featured an unusual selection of switches: the eight small buttons provided a variety of tonal variation; the large switches gave different volume options.

Egmond Solid 7, 1961

Sold in the UK under the Rosetti name, the Egmond Solid 7 was an unorthodox-looking guitar that owed little – except perhaps the Fender-style headstock – to the US classics of the 1950s. Evolving from an earlier model (also called the Solid 7), in spite of the name it was, in fact, a lightweight, hollowbody instrument. Its most unusual feature was the floating scratchplate behind which all of the electrics were concealed, and which also housed the two pickups, volume and tone controls, as well as the selector switch and the angled audio socket.

The trussrod is adjusted by removing the metal covering on the headstock.

- **DATE** 1961
- **ORIGIN** Best, The Netherlands
- **WOOD**
  Hardwood laminated hollowbody, maple bolt-on neck, rosewood fingerboard.
- **UNUSUAL FEATURE**
  The floating scratchplate that houses the electrics and knobs makes the Solid 7 stand out.

The Solid Seven has a floating scratchplate behind which the electrics are housed.

Framus Strato Deluxe, 1966

Fred Wilfler set up the Framus company in Bavaria after the end of World War II, when Germany was still an occupied nation. Initially producing violins, Framus noted the increasing demand for guitars during the 1950s, and soon became one of Europe's biggest producers. The Strato Deluxe was clearly inspired by Fender's flagship Jaguar, but also it incorporated additional circuitry to create an interesting organ-swell effect. It remains one the finest European instruments of the time.

- **DATE** 1966

- **ORIGIN** Bubenreuth, Germany

- **WOOD**
  Maple sandwich-cut body, maple bolt-on neck, rosewood fingerboard.

- **UNUSUAL FEATURE**
  The inbuilt Orgeleffekte – organ-effect – circuitry is a novel touch.

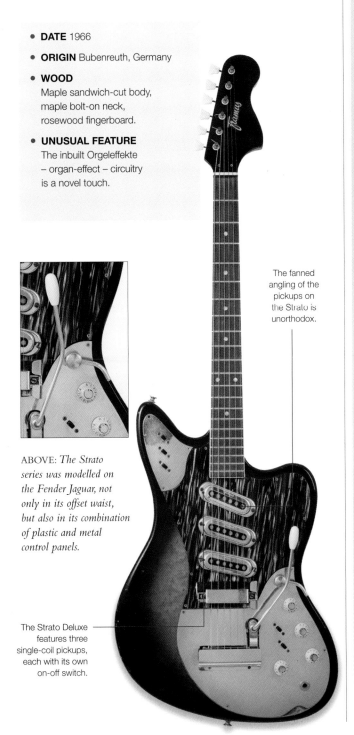

The fanned angling of the pickups on the Strato is unorthodox.

ABOVE: *The Strato series was modelled on the Fender Jaguar, not only in its offset waist, but also in its combination of plastic and metal control panels.*

The Strato Deluxe features three single-coil pickups, each with its own on-off switch.

The cult of Hagström

ABOVE: *Guitarist Pat Smear made his name in US punk band the Germs. He briefly toured with Nirvana prior to the death of Kurt Cobain, and then went on to form the Foo Fighters with Dave Grohl.*

In 1981, no longer able to compete with cheaper Japanese guitars, Karl-Erik Hagström ended production, and the company went into hibernation. The next two decades saw prices for used Hagström guitars on the rise, especially for the early models. Particularly prized was the P46, with its accordion-sparkle finish and reputation as the first production guitar fitted with four pickups – and the 2000s saw it heavily used on stage by the Scottish band Franz Ferdinand.

A key figure in more recent Hagström history is guitarist Pat Smear of US band Foo Fighters. Performing in one of the most popular rock groups in the world, Smear is rarely seen in concert without a Hagström guitar, creating huge interest in a brand largely unknown in America. Smear himself has one of the largest collections of original Hagström guitars in the world, and at one stage even approached Karl-Erik Hagström with plans to fund the revival of the brand.

In 2005, Hagström's son, Karl-Erik Jr, took over the business, and is once again producing some of the best-known models, this time built in China.

Double-neck guitars

It became clear from the earliest days of the electric guitar that there would be times when a performer would want to create different sounds from the same instrument within the same song, either in concert or in a recording studio. In an era that pre-dated multitrack recording and multiple-effect units, one solution was to create a guitar with more than one neck.

Stratosphere Twin, 1955

The classic double-neck guitar configuration was to combine six and twelve strings. The Stratosphere Twin was the first production guitar of this type. Curiously, the maker's recommended 12-string tunings were unorthodox, geared towards playing harmony lead lines rather than chords. Although country star Jimmy Bryant championed this pioneering guitar, even creating the instrumental "Stratosphere Boogie" for its use, it was generally viewed as a novelty instrument.

- **DATE** 1955

- **ORIGIN** Springfield, Missouri, USA

- **WOOD**
  Sap gum body, two set one-piece maple neck/fingerboards.

- **UNUSUAL FEATURE**
  Sap gum is an unorthodox wood for use in guitar construction; it is widely used for wall panelling and furniture.

Danelectro 3923 Short Horn Double Neck, 1958

Unlike the Stratosphere, the Danelectro 3923 combined six-string and bass necks. Construction was typical of Danelectro, the body built from a pine frame covered top and bottom with Masonite. Thus, existing single-neck Short Horn circuitry could be used, and each 'guitar' had just one pickup. The guitar/bass double-neck combo would later find favour with progressive rock bands in the 1970s.

- **DATE** 1958

- **ORIGIN** Neptune, New Jersey, USA

- **WOOD**
  Pine frame, Masonite top and back, maple bolt-on neck, rosewood fingerboard.

- **UNUSUAL FEATURE**
  This was the first example seen of a guitar/bass combination.

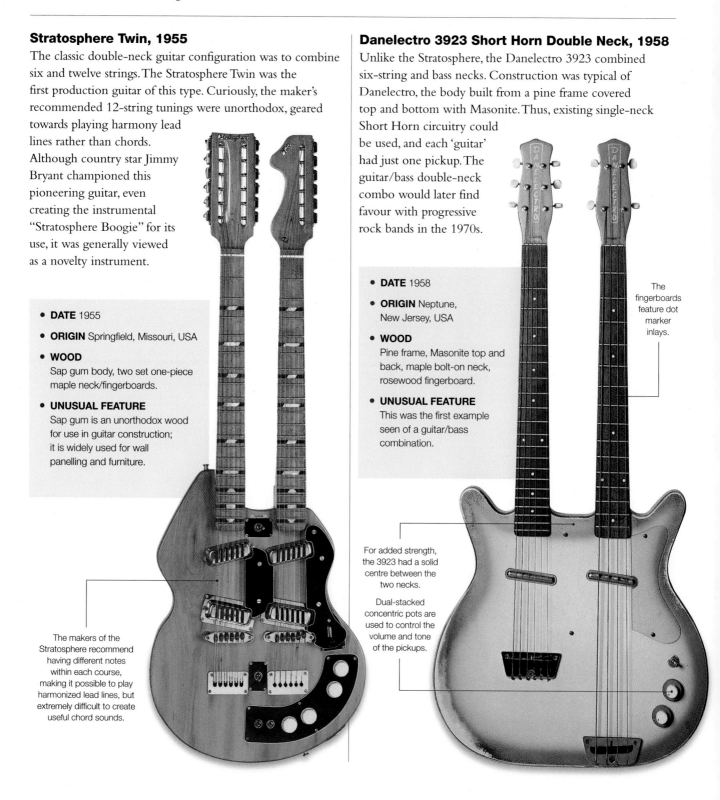

The makers of the Stratosphere recommend having different notes within each course, making it possible to play harmonized lead lines, but extremely difficult to create useful chord sounds.

For added strength, the 3923 had a solid centre between the two necks.

Dual-stacked concentric pots are used to control the volume and tone of the pickups.

The fingerboards feature dot marker inlays.

Gibson EDS-1275, 1963

Something of a niche among guitarists, double-necks are prized by some for their versatility, but many have also struggled with their bulk and top-heavy balance. Gibson had experimented with multi-necks in the late 1950s, notably with a mandolin/guitar, the EMS-1235. In 1963, Gibson produced what has since become the best-known example of its type – the SG-inspired EDS-1275. The instrument's continued popularity can largely be attributed to its use by Led Zeppelin's Jimmy Page during the first half of the 1970s.

- ● **DATE** 1963

- ● **ORIGIN** Kalamazoo, Michigan, USA

- ● **WOOD**
  Mahogany body, two mahogany set necks, rosewood fingerboards.

- ● **UNUSUAL FEATURE**
  The pearloid split-parallelogram fingerboard marker inlays are integral to the look.

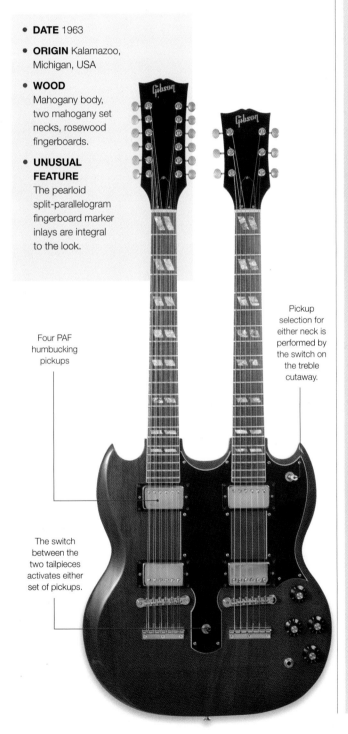

Four PAF humbucking pickups

Pickup selection for either neck is performed by the switch on the treble cutaway.

The switch between the two tailpieces activates either set of pickups.

Jimmy Page

From the early 1960s, Jimmy Page (b. 1944) had been one of the leading studio session guitarists on the London scene, used anonymously on recordings by diverse artists such as The Kinks, The Rolling Stones, Petula Clark, Johnny Halliday and Donovan. Unwilling for years to give up his lucrative career to join a band, after a brief stint with the Yardbirds (following Eric Clapton and Jeff Beck), he formed Led Zeppelin in 1968. Within three years, they were arguably the biggest band in the world, and Page was widely touted as the greatest rock guitarist of them all.

Page's choice of guitars was sometimes odd. Early film of Led Zeppelin live shows sees him coaxing the heaviest of the band's classic lead lines out of a Fender Telecaster. He would also sometimes use a cheap 1960s Danelectro in concert. He is, however, perhaps most famously associated with the Gibson EDS-125 double-neck.

ABOVE: *On stage, Jimmy Page frequently switched between six and twelve strings. In the 1976 concert film* The Song Remains the Same *we see the Gibson EDS-1275 being used on the band's anthem "Stairway to Heaven", as Page picks out the delicate opening on the lower, six-string neck, before flicking the selector switch to 12-string mode. The popularity of the double-neck guitar peaked in the 1970s, although, in recent years, it has begun to reappear with the resurgence of interest in progressive rock.*

Guitars from the Eastern Bloc

The Cold War between the West and the Soviet Union and other Communist Eastern European states saw limited cross-cultural contact between the two sides. Yet, even though rock 'n' roll music was actively discouraged by the authorities in the Eastern Bloc, the limited production of electric guitars did, nonetheless, take place, some results of which were exported to other parts of Europe.

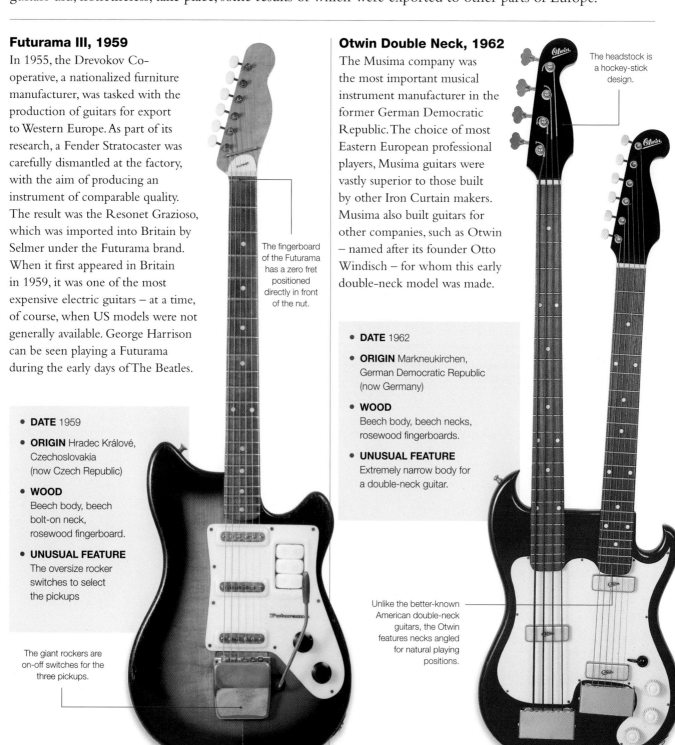

Futurama III, 1959

In 1955, the Drevokov Co-operative, a nationalized furniture manufacturer, was tasked with the production of guitars for export to Western Europe. As part of its research, a Fender Stratocaster was carefully dismantled at the factory, with the aim of producing an instrument of comparable quality. The result was the Resonet Grazioso, which was imported into Britain by Selmer under the Futurama brand. When it first appeared in Britain in 1959, it was one of the most expensive electric guitars – at a time, of course, when US models were not generally available. George Harrison can be seen playing a Futurama during the early days of The Beatles.

- **DATE** 1959
- **ORIGIN** Hradec Králové, Czechoslovakia (now Czech Republic)
- **WOOD** Beech body, beech bolt-on neck, rosewood fingerboard.
- **UNUSUAL FEATURE** The oversize rocker switches to select the pickups

The giant rockers are on-off switches for the three pickups.

The fingerboard of the Futurama has a zero fret positioned directly in front of the nut.

Otwin Double Neck, 1962

The Musima company was the most important musical instrument manufacturer in the former German Democratic Republic. The choice of most Eastern European professional players, Musima guitars were vastly superior to those built by other Iron Curtain makers. Musima also built guitars for other companies, such as Otwin – named after its founder Otto Windisch – for whom this early double-neck model was made.

- **DATE** 1962
- **ORIGIN** Markneukirchen, German Democratic Republic (now Germany)
- **WOOD** Beech body, beech necks, rosewood fingerboards.
- **UNUSUAL FEATURE** Extremely narrow body for a double-neck guitar.

The headstock is a hockey-stick design.

Unlike the better-known American double-neck guitars, the Otwin features necks angled for natural playing positions.

Aelita 1, 1978

More isolated from the West than the other states of Eastern Europe, the Soviet Union was the last among the Iron Curtain countries to mass-produce electric guitars. The Kavkaz factory in the city of Rostov-on-Don had formerly built furniture and balalaikas, but introduced a pair of electric guitars during the 1970s – the Aelita and the Bas. Although it was one of the better guitars produced during this period in the Soviet Union, by Western standards the primitive Aelita was a good 15 years out of date.

- **DATE** 1978

- **ORIGIN** Rostov-on-Don, USSR (now Russia)

- **WOOD**
  Front/Back & Sides
  Unspecified hardwood body, beech bolt-on neck, beech fingerboard.

- **UNUSUAL FEATURE**
  The Aelita uses a six-pin DIN output socket, not a jack plug.

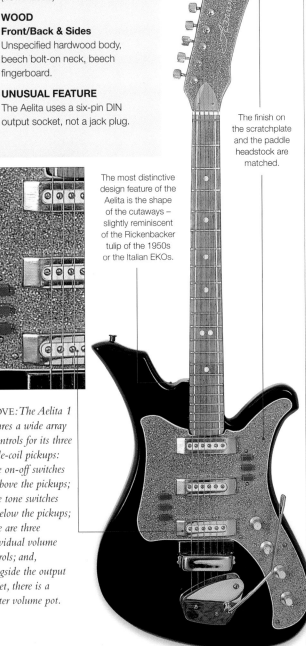

The most distinctive design feature of the Aelita is the shape of the cutaways – slightly reminiscent of the Rickenbacker tulip of the 1950s or the Italian EKOs.

The finish on the scratchplate and the paddle headstock are matched.

ABOVE: *The Aelita 1 features a wide array of controls for its three single-coil pickups: three on-off switches sit above the pickups; three tone switches sit below the pickups; there are three individual volume controls; and, alongside the output socket, there is a master volume pot.*

Communism and the electric guitar

The arrival of rock 'n' roll was not at all welcomed in the Communist Eastern Bloc. Cold War sensibilities ensured there was distrust in all forms of popular culture that emanated from the West. Unsurprisingly, the Soviet Union took the strongest line, and with such a strong connection between rock music and the electric guitar, it was not until the 1970s that guitars were produced by state-owned factories. Rock music was not in itself against the law, but the legal framework was such that musicians had to be accepted by the State Concert Agency in order to gain professional status and earn money.

There was greater tolerance of Western culture in other Eastern European countries, and during the 1960s electric guitars were being produced in Hungary, Poland, Bulgaria, Czechoslovakia and East Germany (DDR). In some cases, these were exported across the Iron Curtain to help satisfy demand during the beat boom.

Although they were generally poorly made – not to mention unpleasant to play – Communist-era guitars are increasingly of interest to modern-day collectors.

ABOVE: *Stas Namin was the leader of the groundbreaking band Tvesty (which translates as Flowers). Often referred to as the 'Russian Beatles', they achieved enormous popularity throughout the Soviet Union during the 1970s; much of their following came about by the distribution of cassette tapes at their concerts. Namin himself is one of the most influential figures in the creation of an indigenous Russian rock-music scene.*

Rickenbacker 12-string electrics

It was during the 1920s that the 12-string guitar first achieved popularity. The twelve strings were grouped into six groups of pairs, each tuned either in unison or an octave apart, enabling one guitar to achieve the rich depth of two. It was with the early 1960s folk revival that a new generation of musicians became interested in the instrument, which itself led to the development of the first electric 12-string guitars.

360/12, 1964

By 1964, both Gibson and Danelectro had already dabbled with the idea of an electric 12-string guitar – with limited success. Rickenbacker's attempt took a standard hollowbody Model 360 and created a radical new headstock design that enabled all 12 machine heads to fit on to a regular-sized headstock. Rickenbacker owner Francis C. Hall presented a prototype to George Harrison, who used it on the opening chords of "A Hard Day's Night". The example here has rounded horns and no binding.

- **DATE** 1964

- **ORIGIN** Santa Ana, California, USA

- **WOOD**
  Carved maple body, three-ply maple set neck, rosewood fingerboard.

- **UNUSUAL FEATURE**
  The headstock design is a radical solution to the problem of accommodating 12 pegs.

Combining a regular electric guitar peghead with the slotted style used on classical guitars, it was possible to fit all 12 tuners into a regular-sized headstock.

450/12, 1965

With Rickenbacker's stock riding high on the popularity of The Beatles and the new jangly folk-rock sound spearheaded by The Byrds, other standard Rickenbacker models were successfully given the 12-string treatment. The Model 450, with its cresting wave body, had been introduced in 1958. Seven years later it appeared as a 12-string electric. The majority of Rickenbackers were finished in what was called Fireglo sunburst, black, or – as with the model shown here – natural maple.

- **DATE** 1965

- **ORIGIN** Santa Ana, California, USA

- **WOOD**
  Maple body, maple straight-through neck with wings bolted and glued, rosewood fingerboard.

- **UNUSUAL FEATURE**
  The headstock is unique as it combines electric and acoustic designs.

Note the ingenious Rickenbacker configuration of horizontal and vertical machine heads used on the company's 12-string electric guitars.

For each pickup there are dedicated volume and tone controls – the smallest knob is a balance mixer between the two.

Rickenbacker's characteristic cat's-eye soundhole

The cresting wave refers to the shape of the double cutaway.

The 450/12 is fitted with an all-in-one fixed bridge unit.

336/12, 1966

In production for ten years after it first appeared in 1966, the 336/12 is identical to the pointed-horn version of the 360/12, with one very curious exception: it was fitted with a metal contraption referred to as the 12/6 converter unit. Patented by James Gross, the device was fixed alongside the neck pickup, and when engaged by the lever would push one of the strings from each pair down against the fingerboard. This enabled the player to switch quickly between six and twelve strings. It was of limited use, however, since it made string bending and other playing techniques extremely difficult to execute.

- **DATE** 1966
- **ORIGIN** Santa Ana, California, USA
- **WOOD** Carved maple body, three-ply maple set neck, rosewood fingerboard.
- **UNUSUAL FEATURE** The 12/6 converter unit – widely known as the comb – was used to turn it into a six-string.

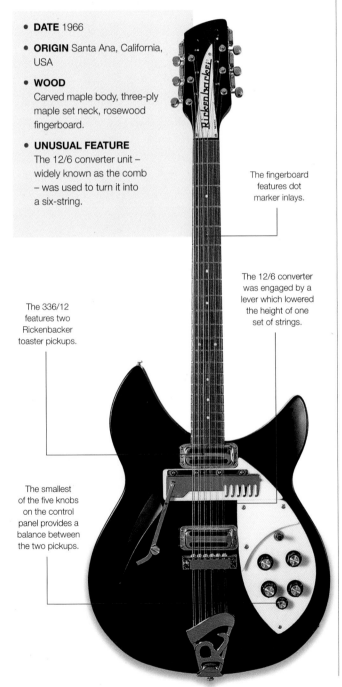

The fingerboard features dot marker inlays.

The 12/6 converter was engaged by a lever which lowered the height of one set of strings.

The 336/12 features two Rickenbacker toaster pickups.

The smallest of the five knobs on the control panel provides a balance between the two pickups.

370/12 RME1, 1988

Much of the enduring popularity of Rickenbacker 12-string electrics was down to the similarly timeless appeal of the pioneering folk-rock band The Byrds. Their 1965 worldwide hit single "Hey Mr Tambourine Man" and their subsequent recordings largely revolved around the Rickenbacker 12-string sound. In 1988, Roger McGuinn of The Byrds was honoured by Rickenbacker with his own limited-edition signature version of the three-pickup 370/12, the guitar with which he was most strongly identified.

- **DATE** 1988
- **ORIGIN** Santa Ana, California, USA
- **WOOD** Carved maple body, three-ply maple set neck, rosewood fingerboard.
- **UNUSUAL FEATURE** The scratchplate carries Roger McGuinn's signature.

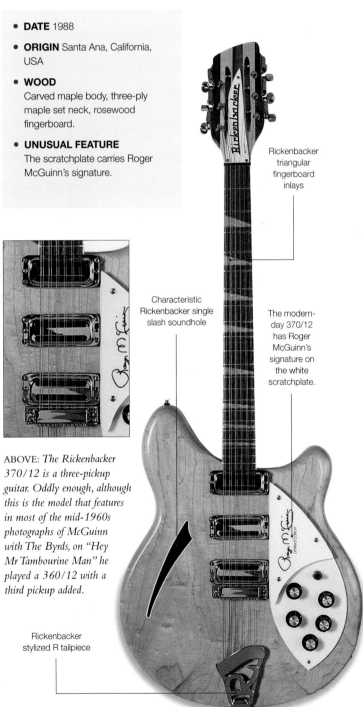

Rickenbacker triangular fingerboard inlays

Characteristic Rickenbacker single slash soundhole

The modern-day 370/12 has Roger McGuinn's signature on the white scratchplate.

ABOVE: *The Rickenbacker 370/12 is a three-pickup guitar. Oddly enough, although this is the model that features in most of the mid-1960s photographs of McGuinn with The Byrds, on "Hey Mr Tambourine Man" he played a 360/12 with a third pickup added.*

Rickenbacker stylized R tailpiece

Fender in the 1960s

By the 1960s, Fender was a well-established leader in the electric guitar market. Leo Fender, however, soon found himself facing a new problem – his health. The gradual worsening of a long-standing sinus problem led him to believe – wrongly as it happened – that he was seriously ill, and in 1965 he decided to sell his company. The buyer was Columbia Broadcasting Systems (CBS), which paid Fender $13 million.

Stratocaster, pre-1965

There has been a great deal of debate about the impact of the CBS buyout on Fender guitars. When the new management took over, cost-cutting measures were implemented. Rather than adversely affecting the quality of the guitars overnight, there seems to have been a very slow deterioration, which becomes much more noticeable in models produced in the 1970s. As a consequence, what are now known as pre-CBS Fenders – such as the example shown here – are highly collectible instruments.

- **DATE** Pre-dating CBS takeover in 1965
- **ORIGIN** Fullerton, California, USA
- **WOOD**
  Ash body, maple bolt-on neck, rosewood or maple fingerboard.
- **UNUSUAL FEATURE**
  Pre-CBS Stratocasters have solid steel inertia blocks at the bridge.

Coronado II, 1966

Designed by legendary luthier Roger Rossmeisl, the Coronado was a thinline, hollowbody guitar with two rounded cutaways. Rossmeisl had created many of Rickenbacker's classic designs and had been engaged by Fender to capitalize on the mid-1960s vogue for semi-acoustic guitars. Unlike the Gibson ES-335, which it superficially resembled, the Coronado was a genuine hollowbody instrument with a gently arched top – something of a departure for Fender.

- **DATE** 1966
- **ORIGIN** Fullerton, California, USA
- **WOOD**
  Beechwood back and sides, maple top, maple bolt-on neck, rosewood fingerboard.
- **UNUSUAL FEATURE**
  Available in Wildwood finish, made by injecting dye into the tree.

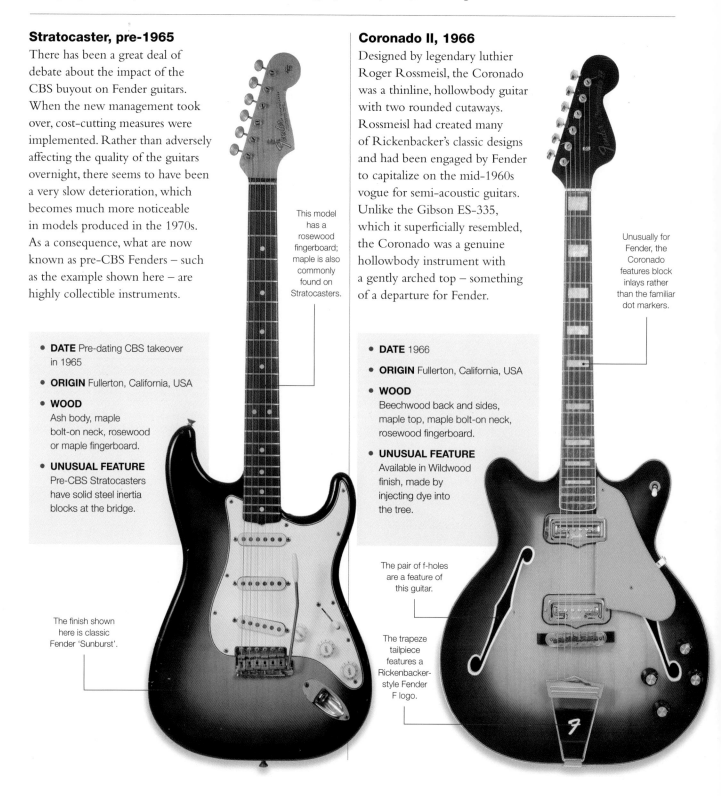

This model has a rosewood fingerboard; maple is also commonly found on Stratocasters.

Unusually for Fender, the Coronado features block inlays rather than the familiar dot markers.

The finish shown here is classic Fender 'Sunburst'.

The pair of f-holes are a feature of this guitar.

The trapeze tailpiece features a Rickenbacker-style Fender F logo.

Telecaster, 1968

In December 1968, a custom-built Fender Telecaster with a solid rosewood body was flown across the Atlantic and delivered by hand to George Harrison of The Beatles. It would be used extensively throughout the band's *Let It Be* sessions and at their final live performance – filmed on the roof of their Apple HQ. In 1969, Harrison gave the guitar to his friend Delaney Bramlett, who treasured the guitar until 2003 when he sold it at auction for $434,750. The buyer was later revealed to be Olivia Harrison, George's widow. This model went into general production in 1969.

- **DATE** 1968

- **ORIGIN** Fullerton, California, USA

- **WOOD**
  Maple and rosewood body, rosewood bolt-on neck, separate rosewood fingerboard.

- **UNUSUAL FEATURE**
  Rosewood is very rarely used for solid guitar bodies.

The body of this instrument is built from two pieces of rosewood sandwiching a thin piece of maple. The guitar went into general production between 1969 and 1972.

ABOVE: *The original Telecaster bridge mechanism contained three saddles, two strings resting on each; they were fully height-adjustable, but intonation could only be altered in pairs.*

Jimi Hendrix

ABOVE: *Jimi Hendrix played a variety of different guitars, but he was most readily associated with the Fender Stratocaster. Although he was a left-handed player, Hendrix preferred to play on a restrung right-handed guitar.*

In a career that lasted barely four years in the limelight, Jimi Hendrix (1942–1970) took the electric guitar into new territory, setting new standards for blues and rock improvisation.

Hendrix first picked up the guitar at the age of 12, and learnt by listening to the great electric blues players of the period, such as Muddy Waters and Elmore James. After a brief period in the US Army, Hendrix found work as a back-up musician for touring R&B artists, among them the Isley Brothers, Ike and Tina Turner and Little Richard. Spotted in a New York blues club, he was brought over to the UK, where he formed the Jimi Hendrix Experience. Together, this incredible rock trio produced landmark albums such as *Axis: Bold as Love* and *Are You Experienced?* and gave concert performances of startling virtuoso musicianship. Although he died in 1970, Hendrix's playing has continued to influence successive generations of young rock musicians.

Other 1960s US solidbodies

It is easy to form the view that the likes of Fender, Gibson, Gretsch, Epiphone and Rickenbacker *were* the American guitar industry. In fact, there were numerous less auspicious brands available. Some, like the Harmony brand, sold huge numbers of cheaper instruments, but the 1960s also saw the early days of the independent boutique guitar brands that would begin to flourish a decade later.

Alamo Fiesta 2568R, 1964

After the end of World War II, an electronics engineer Charles Eilenberg was recruited by the Southern Music chain of stores to set up a manufacturing workshop. Based in San Antonio, Texas, Alamo Electronics provided amplifiers and guitars to the cheaper end of the market. The instruments were characterized by thin bodies and rather unusual body shapes. The Fiesta, like others in the range, was not in fact a solidbody instrument, but was comprised of a birch plywood top glued on to a hollow core. Distribution was largely limited to the Southern states and across the Mexico border.

The truss rod cover on the headstock also doubles as guitar's logo display.

- **DATE** 1964
- **ORIGIN** Texas, San Antonio, USA
- **WOOD** Birch ply body, maple bolt-on neck, rosewood fingerboard.
- **UNUSUAL FEATURE** The unusually shaped extended bass horn gives the body a distinctive outline.

The futuristic body design was unusual for its time.

Harmony Bobkat H14, 1963

The Harmony company of Chicago produced more electric guitars than any other US manufacturer in the 1950s and '60s. The Bobkat (1963-71) series was among the finest solidbody electrics it produced. Although available in various guises – including the twin-pickup H15, the blue H16B and the white H16W – the single pickup identifies the Bobkat shown here as an H14. Its original red sunburst finish has been removed and the bare alder varnished for an attractive natural look. The original Harmony logo has also been removed.

- **DATE** 1963
- **ORIGIN** Chicago, Illinois, USA
- **WOOD** Alder body, maple bolt-on neck, rosewood fingerboard.
- **UNUSUAL FEATURE** The pickup is oddly positioned and angled.

The body is based broadly on the Fender Jaguar shape.

Floating wooden bridge

Bobkats with a V suffix have a vibrato tailpiece – this option was not available on the single-pickup H14.

Silvertone 1477, 1963

Produced by Harmony for Sears, Roebuck, the Silvertone 1477 is based on Harmony's own Bobkat H15. It featured a slimline three-quarter-scale-length neck, meaning that it was probably targeting the youth end of the market. The electronics were a notch up from other budget models, the pair of DeArmond Goldtone pickups being capable of producing a classic 1960s-style single-coil bite. With the ordinary guitar collector now priced out of the high end of the market, there is growing interest in models like this today.

- **DATE** 1963

- **ORIGIN** Chicago, Illinois, USA

- **WOOD**
  Alder or maple body, maple bolt-on neck, rosewood fingerboard.

- **UNUSUAL FEATURE**
  The use of upmarket DeArmond Goldtone pickups on a budget instrument was unusual.

Differentiating it from the Harmony Bobkat, the 1477 features block fingerboard inlays.

ABOVE: *The 1966 Harmony catalogue describes the Bobkat H15/Silvertone 1477 as having "Torque Lok adjustable dual reinforcing rods". This refers to the adjustable twin truss rods that support the neck, and which are accessed via the truss-rod cover on the headstock.*

Guitar making in the 1960s

The 1960s was a boom period for the electric guitar in the USA. While every fledgeling guitarist wanted a Fender, Gibson, Gretsch or Rickenbacker, these instruments were not aimed at the masses. For most, the alternative was provided by the Sears, Roebuck catalogue, which advertised and sold enormous volumes of Silvertone guitars – the most expensive of which cost barely 15 per cent of the price of a new Gibson.

These basic, mass-produced instruments were, of course, hardly comparable to the craftsmanship of the luthiers of Kalamazoo, Michigan, but they did provide an essential grounding in the electric guitar for just about every young American during the 1960s and '70s.

A significant proportion of the Silvertone-branded instruments were produced by the Chicago-based Harmony company and, as the examples here illustrate, were usually slightly modified versions of existing models. Harmony was the undisputed king of the production line, and, at its mid-1960s peak, it was building more electric guitars than all of America's other manufacturers put together.

ABOVE: *The Sears, Roebuck catalogue was the source for many a high-school band during the 1960s. At this time, a serviceable Silvertone electric guitar could be bought for around $60, while a Gibson SG Custom would have retailed at around $450.*

Italian electrics

Much of Italy's electric guitar manufacturing took place around Castelfidardo on the country's Adriatic coast. The area had been well known for producing accordions of global renown but had struggled in the aftermath of Italy's wartime defeat, and there was a corresponding decline in the popularity of the instrument. Some workshops saw the emerging popularity of the electric guitar as the way forward.

Wandré Rock Oval, c.1960

Luthier, anti-Fascist partisan fighter and conceptual artist, Antonio Pioli produced some extremely unorthodox guitar designs from the late 1950s to the start of the 1970s. Not only did he employ surreal body shapes – the Rock Oval is based on a Salvador Dalí painting – he also experimented with unorthodox materials; for example, using aluminium necks. The Rock Oval was usually labelled Wandré, Framez or Davoli (named after Pioli's collaborator Athos Davoli).

- **DATE** c.1960
- **ORIGIN** Italy
- **MATERIALS**
  Assorted hardwoods or fibreglass body, aluminium bolt-on neck.
- **UNUSUAL FEATURE**
  The body shape is like no other instrument.

The three-a-side, asymmetrically aligned tuners are positioned on a particularly wide headstock; with no string guides, this places greater stress on the nut.

This was perhaps the most extreme example of a cutaway ever seen in a guitar.

The Rock Oval's body shape is one of the strangest ever made. It seemed a futuristic design by the standards of 1960 when it was first produced, although it was inspired by Salvador Dalí's 1931 painting *The Persistence of Memory*. Despite its striking design, it was not entirely practical – it was almost impossible to play in the sitting position.

Eko 700/4V, 1961

Oliviero Pigini was among the first of Italy's accordion makers to turn to the electric guitar. Taking over his uncle's workshop in 1959, he brought a team of experienced luthiers to the region to make guitars under the Eko brand. In 1961, Pigini launched the 700 range. With its unique triple-cutaway body design and, on many models, the characteristic accordion-maker's sparkly plastic covering, it was an eye-catching instrument, and one that bore little resemblance to the popular classic US designs.

- **DATE** 1961
- **ORIGIN** Castelfidardo, Italy
- **WOOD**
  Mahogany body (other hardwoods were also used), maple set neck, rosewood fingerboard.
- **UNUSUAL FEATURE**
  The 700 featured a curious rear cutaway.

The third cutaway on the rear of the guitar remains an extremely unusual design feature.

The Eko 700/4V features an unusual array of electrics, including four pickups arranged in pairs. The multiple switches are wired for a range of pickup combinations.

Élite 40-V, 1962

The Crucianelli company had been building accordions in Castelfidardo since 1888. During the first half of the 1960s, its Élite range was Pigini's main competitor. Although the body shape of the 40-V is clearly Fender-inspired, the 'Italian' characteristics – the plastic sparkle covering used on accordions and the quirky pickup configuration – remain in place. Both the Crucianelli and Eko factories would later on produce some of the more distinctive models for the British-based Vox company.

- **DATE** 1962

- **ORIGIN** Castelfidardo, Italy

- **WOOD**
  Assorted woods, often basswood, used for the body, set neck.

- **UNUSUAL FEATURE**
  As with other Italian guitars, the Élite has a plastic sparkle finish similar to that used on accordions.

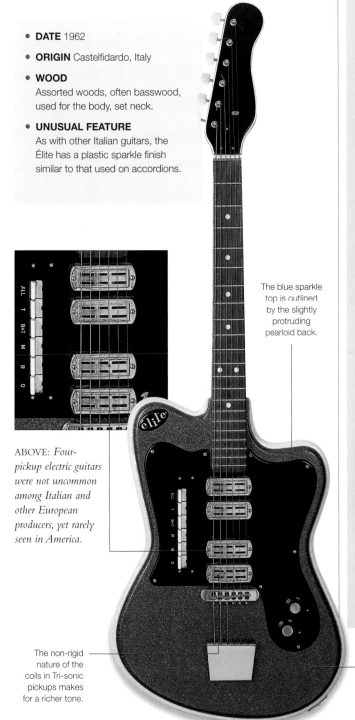

ABOVE: *Four-pickup electric guitars were not uncommon among Italian and other European producers, yet rarely seen in America.*

The blue sparkle top is outlined by the slightly protruding pearloid back.

The non-rigid nature of the coils in Tri-sonic pickups makes for a richer tone.

The Italian cult

The electric-guitar market in Italy thrived during the early 1960s. Like the rest of Europe, the popular US models were largely unobtainable, so a new industry emerged around the coastal town of Castelfidardo – formerly home to the country's celebrated accordion industry. Oliviero Pigini's Eko brand led the way – the Eko 700 range, with its unique rear cutaway, is perhaps the most celebrated Italian-built guitar of all time.

Almost all of the Castelfidardo guitar manufacturers evolved from accordion makers, which led to a number of curious similarities that set their instruments apart from those produced elsewhere, notably the strong tendency to take their decorative cues from the accordion: plain colours or natural finishes were largely eschewed in favour of sparkling plastic coverings. In the case of the Eko brand, Pigini developed a thick plastic protective coating, ensuring that the bodywork on many surviving examples of 50-year-old instruments remains in remarkably good condition. The electrics of these guitars were also unusual compared with models built elsewhere, favouring multiple pickups controlled by panels of large rocker switches.

Italian guitars of the 1960s are now highly collectible. While not in the same league as their famous US counterparts in terms of quality, their frequently eye-catching appearance has huge retro appeal.

ABOVE: *When demand for accordions began to dip, in 1956, 34-year-old Oliviero Pigini began successfully to import cheap guitars produced by the state musical instrument factory in neighbouring communist Yugoslavia. Taking a lead from Swedish accordion maker Hagström, Pigini set up his own manufacturing facilities in 1959, to produce EKO electric guitars.*

The body shape of the V-40 is curiously reminiscent of the 'non-reverse' Gibson Firebirds – even though it actually appeared three years earlier.

Is it a guitar or a bass?

There is a breed of instrument that occupies a kind of borderland between the bass and the guitar. These are six-string instruments designed with a scale length of between 660 and 762mm (26 and 30in), making them longer than a guitar but shorter than standard bass. This group includes baritone guitars and six-string basses, and although they are tuned differently, there is a good deal of crossover between the two.

Fender Bass VI, 1961

Pre-dating the similarly styled Fender Jaguar by a year, the Bass VI – unlike similarly scaled baritone guitars – was designed to be strung using standard pitch intervals, but one octave lower. A genuine curiosity, it is not entirely clear who Fender had in mind when it was created; it more than covered the range of a regular bass guitar and yet featured a vibrato arm and triple-pickup configuration. Perhaps the most notable group of users comprised nimble-fingered bass players such as John Entwistle and Jack Bruce.

- **DATE** 1961

- **ORIGIN** Fullerton, California, USA

- **WOOD**
  Alder body, maple bolt-on neck, rosewood fingerboard.

- **UNUSUAL FEATURE**
  Including a vibrato arm on an instrument mostly used as a bass was highly unorthodox, and rarely used unless playing melodic parts.

Burns Split Sound, 1962

Arguably, the first electric guitar that could be described as a baritone appeared in 1956, when Danelectro produced the UB2. Effectively a guitar with a 762mm (30in) scale length, it was sold as a six-string bass but more commonly used for playing low-pitched melodic lines. Burns produced the similarly ambiguous Split Sound, which was also rarely used as a conventional bass. It made good use of the Split Sound pickups, with the output of the bottom three strings being passed through independent circuitry from the top three.

- **DATE** 1962

- **ORIGIN** London, UK

- **WOOD**
  Mahogany body, maple set neck, rosewood fingerboard.

- **UNUSUAL FEATURE**
  Three-pickup basses are uncommon. The unorthodox Split Sound pickup enabled the bass strings to be given greater presence.

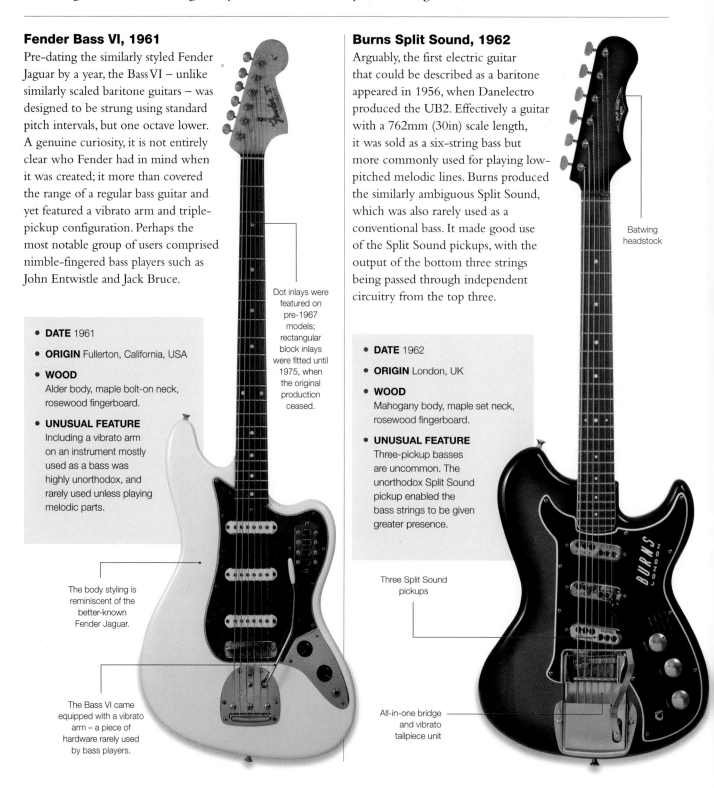

Dot inlays were featured on pre-1967 models; rectangular block inlays were fitted until 1975, when the original production ceased.

Batwing headstock

The body styling is reminiscent of the better-known Fender Jaguar.

The Bass VI came equipped with a vibrato arm – a piece of hardware rarely used by bass players.

Three Split Sound pickups

All-in-one bridge and vibrato tailpiece unit

Teisco VN-4, 1965

One of Japan's biggest guitar makers of the time, Teisco had been one the most prolific early offenders in the cheap-copy market, but by the mid-1960s had begun to produce guitars with a unique character. The VN-4 was marketed as a baritone guitar, although with a scale length of 673mm (26½in) – only 25.4mm (1in) longer than a standard Fender – it is certainly among the shorter baritones. Often rebranded prior to export, the VN-4 can also be found with the Ayer, Demian and Silvertone labels.

- **DATE** 1965

- **ORIGIN** Tokyo, Japan

- **WOOD**
  Plywood body, maple bolt-on neck, rosewood fingerboard.

- **UNUSUAL FEATURE**
  The controls (pickup rocker switches and roll-on volume and tone controls) are quirky.

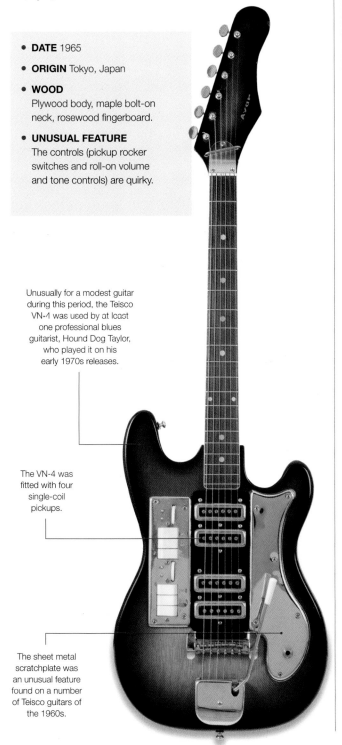

Unusually for a modest guitar during this period, the Teisco VN-4 was used by at least one professional blues guitarist, Hound Dog Taylor, who played it on his early 1970s releases.

The VN-4 was fitted with four single-coil pickups.

The sheet metal scratchplate was an unusual feature found on a number of Teisco guitars of the 1960s.

Baritone tuning

ABOVE: *A standard Gibson Les Paul with a 629mm (24¾in) scale length (left), shown alongside a baritone Les Paul with a 686mm (27in) scale length (right).*

There is no definitive fixed scale length in the world of the guitar or bass. Fenders, for example, are built with a 648mm (25½in) scale length, whereas Gibsons are typically 629mm (24¾in). The same is true with basses, which range from 762–914mm (30–36in). It is therefore difficult to define a baritone guitar by measuring the distance from the bridge to the nut.

The principal difference between a baritone guitar and a six-string bass is largely a matter of string type and tuning. Specialized string sets are generally required. Six-string basses, such as the Fender VI, are typically tuned to E-A-D-G-B-E – standard guitar tuning only one octave lower. It is possible to play them as regular bass guitars with the top two strings offering an extended register. Chords can also be played, although open chords may sound murky.

When using a set of baritone strings, standard tuning intervals are normally used, but taken down in pitch by a perfect fifth (A-D-G-C-E-A) or – more popularly among afficionados – a perfect fourth (B-E-A-D-F#-B).

Curious shapes

The vast majority of guitars ever produced have followed the traditional figure-of-eight Spanish style, later evolving towards single- or double-cutaway styles. However, there were guitar makers ready to look in different directions for inspiration, coming up with new basic shapes or creating personalized detailing. This thinking flourished in the 1980s, when metal guitarists began searching for ever-stranger shapes.

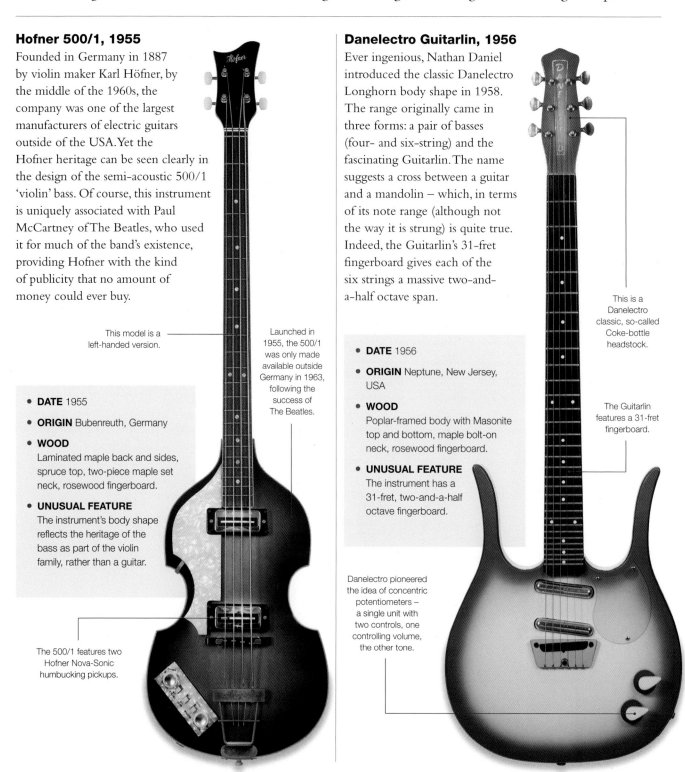

Hofner 500/1, 1955

Founded in Germany in 1887 by violin maker Karl Höfner, by the middle of the 1960s, the company was one of the largest manufacturers of electric guitars outside of the USA. Yet the Hofner heritage can be seen clearly in the design of the semi-acoustic 500/1 'violin' bass. Of course, this instrument is uniquely associated with Paul McCartney of The Beatles, who used it for much of the band's existence, providing Hofner with the kind of publicity that no amount of money could ever buy.

This model is a left-handed version.

- **DATE** 1955

- **ORIGIN** Bubenreuth, Germany

- **WOOD**
  Laminated maple back and sides, spruce top, two-piece maple set neck, rosewood fingerboard.

- **UNUSUAL FEATURE**
  The instrument's body shape reflects the heritage of the bass as part of the violin family, rather than a guitar.

Launched in 1955, the 500/1 was only made available outside Germany in 1963, following the success of The Beatles.

The 500/1 features two Hofner Nova-Sonic humbucking pickups.

Danelectro Guitarlin, 1956

Ever ingenious, Nathan Daniel introduced the classic Danelectro Longhorn body shape in 1958. The range originally came in three forms: a pair of basses (four- and six-string) and the fascinating Guitarlin. The name suggests a cross between a guitar and a mandolin – which, in terms of its note range (although not the way it is strung) is quite true. Indeed, the Guitarlin's 31-fret fingerboard gives each of the six strings a massive two-and-a-half octave span.

- **DATE** 1956

- **ORIGIN** Neptune, New Jersey, USA

- **WOOD**
  Poplar-framed body with Masonite top and bottom, maple bolt-on neck, rosewood fingerboard.

- **UNUSUAL FEATURE**
  The instrument has a 31-fret, two-and-a-half octave fingerboard.

This is a Danelectro classic, so-called Coke-bottle headstock.

The Guitarlin features a 31-fret fingerboard.

Danelectro pioneered the idea of concentric potentiometers – a single unit with two controls, one controlling volume, the other tone.

Harvey Thomas Custom Hollowbody, *c.*1962

Based in Kent, Washington, USA, Harvey Thomas was evidently a very unusual fellow, often seen performing locally during the 1960s with his own triple-neck guitar and an early electronic rhythm and effects device he called the Infernal Music Machine. His guitars were all handbuilt and appeared in a variety of unusual shapes – like the famous Maltese Surfer. The model shown here is particularly unusual in that the archtop body is in fact hollowed out of just a single piece of wood.

- **DATE** *c.*1962

- **ORIGIN** Kent, Washington, USA

- **WOOD**
  Carved maple hollow body, maple set neck, rosewood fingerboard.

- **UNUSUAL FEATURE**
  The body is hollow, but carved from a single piece of wood.

The fretboard marker inlays were made by routing a rectangular hole and inserting a piece of drum pearl – the plastic sparkly material used to cover drum kits.

The body is particularly large.

Harvey Thomas guitars were built in very small quantities, making them an appealing prospect for collectors.

The neck pickup is placed at an angle.

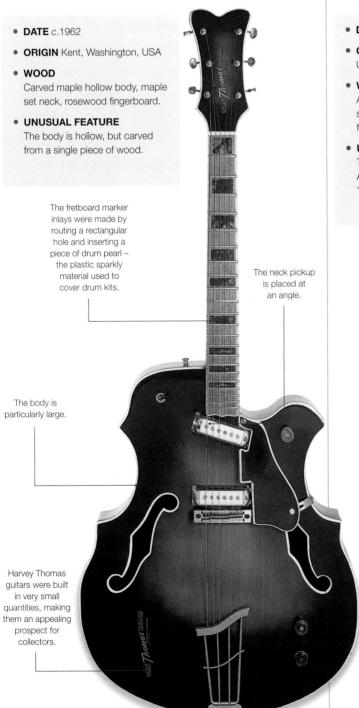

Mosrite Strawberry Alarm Clock, 1967

Semie Moseley had an excellent pedigree as a luthier – having trained under both Paul Bigsby and Rickenbacker's Roger Rossmeisl – and had established his Mosrite brand with the models he created for The Ventures. By 1967, however, surf instrumental bands were out of vogue, which led Moseley to look elsewhere – to America's most popular psychedelic pop group, the Strawberry Alarm Clock. The result was a brightly hand-painted instrument with its bizarre 'exoskeleton' that now looks like a rather curious period piece.

- **DATE** 1967

- **ORIGIN** Bakersfield, California, USA

- **WOOD**
  Alder body/exoskeleton, set maple neck, rosewood fingerboard.

- **UNUSUAL FEATURE**
  The Mosrite Strawberry Alarm Clock has a unique 'exoskeleton' frame design.

These instruments were available as six- and twelve-string guitars, or four-string basses; each came in a different colour.

Each of the Mosrite Strawberry Alarm Clocks was given a psychedelic paint job by surfboard artist Von Dutch (Kenny Howard).

Combined bridge, tailpiece and vibrato unit

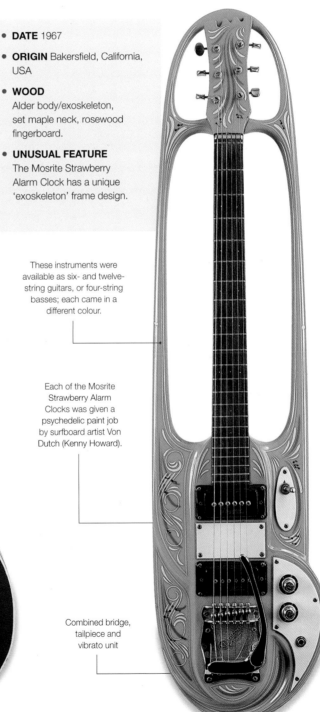

The new Gibson Les Pauls

The Les Paul was produced throughout the 1950s, but when it became apparent that it was unable to stem the growing success of Fender – a company that had barely existed a decade earlier – Gibson decided to replace the line. However, when the popularity of second-hand Les Paul Standards began to bloom during the 1960s, Gibson decided to relaunch the model – and even brought some additions to the range.

Les Paul Deluxe, 1968

Among the first of the new 1968 Les Pauls, the Deluxe featured Gibson New York mini-humbuckers – leftover stock from when Gibson began switching Epiphone production to Japan. In its first incarnation, the Deluxe featured a one-piece body and slim three-piece neck; a year later this was replaced by the so-called pancake body – a thin layer of maple covering two layers of Honduran mahogany. The Les Paul Deluxe did not prove to be anything like as popular as the Standard, but continued until 1985.

The fingerboard features pearled trapezoid marker inlays.

- **DATE** 1968

- **ORIGIN** Kalamazoo, Michigan, USA

- **WOOD**
  Mahogany body (with maple pancake top from 1969), mahogany set neck, rosewood fingerboard.

- **UNUSUAL FEATURE**
  The New York mini-humbuckers set it apart from most other Les Pauls.

The New York mini-humbuckers were fitted to a standard P-90 cavity using an adaptor ring.

Les Paul Recording, 1971

The Les Paul Recording was part of the same controversial range that introduced the low-impedance Les Paul Personal and Professional models. Central to the idea was that these pickups would be suitable for direct input into a mixing board, and capable of a cleaner sound with a wider frequency response and reduction in hum. Unlike the other two models, there was an impedance switch as well on the control panel, which in Hi mode would still make the guitar capable of overdriving an amplifier.

Instead of the usual tone control, the Recording featured tone filter switches and separate bass and treble pots.

- **DATE** 1971

- **ORIGIN** Kalamazoo, Michigan, USA

- **WOOD**
  Clear Honduras mahogany with centre band, three-piece mahogany set neck, rosewood fingerboard.

- **UNUSUAL FEATURE**
  The low-impedance pickups and extensive on-board filter circuitry.

The Decade Control is an 11-position switch that tunes or alters the treble harmonics.

Long travel bridge

Les Paul Studio, 1983

Introduced in 1983, the Les Paul Studio, as the name suggests, was designed with the studio musician in mind. Unlike the early 1970s low-impedance models, however, the Studio features regular Les Paul electrics. The intention was to produce a lower-priced Les Paul stripped of the expensive cosmetics, such as body and neck binding and ornate inlays, but standard in most other ways. The Studio has, nonetheless, been seen frequently on stage – its slightly thinner body, lower weight and frugal appearance is attractive to many modern professional players.

- **DATE** 1983

- **ORIGIN** Kalamazoo, Michigan, USA

- **WOOD**
  Mahogany body, maple top, mahogany set neck, rosewood fingerboard (ebony on later models).

- **UNUSUAL FEATURE**
  The stripped-down look requires no binding on the body or neck.

The Studio is identifiable from the legend on the truss rod cover on the headstock.

Unbound neck

ABOVE: *The Tune-o-matic bridge was designed by Gibson president Ted McCarty, and first appeared in 1954 on the Les Paul Custom. Offering the possibility of altering the intonation for each string, it became standard on all of the company's fixed-bridge guitars.*

The body of the Studio is around 6mm (¹/₄in) thinner than a standard Les Paul.

Frank Zappa

Composer, singer, record producer, film director and dazzlingly brilliant guitarist, Frank Zappa (1940–93) released more than 60 albums over a period of 30 years, either as a solo artist or with his band The Mothers of Invention.

Freak Out!, the debut album by the Mothers, set the tone for his career, combining conventional pop and rock songs – often humorously digging at society, politics and religion – with free jazz improvisations and *musique concrète*-style studio-generated sound collages.

By 1969, although moderately successful, Zappa struggled to finance the nine-piece Mothers of Invention, and the group folded. Throughout the 1970s, he toured and recorded with a succession of small and highly disciplined ensembles, his music becoming increasingly jazz-rock oriented.

From the mid-1980s, Zappa became excited by the compositional possibilities of early digital sampling technology, and his attention switched away from the guitar. Indeed, apart from a brief guitar solo, his Grammy-winning 1986 album *Jazz from Hell* was produced entirely on a Synclavier sampler.

Zappa continued recording until shortly before his death in 1993 from prostate cancer.

ABOVE: *Throughout most of the 1970s, Frank Zappa was most often seen in concert playing a Gibson SG. The following decade he switched to a Les Paul Custom or Fender Stratocaster, both of which he retrofitted with DiMarzio pickups.*

The last Gibson originals

The 1970s and '80s proved to be a trying time for Fender and Gibson alike, their reputations both on the wane. The problem was a perceived fall in quality resulting from corporate takeovers, as well as competition from small independent manufacturers – some of which were producing instruments that made the American classic designs that had emerged in the 1950s seem increasingly dated.

S-1, 1976

Seth Lover had designed the first humbucking pickup in 1955, and from the end of the decade it was fitted to almost all Gibson electrics. Yet, into the 1970s, Gibson still made the occasional foray into traditional Fender single-coil territory. The 1975 S-1 was noted for its electrics, with the three 'see-thru' single-coil pickups designed by Bill Lawrence and backed by some of the most elaborate circuitry seen in a non-active guitar. A very versatile instrument, it remained in production for only four years, in spite of endorsements from Carlos Santana and The Rolling Stones.

- **DATE** 1976
- **ORIGIN** Kalamazoo, Michigan, USA
- **WOOD** Alder body, maple bolt-on neck, rosewood fingerboard.
- **UNUSUAL FEATURE** Single-coil pickups and a bolt-on neck were unusual on post-1960s Gibsons.

The headstock is modelled on that of the Flying V.

The complex wiring of the S-1 comes together on the four-position chicken-head phase switch. This, combined with other on-board switching, makes it possible to produce a wide range of single- and twin-coil sounds.

The S-1 features an adjustable bridge with a stop tailpiece.

RD Artist, 1977

Launched in 1977, the RD series of maple-bodied instruments were designed to create a brighter sound than existing Gibson models. They feature active electronics designed by synth pioneer Dr Robert Moog. In a further nod towards Fender, the RD guitars were built with a 648mm (25½in) scale length – 19mm (¾in) longer than Gibson's long-established standard. The flagship model, the RD Artist, features an electronic circuitboard that runs the full length of the body, and is powered by a 9-volt battery that is accessible from the back cover.

- **DATE** 1977
- **ORIGIN** Kalamazoo, Michigan, USA
- **WOOD** Maple body, laminated maple set neck, ebony fingerboard.
- **UNUSUAL FEATURE** The Fender-proportioned scale length on early models was new for Gibson, and the circuitry designed by Bob Moog was unique.

The tuners, like the rest of the hardware, are gold-plated.

The RD Artist has a pair of gold-plated Series VI humbucking pickups.

The body shape is based broadly on the 'reverse' Firebirds of the early 1960s.

Victory MVX, 1981

Launched in 1981, the two models in Gibson's Victory MV (multi-voice) range were created as direct competitors to Fender's big two. While the twin-pickup MVII was marketed towards Telecaster-toting country players, the MVX, with its "myriad of separate and distinct electric guitar tonalities" (according to the marketing literature), was pitched against the Stratocaster. The MVX was kitted with two newly designed magnet/iron-loaded humbuckers in the neck and bridge positions, and a Super Stack humbucker in the centre.

- **DATE** 1981

- **ORIGIN** Kalamazoo, Michigan, USA

- **WOOD**
  Maple body, three-piece bolt-on maple neck, rosewood fingerboard.

- **UNUSUAL FEATURE**
  Bolt-on necks are unusual on Gibson guitars.

ABOVE: *The Gibson Victory MV range was more than a little Fender-like in its appearance — both in body shape and six-in-a-line tuners on the headstock.*

Uniquely for Gibson, the dot markers are positioned along the side of the fingerboard.

The Victory MVX shown here has been modified, its original Gibson pickups having been replaced.

Corvus III, 1982

The 1980s saw the ascendency of a new breed of American guitar maker. Brands such as Kramer, B. C. Rich and Jackson began to capture the imagination of a new generation of rock guitarists, with their futuristic, angular body shapes and high-end hardware. Gibson's response to this trend was the curiously retro-looking Corvus series, its body widely known as 'the can opener'. The three Corvus models, kitted out with different pickup configurations, probably represent Gibson's last attempt at creating an original design.

- **DATE** 1982

- **ORIGIN** Kalamazoo, Michigan, USA

- **WOOD**
  American alder, maple bolt-on neck, rosewood fingerboard.

- **UNUSUAL FEATURE**
  Its body shape turned heads, with many describing it as 'the can opener'.

The Corvus III shown here has three single-coil pickups with a five-way selector switch; the Corvus I is equipped with a single high-output Alnico V humbucker; while the Corvus II has an Alnico V at the bridge and a regular Gibson humbucker at the neck.

Although an attempt at a 1980s reinvention, the Corvus rather recalls early 1970s guitars, such as the Ovation solidbodies – even down to the selection of colour finishes.

The rear cutaway gives the Corvus its 'can opener' soubriquet.

Yamaha

Appearing relatively late on the scene, Yamaha's first electric guitars did not emerge until 1966. In contrast to other Japanese guitar makers of the period, these were well-built instruments, which often exhibited interesting design features. It is perhaps unsurprising that, a decade later, Yamaha would be in the vanguard of the first wave of high-end Japanese guitar production.

SG60T, 1972

The first generation of Yamaha electrics, the so-called Flying Samurai models, made little impact in the West – a surf guitar launched in 1967 had limited appeal outside of Japan – and it was not until the 1970s that Yamaha established its credentials as a serious guitar maker. An early indication of intent came in 1972 with the second-generation SG60T, a twin-humbucker model with a bolt-on neck and a body shape, and an unorthodox German carve, influenced by both Gibson and Mosrite. There are two models: the hardtail SG60 and the SG60T, which has a vibrato unit.

The scale length is 628mm (24½in).

- **DATE** 1972
- **ORIGIN** Hamamatsu, Japan
- **WOOD**
  Mahogany body, mahogany bolt-on neck, rosewood fingerboard.
- **UNUSUAL FEATURE**
  German-carve body contour.

Like the earlier Flying Samurais, the neck pickup is set at an extreme angle – although, strangely, slanted in the opposite direction.

SG2000, 1976

Aware that the classic US brands had lost some of their reputation, by the mid-1970s Yamaha felt it was time to make a bold statement and produce a Japanese-built guitar with the same high production values as Gibson and have it endorsed by a celebrity. They came up with the SG2000, which bears more than a passing resemblance to a Gibson SG, but has such luxury features as a straight-through neck and gold-plated hardware. With Carlos Santana the willing endorsee, the SG2000 showed beyond any doubt that Japan was capable of producing world-class instruments.

Each pickup has dedicated tone and volume controls.

- **DATE** 1976
- **ORIGIN** Hamamatsu, Japan
- **WOOD**
  Mahogany back, carved maple top, mahogany and maple straight-through neck, rosewood fingerboard.
- **UNUSUAL FEATURE**
  T-cross neck construction.

There are two covered Alnico V humbucking pickups.

Yamaha T-O-M bridge unit

Pacifica, 1989

The Yamaha Pacifica range is one the company's most enduring lines, having remained in production for over two decades. Designed as a test project at Yamaha's California custom shop, they went into production in Japan, the entry-level models proving to be particularly successful. The Pacifica range was clearly Fender-influenced, the double-cutaway – shown here – appearing as an elongated Stratocaster. There is also a Telecaster-type single-cutaway model. The budget models are all bolt-on neck constructions; however, early Pacificas, such as the PAC1412 models, had set necks and and other high-end features that ultimately proved too costly for Yamaha's market.

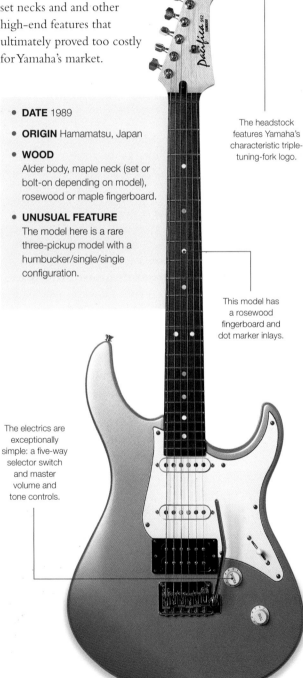

- **DATE** 1989

- **ORIGIN** Hamamatsu, Japan

- **WOOD**
  Alder body, maple neck (set or bolt-on depending on model), rosewood or maple fingerboard.

- **UNUSUAL FEATURE**
  The model here is a rare three-pickup model with a humbucker/single/single configuration.

The headstock features Yamaha's characteristic triple-tuning-fork logo.

This model has a rosewood fingerboard and dot marker inlays.

The electrics are exceptionally simple: a five-way selector switch and master volume and tone controls.

The new wave of Japanese manufacturers

The Yamaha guitars produced from the early 1970s brought about a change in the perception of instruments built in Japan. They were quickly joined by Ibanez, who, after Gibson's legal threats, began to produce a range of respectable originals such as the Iceman and the Axstar, through to the Steve Vai-developed Jem superstrats. Into the 1980s, Aria Pro II and the Westone brand (built at the Matsumoku factory) also made a mark with innovative and interesting instruments, and copies produced by Tokai were suddenly seen as serious rivals to the originals.

Such a rise in production values naturally meant higher manufacturing costs. As a consequence, low-end models or diffusion ranges were gradually brought in from countries with a cheaper labour force, such as South Korea, Mexico, Indonesia and more recently China. This has resulted in an upsurge of interest in Japanese-built instruments from the 1970s and '80s. For example, although they still don't enjoy the same brand cachet, the first Squier Stratocasters, produced from 1982 by Fender Japan, are now generally viewed as at least comparable to the more expensive 'real' Strats being built at the same time in the USA.

ABOVE: *Carlos Santana was the first major Western artist to endorse a Japanese-built guitar. He's seen here with a Yamaha SG2000, which he played a major role in popularizing. During the 1980s, he switched allegiance to the US Paul Reed Smith brand, and was an important figure in its early successes.*

1970s American solidbodies

From the end of the 1960s, a number of small American companies emerged to challenge the major names in guitar manufacture. Some, such as Ovation and Travis Bean, appeared on the scene with radical new ideas in construction and design; others, including Alembic and Peavey, came to guitar production from a successful background in electronics design.

Alembic Series 1, c.1971

Emerging from the late 1960s Californian music scene, Alembic initially supplied exclusive high-end sound equipment to top West Coast bands Jefferson Airplane and the Grateful Dead. They moved towards instrument manufacture, having pioneered a system of active on-board circuitry that gave their pickups a much wider audio bandwidth than traditional passive units. Although Alembic has produced six-string models, the company's reputation is based on having producing some of the finest basses ever.

The technology behind the early Alembics made them among the most advanced guitars on the market at that time.

- **DATE** c.1971

- **ORIGIN** Santa Rosa, California, USA

- **WOOD**
  Assorted woods, commonly maple/purpleheart straight-through neck with mahogany body 'wings' and ebony fretboard.

- **UNUSUAL FEATURE**
  The protrusion at the bottom of the body is a signature feature, as is the active circuitry.

Low-impedance pickups boosted by active circuitry gave the Alembic a wider dynamic range than passive pickups.

The pointed protrusion at the bottom was said to have been to encourage players to use a guitar stand.

Ovation Viper, 1973

With its reputation forged on groundbreaking electro-acoustic guitars, Ovation fared less well in the solidbody market. Its first attempt, 1971's Breadwinner, was simply too odd-looking for its time (and is now something of a cult instrument). Two years later, a more conventional model appeared, the Viper, which clearly resembles a scaled-down Ovation acoustic with a single cutaway. An outstanding guitar with biting high-output pickups, the Viper remained in production until the early 1980s.

The alder body followed the contours of a standard Ovation acoustic guitar; a single cutaway would later become commonplace on Ovation acoustics.

- **DATE** 1973

- **ORIGIN** New Hartford, Connecticut, USA

- **WOOD**
  Alder body, one-piece maple bolt-on neck and fingerboard.

- **UNUSUAL FEATURE**
  The high-output pickups, which were a selling point of the instrument.

Ovation advertising literature of the time claimed that the Viper's single-coil pickups had 30 per cent more windings than other similar models, resulting in a 6dB boost in output.

Kramer 450T, 1976

Gary Kramer set up his Neptune, New Jersey, factory in 1976 with the sole intention of making aluminium-necked guitars, an idea that he and his former business partner Travis Bean had pioneered earlier in search of greater sustain. The Travis Bean-branded models had used a straight-through neck design, which created an excellent sound, but they were extremely heavy and could react badly to temperature change. Kramer adapted the neck principle by using a T-shaped aluminium block filled with a walnut inlay on either side, reducing it to a more manageable weight.

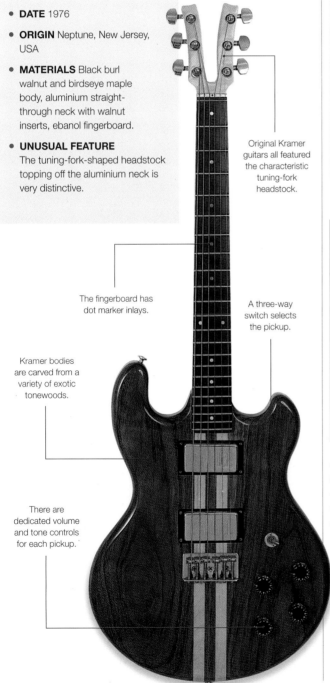

- **DATE** 1976

- **ORIGIN** Neptune, New Jersey, USA

- **MATERIALS** Black burl walnut and birdseye maple body, aluminium straight-through neck with walnut inserts, ebanol fingerboard.

- **UNUSUAL FEATURE** The tuning-fork-shaped headstock topping off the aluminium neck is very distinctive.

Original Kramer guitars all featured the characteristic tuning-fork headstock.

The fingerboard has dot marker inlays.

A three-way switch selects the pickup.

Kramer bodies are carved from a variety of exotic tonewoods.

There are dedicated volume and tone controls for each pickup.

Peavey T-60, 1978

Having designed and built his first guitar amplifier while still in high school, Hartley Peavey set up a small company in the basement of his home in 1965. Within a decade, Peavey was one of the biggest names in the world of music electronics. The first Peavey electric guitar, the T-60, launched in 1978, found an immediate place in guitar history as the first production model to be built using computer-controlled carving machines. The T-60 and its bass counterpart, the T-40, were both well regarded mid-market guitars in their day.

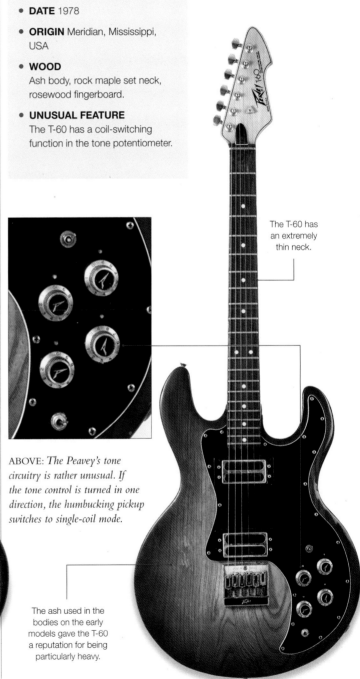

- **DATE** 1978

- **ORIGIN** Meridian, Mississippi, USA

- **WOOD** Ash body, rock maple set neck, rosewood fingerboard.

- **UNUSUAL FEATURE** The T-60 has a coil-switching function in the tone potentiometer.

The T-60 has an extremely thin neck.

ABOVE: *The Peavey's tone circuitry is rather unusual. If the tone control is turned in one direction, the humbucking pickup switches to single-coil mode.*

The ash used in the bodies on the early models gave the T-60 a reputation for being particularly heavy.

Britain in the 1970s

The last decade in which British electric guitars were built in any great quantity, the 1970s saw the brief emergence of Shergold, which evolved from the Hayman brand, a key figure in which had been none other than Jim Burns, the 'British Leo Fender'. The second half of the decade saw Burns embark on two final ill-fated business projects, Burns UK and Jim Burns Actualizers.

Ned Callan Cody, 1973

London luthier Peter Cook had been well known for custom-building instruments for the likes of B. B. King and The Who when he agreed to develop a range of guitars for the Shaftsbury brand. Adopting the pseudonym Ned Callan, Cook designed the Western-styled Cody and Hombre models, which were built at the East London Shergold factory. With its curious double-cutaway horns, the Cody became widely known as the Nobbly Ned.

- **DATE** 1973
- **ORIGIN** London, UK
- **WOOD**
  Obeche body, maple bolt-on neck, rosewood fingerboard.
- **UNUSUAL FEATURE**
  The circular scratchplate and winged bridge cover plate both add to the singular appearance of this guitar.

Unusual unsculpted headstock design

The circular scratchplate of Nobby Ned houses a pair of soapbar pickups.

Basic electrics – a master volume and tone control and a three-way selector switch

Shergold Masquerader, 1975

Like much of the British guitar industry, Shergold's roots were linked to Jim Burns. Founded in 1967 by Jack Golder and Norman Houlder, two former Burns employees, Shergold initially produced woodwork for other guitar manufacturers. When Hayman, one of their clients, collapsed in 1974, Shergold continued operations, launching a range of guitars that drew heavily on the four Hayman models. The last significant British mass-producer of electric guitars, the final Shergolds came off the production line in 1982.

- **DATE** 1975
- **ORIGIN** London, UK
- **WOOD**
  Obeche body, maple bolt-on neck, maple fingerboard.
- **UNUSUAL FEATURE**
  This, like most Shergold guitars and basses, has a body made from obeche, a West African tree that produces a lightweight wood.

Unusually, the headstock features string guides for the A, D, G and B strings.

'Apple Green' is the most popular finish among Shergold collectors.

The Masquerader's circuitry was extremely versatile: pickups could be switched from humbucker to single coil and out of phase.

The lacquer used on Shergold guitars does not age well – examples with no cracking are rare.

Burns UK Mirage, 1976

Jim Burns had always been more of an innovator than a businessman. Having been forced to sell the original Burns brand in 1965, he had been engaged by Dallas Arbiter to work on designs for the short-lived Hayman range. In 1974, he reappeared with the Burns UK brand and a small range of curious-looking instruments. These included the Flyte – a model based on the shape of the Concorde supersonic jet – and its close relative, the more obscure Mirage, described in the company literature as a "colourful swinging axe".

- **DATE** 1976

- **ORIGIN** Newcastle upon Tyne, UK

- **WOOD**
  Selected hardwood body, Canadian rock maple bolt-on neck, maple fingerboard.

- **UNUSUAL FEATURE**
  Both the body shape and the curiously positioned tuners are unique to this instrument.

ABOVE: *The positioning of the tuners on the headstock is quite extraordinary – they are both asymmetrically and inconsistently spaced.*

The pickups are the unusually shaped Burns Mach One Humbusters, featuring Alcomax four-bar magnets.

The scratchplate follows the contour of the body and secures the electrics.

Gordon-Smith Gypsy 60 SS, 1980

The largest guitar maker in Britain today, Lancashire-based Gordon-Smith is very well known for producing quality instruments based on classic US designs. The Gypsy range comprises both solid and semi-solid (SS) models, with single and twin cutaways, and resembles the Gibson Les Paul Junior. The Gypsy 60 SS is an attractive mahogany-bodied semi-solid with distinctively large twin f-holes.

- **DATE** 1980

- **ORIGIN** Partington, UK

- **WOOD**
  Mahogany body, mahogany set neck, rosewood fingerboard.

- **UNUSUAL FEATURE**
  The oversize f-holes are a feature of this instrument.

The headstock shape, like the body, echoes the lines of the original Gibson Les Paul.

The model shown here has two single-coil pickups – humbucking models are also available. The company make its own pickups, and was the first to offer coil-tapped humbuckers.

Distinctive dolphin soundholes

The new Fender classics

Fender was never a company to tinker too much with a winning formula. Amendments over the years to the already iconic Stratocaster and Telecaster models had thus far been subtle. In the 1970s, however, Fender decided to introduce a new range of three Telecasters: the hollowbody Thinline, and two models armed with Fender's state-of-the-art range of humbucking pickups.

Telecaster Deluxe, 1972

The histories of the Fender and Gibson brands is peppered with one of them responding to the other's successes. The popularity of the Gibson SG and the 1968 relaunch of the Les Paul pushed the humbucking pickup centre stage. One reaction by Fender was to hire Seth Lover, the ex-Gibson man who, in the 1950s, had developed the PAF humbucker. The result was the Fender Wide Range pickup. The new flagship Telecaster, the Deluxe, was the first instrument to be kitted out with these powerful new pickups.

- **DATE** 1972
- **ORIGIN** Fullerton, California, USA
- **WOOD**
  Ash body, maple bolt-on neck, maple fingerboard.
- **UNUSUAL FEATURE**
  Curiously for Telecaster, this model features a Stratocaster-style headstock.

Telecaster Custom, 1972

Often referred to as the 72 Custom – to avoid confusion with the Custom Telecaster produced between 1959 and 1968 – the new model was an attempt to retain the characteristic bite of the traditional Telecaster bridge pickup with a humbucking sound at the neck. The Custom was noteworthy for having been built using dense ash for the body. This resulted in a substantially heavier instrument – by almost 30 per cent – but one with a thicker sound and arguably capable of greater sustain.

- **DATE** 1972
- **ORIGIN** Fullerton, California, USA
- **WOOD**
  Ash body, maple bolt-on neck, maple fingerboard.
- **UNUSUAL FEATURE**
  This Telecaster features a rare combination of both a single-coil pickup and a humbucker.

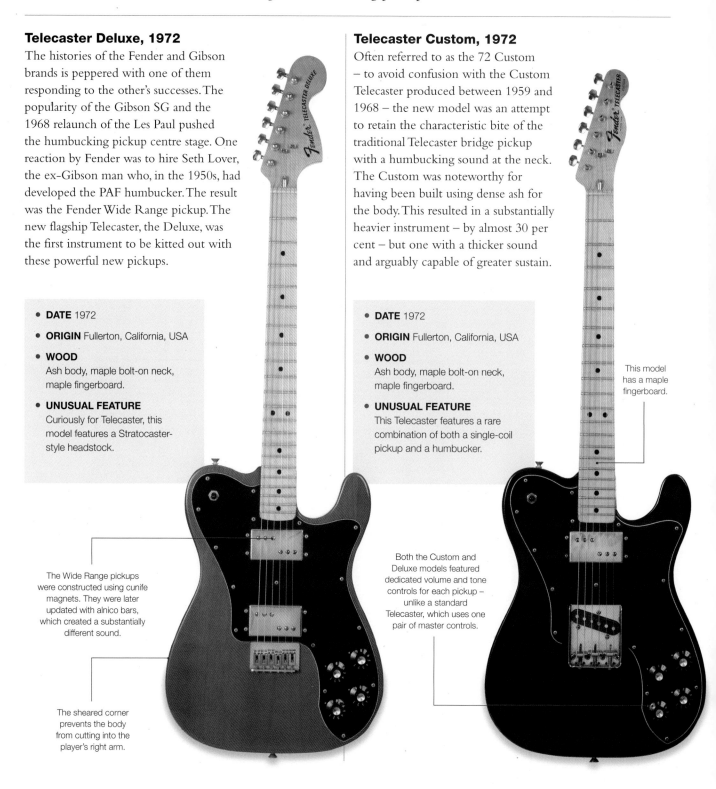

This model has a maple fingerboard.

The Wide Range pickups were constructed using cunife magnets. They were later updated with alnico bars, which created a substantially different sound.

The sheared corner prevents the body from cutting into the player's right arm.

Both the Custom and Deluxe models featured dedicated volume and tone controls for each pickup – unlike a standard Telecaster, which uses one pair of master controls.

Stratocaster, 1965

By the middle of the 1970s, the Stratocaster was still the most popular solidbody electric guitar in the world. However, there was a wide perception that production standards had dropped, and a growing market for used pre-CBS Stratocasters – those made before the CBS takeover in 1965. The basic Stratocaster has altered little since then: the most significant change took place in 1977 with the introduction of the five-way selector switch. This eradicated the age-old Stratocaster players' technique of wedging the original three-way switches to produce a greater variety of tones.

- **DATE** From 1965

- **ORIGIN** Fullerton, California, USA

- **WOOD**
  Ash body (variations have included alder, poplar, bass-wood, mahogany and koa), maple bolt-on neck, maple or rosewood fingerboard.

- **UNUSUAL FEATURE**
  Early Strats had a three-way selector switch, but since 1977, a five-way switch has been used.

Strat players discovered that the standard three-way pickup selector switch could be wedged into position between settings, using objects such as matchsticks to provide greater tonal variety. From 1977, the Strat was fitted with a notched five-way switch for these in-between settings, as seen here.

Like most standard Fenders, the Stratocaster comes with a rosewood or maple fingerboard.

Eric Clapton

One of Britain's most noted guitarists, Eric Clapton (b. 1945) first came to attention as an 18-year-old member of the Yardbirds, an R&B band that played on the same club circuit as the young Rolling Stones. Leaving the band in 1965, when its sound shifted towards pop, Clapton joined John Mayall's Bluesbreakers, where he quickly established himself as one of the country's most gifted electric players.

In 1966, Clapton, with bassist Jack Bruce and drummer Ginger Baker, formed Cream, generally thought to be the first rock/blues power trio. Hugely popular on both sides of the Atlantic, Cream provided a template for much of the heavy-riffing rock that followed, particularly during the 1970s.

When Cream broke up, Clapton engaged in projects of varying note, among them Derek and the Dominoes, which recorded "Layla", one of rock's all-time great anthems.

Throughout the 1980s, he established a niche for easy-listening rock, which saw his guitar skills taking a back seat. He has since taken on the role of elder statesman of blues, famously performing unplugged.

ABOVE: *Eric Clapton playing Blackie, a composite Stratocaster he built in 1970 using parts taken from three 1956–57 models. He used it extensively live and in the studio until the early 1990s. In 2004, Blackie was sold at auction for $959,500 to raise funds for the Crossroads Centre, a drug-rehabilitation centre that Clapton himself had founded.*

Alternative materials

The early days of guitar electrification saw Rickenbacker experimenting with aluminium and Bakelite, and Dobro/National with metal bodies. Yet, as the electric guitar gained popularity, it was clear that guitarists were more interested in guitars built traditionally – using wood. This has not, however, prevented a number of maverick luthiers from experimenting successfully with other materials.

Ampeg Dan Armstrong, 1969

The Ampeg brand was founded in the 1940s, its sole aim back then to provide amplification for jazz acoustic-bass players. In 1968, under new ownership, Ampeg engaged young luthier Dan Armstrong as a consultant to improve its Grammer line of guitars. Armstrong instead came up with an altogether new line, a see-through guitar built from a strong, clear acrylic plastic called Plexiglass. The material was chosen because the density of the material would give the instrument greater sustain. Armstrong also produced a bass model, famously used on stage during the early 1970s by Bill Wyman of The Rolling Stones.

- **DATE** 1969
- **ORIGIN** Linden, New Jersey, USA
- **MATERIALS**
  Plexiglass body, maple bolt-on neck, rosewood fingerboard.
- **UNUSUAL FEATURE**
  The body materials and modular pickup design single this guitar out.

The pickups were specially developed by Bill Lawrence.

There were six different quick-change slot-in pickup options available.

Two strap buttons at the base of the body

Travis Bean TB1000, 1974

Between 1974 and 1979, Travis Bean produced around 3,600 guitars and basses, each one fitted with a revolutionary aluminium straight-through neck. Expensive to manufacture and created with unusually high production values, Travis Beans were too costly for most non-professional players. Aluminium was used because, in theory, its density would allow for greater sustain. The downside was that the guitars were heavy, slightly unbalanced and could result in tuning problems when room temperature or humidity changed.

- **DATE** 1974
- **ORIGIN** Sun Valley, California, USA
- **WOOD**
  Koa body, aluminium set neck, rosewood fingerboard.
- **UNUSUAL FEATURE**
  Its characteristic open-T headstock design and its aluminium neck and scratchplate.

Travis Bean guitars are immediately recognizable from the cut-out T in the headstock; when Gary Kramer left the company, he adapted the idea for his own tuning-fork headstocks.

The Travis Bean's body is carved from costly Hawaiian koa. When Bean's investors pressurized him to try to reduce prices, refusing to compromise on quality, he simply chose to cease production.

Ovation Adamas, 1977

Aeronautical engineer Charles Kaman enjoyed a successful career designing helicopters and aviation components. He was also a keen guitarist who, during the 1960s, used the cutting-edge technological capabilities of the Kaman Corporation to produce a new type of guitar. Accepting the orthodox view that the key to the quality of an acoustic guitar was in the design and tonewoods used in the soundboard, Kaman turned his attention to the back and sides. For this he created a bowled shape made from Lyrachord, a type of fibreglass which combined light weight with great strength, meaning that internal bracing – which interfered with the natural flow of the soundwaves – was no longer needed.

- **DATE** 1977

- **ORIGIN** New Hartford, Connecticut, USA

- **WOOD**
  Spruce top, Lyrachord bowled back and sides, set maple neck, rosewood fingerboard.

- **UNUSUAL FEATURE** The body shape and material, the decoration around multiple soundholes and piezo bridge transducer pickup all distinguish this instrument.

Multiple soundholes in the upper bout of the body

ABOVE: *The Kaman Corporation also developed a revolutionary piezo pickup housed inside the bridge and mounted on the underside of the soundboard. This went some way to solving the problem of amplifying an acoustic guitar in concert without using a microphone, while still maintaining the natural sound of the acoustic instrument.*

The pre-amp and controls are fitted to top side of the guitar.

Why wood?

ABOVE: *Aerosmith is one of the biggest-selling rock bands of all time, with global sales of over 150 million albums. Lead guitarist Joe Perry was one of the most prominent users of the Dan Armstrong Plexiglass model.*

There is no question that the materials used to make an acoustic guitar have an enormous impact on its sound – different types of wood produce different tonal qualities. The same is true for an electric guitar, except that the design of the magnetic pickup is perhaps the biggest single factor affecting the way it sounds. This has led some to question as to whether wood is necessarily the best material to use. Alternative body materials, such as different types of plastic, have been shown to have little negative impact on sound. The most successful experiments have tended to concentrate on the area of scale length – from the fingerboard to the bridge. Materials that rival or surpass hardwoods in density, such as aluminium – or the graphite and carbon-fibre blend used successfully on Steinberger guitars in the 1980s – can often provide greater levels of sustain. It is notable that experiments in this area have been more readily taken on board in the four-string field, since bass guitarists seem more prepared to experiment than their six-string cousins are.

Curiosities

Over the years, guitars have appeared in all shapes and sizes. Some have been built to reflect the eccentricities of their makers, others – such as the Framus Super Yob – were built at the whim of wealthy and successful pop stars. Some have existed simply to market a band or its music. These curious designs, however, serve to illustrate the rich variety that exists in the electric guitar world.

Zemaitis, 1971

Tony Zemaitis produced guitars for the top end of the market, famously The Rolling Stones. During the 1960s, his London-based workshop had a clientele that included George Harrison, Jimi Hendrix and Eric Clapton. In 1970, attempting to combat feedback, he experimented with placing a metal shield over the body; the metalwork was then intricately hand-engraved. Since his death in 2002, his highly collectible guitars – all of which he personally handbuilt – have been fetching values as much as $30,000 at auction.

- **DATE** 1971

- **ORIGIN** Chatham, UK

- **WOOD**
  Mahogany body with hand-etched duralumin top, mahogany set neck, ebony fingerboard.

- **UNUSUAL FEATURE**
  The guitar has a hand-etched metal shield.

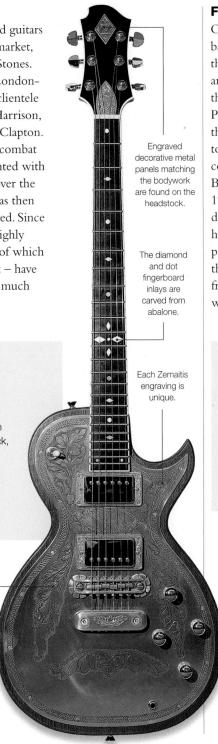

Engraved decorative metal panels matching the bodywork are found on the headstock.

The diamond and dot fingerboard inlays are carved from abalone.

Each Zemaitis engraving is unique.

Although outstanding instruments in their own right, the guitars produced by Tony Zemaitis after 1971 are prized as much for their ornate visual appearance. The duralumin shield on the front of each guitar was hand-etched by Danny O'Brien, a celebrated gun engraver.

Framus Super Yob, 1974

One of the most popular British bands of the 1970s, Slade topped the charts with raucous terrace anthems such as "Cum On Feel the Noize" and "Skweeze Me, Pleeze Me". Guitarist Dave Hill, the only member of the band truly to embrace the glam-rock ethos, commissioned British luthier John Birch to produce a guitar styled as a 1950s sci-fi ray gun. Hill loved the design but disliked the guitar, and had German manufacturer Framus produce a new version. Christened the Super Yob, the guitar was frequently seen in concert as well as on British TV.

- **DATE** 1974

- **ORIGIN** Bubenreuth, Germany

- **WOOD**
  Alder body, maple set neck, maple fingerboard.

- **UNUSUAL FEATURE**
  The body shape is like no other instrument ever made.

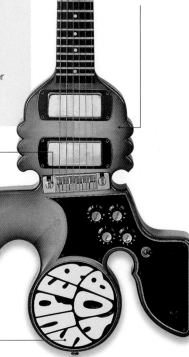

The finish mimics the famous Rickenbacker Fireglo effect.

The gun shape necessitates positioning the bridge close to the centre of the body, causing the instrument to be neck-heavy.

The Super Yob moniker was a remnant from Slade's early days, when the members of the band presented themselves as aggressive skinheads.

Rob Armstrong Cornflake, 1978

Custom-guitar builder Rob Armstrong came up with this unique design for Simon Nicol, a guitarist with the British folk-rock band Fairport Convention. Although built around a Kellogg's packet, it bears more than a passing resemblance to a South African oil-can guitar. Hardly intended as a serious instrument, this whimsical design was built using parts from a low-quality Japanese Columbus Les Paul copy, and it features two humbucking pickups with dedicated volume and tone controls mounted on the top side of the body.

- **DATE** 1978

- **ORIGIN** Coventry, UK

- **WOOD**
  Unidentified wooden body covered with cardboard box, maple neck, rosewood fingerboard.

- **UNUSUAL FEATURE**
  The Bo Diddly-style rectangular body shape is cut to fit a breakfast cereal packet.

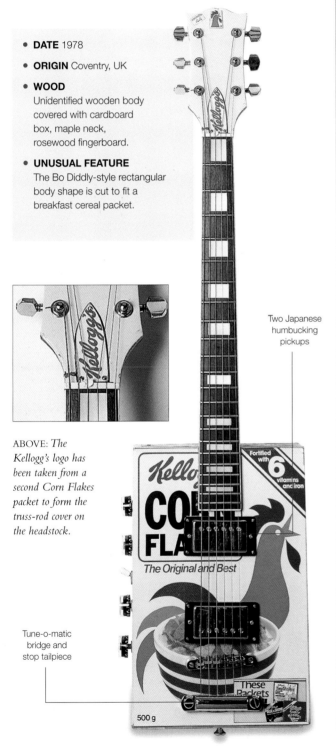

ABOVE: *The Kellogg's logo has been taken from a second Corn Flakes packet to form the truss-rod cover on the headstock.*

Two Japanese humbucking pickups

Tune-o-matic bridge and stop tailpiece

Eastwood Blue Moon, 1980

Creating a bespoke guitar to publicize a single might seem like an extreme measure, but that's just what British rock 'n' roll 'revival' band Showaddywaddy did in 1980 for their cover of the song "Blue Moon". Luthier Brian Eastwood was approached, and he quickly came up with this novelty instrument that sees the man in the moon emerging from behind a fluffy white cloud. The guitar was featured on the band's TV promotional events, and the single became a Top 40 hit. More recently, Eastwood has built an acoustic version.

- **DATE** 1980

- **ORIGIN** Rochdale, UK

- **WOOD**
  Laminated hardwood body and neck.

- **UNUSUAL FEATURE**
  The Blue Moon has a totally unique body shape, like several of Brian Eastwood's creations.

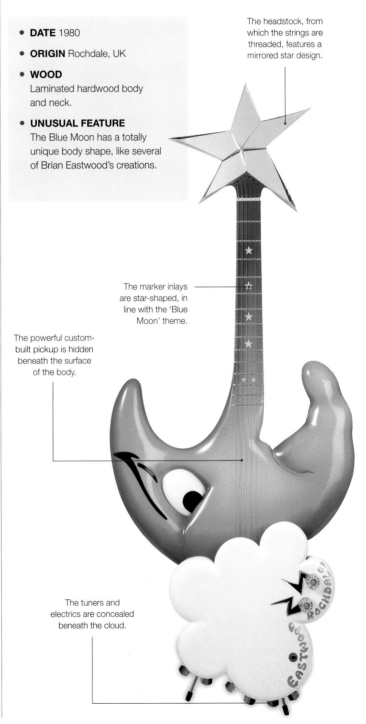

The headstock, from which the strings are threaded, features a mirrored star design.

The marker inlays are star-shaped, in line with the 'Blue Moon' theme.

The powerful custom-built pickup is hidden beneath the surface of the body.

The tuners and electrics are concealed beneath the cloud.

B. C. Rich

For a brand name that instantly conjures up images of the 1980s metal scene, B. C. Rich came from what would seem to be the unlikeliest of sources. Bernardo Chavez Rico was a highly accomplished acoustic player who, in 1966, began building flamenco guitars from his base in Los Angeles, California. Six years later, the first of B. C. Rich's visually distinctive electric models emerged.

Mockingbird, 1975

Rico's first electric guitars were surprisingly conservative by his later standards, designed clearly on the lines of Gibson Les Paul and EB-3 bass models, but in 1975, the Mockingbird appeared. The first B. C. Rich to achieve widespread recognition, it was based on a drawing by Johnny 'Go Go' Kallas and built by Neal Moser, one of Rico's talented luthiers. An enduring design, as late as 2010, *Guitar World* magazine ranked it as "the coolest guitar of all time".

- **DATE** 1975

- **ORIGIN** Los Angeles, California, USA

- **WOOD**
  Mahogany body, maple straight-through neck, rosewood body.

- **UNUSUAL FEATURE**
  Its radical body design was like nothing ever seen at the time of its launch.

The stylized R appears on the headstock of early B. C. Rich guitars.

Early US-built B. C. Rich models feature straight-through neck designs, as shown here. These 1970s models are now increasingly collectible.

With its built-in pre-amp and switching options, the Mockingbird was capable of a wide variety of tones.

Bich, 1977

Neal Moser was also responsible for the Bich, B. C. Rich's most radical instrument, the prototype of which was built – much to his annoyance – while Rico was on a visit to Japan. The revolutionary concept here was in the doubling up of the top four strings but leaving the two bass strings single, so there was a total of ten strings. Known widely as the 'Rich Bich', a more conventional six-string version (as shown here) was added, which proved to be extremely popular with metal bands.

- **DATE** 1977

- **ORIGIN** Los Angeles, California, USA

- **WOOD**
  Mahogany body, maple straight-through neck, rosewood body.

- **UNUSUAL FEATURE**
  The original concept has ten strings (six-string version shown here).

The 'Rich Bich' was one of the first models to feature the pointed headstocks that would soon characterize metal guitars.

The Bich shown here features the cloud fingerboard inlays used on early B.C. Rich models.

The cutaway beneath the bridge is a practical design feature of this guitar.

Warlock, 1981

Emerging in 1981, the Warlock is often thought of as the final one of B. C. Rich's classic five shapes, its claw-like design proving highly popular among metal players – both guitar and bass. By this time the brand had become so well known that high-end Japanese brands such as Aria began to produce imitations. Taking Fender's lead, Rico set up a Japanese operation, B. C. Rich NJ ('Nagoya, Japan', where the guitars were built). The vogue for unorthodox body shapes endured throughout the 1980s – and still has a niche following in the metal world – many of which could be traced back to B. C. Rich originals.

- **DATE** 1981

- **ORIGIN** Los Angeles, California, USA

- **WOOD**
  Agathis body, maple straight-through neck, rosewood fingerboard.

- **UNUSUAL FEATURE**
  Gothic-styled body design.

All B.C. Rich four-string basses feature two-a-side tuner configurations.

With their gothic body shapes, B.C. Rich guitars remain popular with the heavy rock and metal fraternities. The company has been happy to play up to this image, offering accessories such as coffin-shaped guitar cases.

864mm (34in) fingerscale

Single split P-style pickup

Changing shape of the guitar

The guitar is a practical instrument that has evolved slowly over the centuries. The narrow-waisted figure-of-eight body shape of an acoustic guitar came about because the instrument needed to sit comfortably on the lap of the seated player. The vogue for playing the guitar standing up is a relatively recent one, only becoming the predominant mode since the early 1950s. The electrification of the guitar played a fundamental role in this evolution: on stage, for example, the player need not stay in one position, close to a microphone, but by using a long cable or wireless transmitter, is free to roam the stage. Theoretically, then, these practical considerations are no longer so important.

Since the first electric guitars were little more than acoustic guitars with a pickup fitted, the slow evolution of electric body shape is perhaps not so surprising. Gibson attempted to challenge the figure-of-eight orthodoxy in the late 1950s with its Modernistic series, which included the famous Flying V, but customer reaction was negative, and they were withdrawn. During the 1960s, others emerged with unusual designs, such as the teardrop-shaped Vox Mark III, but these were generally viewed as niche instruments.

It was only in the 1980s that strange and exotic shapes, often inspired by late-1970s B.C. Rich designs, were more commonly seen, often in the hands of dark-metal players. However, the continued popularity of the early Fender and Gibson models, or modern-day derivatives such as those produced by Paul Reed Smith, would seem to provide strong evidence that guitarists are a pretty conservative bunch.

LEFT: *The Rebeth Gothic Cross was built as a one-off in 1982 by British luthier Barry Collier.*

Fenders from the 1980s

The major US guitar manufacturers have realized that when it comes to guitar design, the consumer is rarely interested in embracing innovation. The 1980s was the last decade that saw both the Fender and Gibson companies attempting to come up with original designs, before concentrating on turning their classic models into the high-end heritage brands they are today.

Bullet, 1981

The Bullet was introduced in 1981 as a student guitar to replace the outgoing Mustang and Musicmaster models. In its original form, the Bullet was a cut-down version of the Telecaster, fitted with very basic hardware, an all-in-one bridge and tailpiece, and twin single-coil pickups covered with a plastic sheathing. A year after its launch, the Bullet was given a restyling, this time based on the Stratocaster. From 1984, the Bullet was switched from Fender to the Japanese-built Squier brand instead.

- **DATE** 1981
- **ORIGIN** Fullerton, California, USA
- **WOOD**
  Ash body, maple bolt-on neck, rosewood fingerboard.
- **UNUSUAL FEATURE**
  The original model was available only with a red body and black or white scratchplate, or an off-white body with white scratchplate.

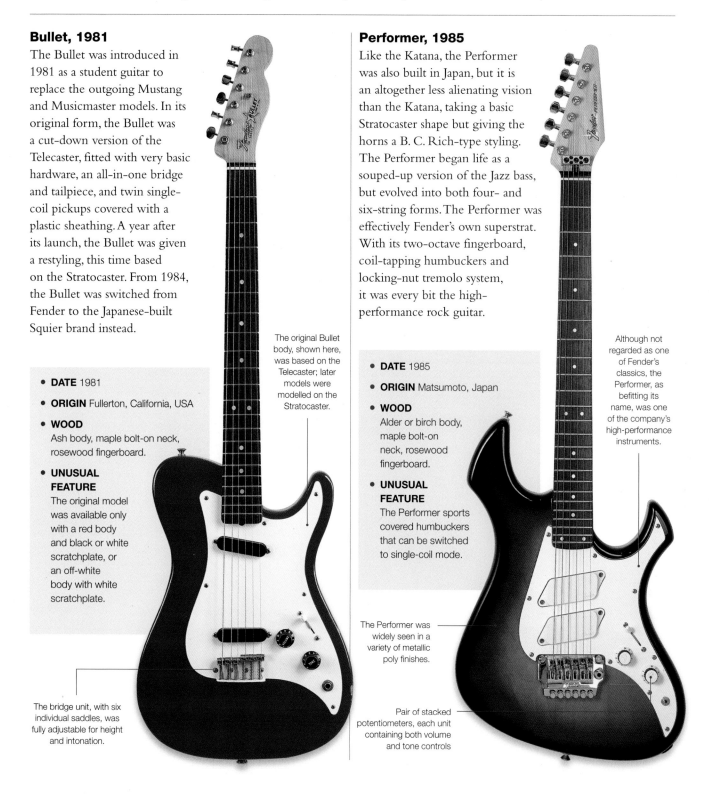

The original Bullet body, shown here, was based on the Telecaster; later models were modelled on the Stratocaster.

The bridge unit, with six individual saddles, was fully adjustable for height and intonation.

Performer, 1985

Like the Katana, the Performer was also built in Japan, but it is an altogether less alienating vision than the Katana, taking a basic Stratocaster shape but giving the horns a B. C. Rich-type styling. The Performer began life as a souped-up version of the Jazz bass, but evolved into both four- and six-string forms. The Performer was effectively Fender's own superstrat. With its two-octave fingerboard, coil-tapping humbuckers and locking-nut tremolo system, it was every bit the high-performance rock guitar.

- **DATE** 1985
- **ORIGIN** Matsumoto, Japan
- **WOOD**
  Alder or birch body, maple bolt-on neck, rosewood fingerboard.
- **UNUSUAL FEATURE**
  The Performer sports covered humbuckers that can be switched to single-coil mode.

Although not regarded as one of Fender's classics, the Performer, as befitting its name, was one of the company's high-performance instruments.

The Performer was widely seen in a variety of metallic poly finishes.

Pair of stacked potentiometers, each unit containing both volume and tone controls

Katana, 1986

The year 1985 was a strange one for Fender. An employee buyout saw the formation of the Fender Musical Instrument Corporation, and during the inevitable period of transition that followed, a number of curious models emerged, and none more so than the Katana, by some distance the oddest-looking Fender ever. The impetus to come up with a radical new shape came from Fender dealers, who had seen their market gradually eroded by contemporary designs from new companies like Jackson. So the Katana was born out of duress, designed by a marketing man fiddling with an art program on a Macintosh, built in Japan and halfheartedly launched by a company that disliked the product. It was dropped within a year.

- **DATE** 1986

- **ORIGIN** Matsumoto, Japan

- **WOOD**
  Ash body, maple glued-in neck, rosewood fingerboard.

- **UNUSUAL FEATURE**
  The Katana featured the Fender System 1 locking vibrato unit.

Note the tiny offset triangle inlays on the fingerboard.

The body is an unusual wedge shape with a bevelled edge.

Unlike traditional Fenders, the Katana had a glued-in neck.

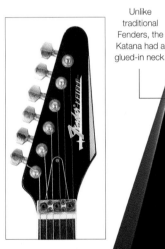

ABOVE: *The Katana was named after a Japanese broadsword – the design of the logo makes this relationship quite evident.*

The Katana was designed to compete with metal guitars, such as the Jackson Randy Rhoads model.

A return to the classics

The Katana and Performer were the last genuinely unusual guitars to bear the Fender name. It was all too clear to Fender that the vast majority of their customer base wanted the classics – the Strats, Teles, Jaguars and Jazzmasters – and if they wanted odd-shaped superstrats, then they probably didn't want one produced by Fender. Since the beginning of the 1990s, Fender has concentrated on producing variations on original designs at every possible price point. So, beautifully crafted exact replicas of early Stratocasters are available – at a premium – from Fender in the USA; cheaper, workmanlike Fender Strats are built in Mexico or Japan; and quality starter Strats produced in Korea or China are labelled with Fender's Squier brand.

This does not give a complete picture, however. Now one of the biggest musical-instrument corporations in the world, since the early 1990s Fender has bought out, among others, the Jackson, Charvel and Hamer brands, so non-standard-shaped metal-style guitars *are* being produced by Fender, just under different names.

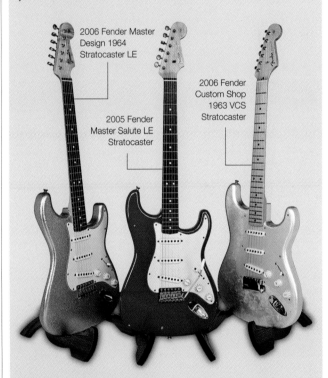

2006 Fender Master Design 1964 Stratocaster LE

2005 Fender Master Salute LE Stratocaster

2006 Fender Custom Shop 1963 VCS Stratocaster

ABOVE: *By the end of the 1980s, Fender had all but ceased producing new designs, concentrating instead on selling its illustrious history, producing heritage versions of its classics, original examples of which were increasingly being sought by wealthy collectors. Many of these were limited-edition models that were produced by the Fender Custom Shop in California.*

Gibsons from the 1980s

Like Fender, Gibson's popularity was at a low by the mid-1980s, with a perception, rightly or wrongly, that quality had slipped. At the time, the vogue for high-performance guitars saw some leading players looking elsewhere, to the superstrats produced by Charvel, Jackson and Ibanez, or to the craftsmanship of Paul Reed Smith, whose Maryland factory produced guitars that combined the best of Gibson *and* Fender.

Nighthawk, 1993

While the short-lived Nighthawk superficially resembles a Les Paul, some elements of its design and sound are more reminiscent of Fenders. Not only does it feature a 648mm (25½in) scale length (like a Fender), but it also uses a slanted bridge pickup like a Telecaster. Although this was a humbucker, its low output gave it a cleaner, brighter tone more redolent of a Tele. Similarly, the Gibson mini-humbucker at the neck had a warm, mellow tone closer in character to a Stratocaster than a regular Gibson PAF. The Nighthawk could be considered a response to the versatility of the Paul Reed Smith models produced during the late 1980s.

- **DATE** 1993
- **ORIGIN** Kalamazoo, Michigan, USA
- **WOOD**
  Maple body with mahogany top, mahogany set neck, rosewood fingerboard.
- **UNUSUAL FEATURE**
  The Nighthawk's pickups are switchable between single-coil and humbucker.

The Nighthawk was made available in a number of variations: the model shown here features an NSX single-coil centre pickup.

The electrics feature a push/pull tone control: when pulled up, the humbuckers function as single-coil pickups. Using the selector switch, this gives the guitar ten different tonal possibilities.

Alpha Q-3000, 1985

By 1984, Eddie Van Halen was well established as rock god *du jour*. His eponymous band was one of the most popular in the USA, and he'd reached a global mainstream audience with his astonishing tapped solo on Michael Jackson's "Beat It". He was also the first major player associated with the superstrat – his influential self-built Charvel 'Frankenstein'. Gibson struggled to compete with these new instruments, producing a Q range of its own with a Strat-style body and a mix of single and humbucking pickups. Although excellent rock guitars, they failed to capture their intended market.

- **DATE** 1985
- **ORIGIN** Kalamazoo, Michigan, USA
- **WOOD**
  Mahogany body straight-through neck, ebonite fingerboard.
- **UNUSUAL FEATURE**
  'Fender'-style Gibson; ebonite fingerboard.

Explorer-style headstock, which had originally influenced the Charvel superstrat designs

The fingerboard is made from ebonite, a material created from vulcanizing rubber and commonly used to make bowling balls.

The Q series features a Kahler locking vibrato system.

Spirit II XPL, 1985

Modelled after the Les Paul Junior, Gibson's diverse Spirit range was introduced in 1982. While models differ greatly, all are characterized by a flat, slimline body. The XPL appeared three years later and was an attempt to combine the classic Gibson heritage with features more readily identified with the superstrats, such as a locking vibrato unit and an S/S/H pickup configuration. Some Spirits were also sold as Epiphones, but these did not sell well, and the remainder were rebranded – the original headstock logo can sometimes be seen faintly beneath the Gibson logo.

- **DATE** 1985
- **ORIGIN** Kalamazoo, Michigan, USA (some Spirits were built at Gibson's plant in Nashville, Tennessee)
- **WOOD** Mahogany body, mahogany set neck, rosewood fingerboard.
- **UNUSUAL FEATURE** A locking vibrato system, unusual on Gibson guitars.

Simple dot marker inlays

ABOVE: *Like the classic 1980s superstrats, the XPL is fitted with a locking vibrato system – the model shown here features a Kahler Flyer. These units enabled the guitarist to perform dive-bomb pitch bends and return to perfect tuning.*

Master volume and tone controls, and a variety of coil tap/series-parallel switching options

US-1, 1986

In 1986, with the company struggling, Gibson was bought by three investors looking for opportunities. One of the first instruments under the new ownership was the US-1, Gibson's first out-and-out superstrat. The most unorthodox aspect of the US-1 was its body construction, with a lightweight balsa core surrounded by curly maple. Poor sales once again illustrated that buyers wanted traditional instruments, as one of the owners later admitted, "Every time we strayed from what customers thought we should be we failed. What they wanted were the classic, good guitars."

- **DATE** 1986
- **ORIGIN** Kalamazoo, Michigan, USA
- **WOOD** **Front/Back & Sides** Balsa core surrounded by curly maple, set mahogany neck, rosewood fingerboard.
- **UNUSUAL FEATURE** The use of balsa wood in the body construction.

ABOVE: *In spite of their appearance, all three pickups are humbuckers; the front two are stacked.*

The fingerboard features split-diamond marker inlays.

The body is broadly Stratocaster-shaped, but without the smooth, contoured edges of the Fender.

Music Man and G&L

In 1971, two disillusioned Fender employees, Forest White and Tom Walker, formed a new company with Leo Fender as a silent partner, Music Man. In 1975, Fender was voted president by the board, and a year later the first Music Man guitars appeared. However, in 1979, disagreements surrounding business arrangements led to Fender forming a new company, G&L, with former colleague, George Fullerton.

Music Man StingRay Bass, 1976

In 1976, having first concentrated on a new hybrid valve/solid-state amplifier, Music Man produced its first range of instruments, the StingRay 1 and the StingRay bass. More than a little reminiscent of a Fender Precision, the bass featured a soapbar humbucker and a built-in active pre-amp – the first production guitars to use active circuitry to boost frequencies. The circuitboard inside the body was coated with epoxy to prevent it being reverse-engineered and copied.

- **DATE** 1976
- **ORIGIN** Fullerton, California, USA
- **WOOD**
  Ash body (alder used on some models), maple bolt-on neck, rosewood, maple or pau ferro fingerboard.
- **UNUSUAL FEATURE**
  The ovaloid scratchplate gives the instrument a distinctive look.

G&L Cavalier, 1983

In 1979, Leo Fender formed a new alliance with another name from his distant past, George Fullerton, with whom Fender had designed the Telecaster. G&L ('George and Leo') was formed with an agenda to build classic Fender-style guitars to the same high standard as those on which their reputation had originally been built – and which, throughout the 1970s, had diminished. Although Leo Fender and George Fullerton have both since passed on, G&L continues to produce instruments in the tradition of its founders.

- **DATE** 1983
- **ORIGIN** Fullerton, California, USA
- **WOOD**
  Ash body, rock maple bolt-on neck, rosewood or maple fingerboard.
- **UNUSUAL FEATURE**
  Unusual variation on the Stratocaster headstock design.

Unusual three-and-one configuration of tuners – with the G string on the treble side of the headstock

This sculpted headstock shape was introduced in 1982, and has been used on various G&L models since.

Pair of slanted MFD humbuckers

The StingRay was available as a single- or twin-pickup model, with an optional piezo pickup built into the bridge.

The Cavalier was a clear attempt by Fender and Fullerton to update the classic Stratocaster design they had come up with 30 years earlier.

Ernie Ball Music Man Axis Supersport, 1995

In 1984, five years after Leo Fender acrimoniously parted company from Music Man, the company was sold to Ernie Ball, the leading string manufacturer, who resumed guitar and bass production. In 1990, the company achieved an impressive coup, creating the Music Man EVH – a signature instrument for Eddie Van Halen. With its sumptuous quilted maple body and birdseye maple neck, the EVH was one of the instruments of the decade. When Van Halen's endorsement deal was over in 1995, the EVH was modified, rechristened the Axis and given a range of its own.

- **DATE** 1995

- **ORIGIN** San Luis Obispo, California, USA

- **WOOD**
  Basswood body with figured maple top, birdseye maple bolt-on neck, birdseye maple fingerboard.

- **UNUSUAL FEATURE**
  The Axis evolved from the EVH signature model built for rock guitarist Eddie Van Halen.

Curious four-and-two configuration of tuners on the headstock

Unusually tiny dot marker inlays on the fingerboard

The HH version of the Axis Super Sport (shown here) features DiMarzio humbuckers; the MM90 version uses a pair of Music Man soapbar pickups.

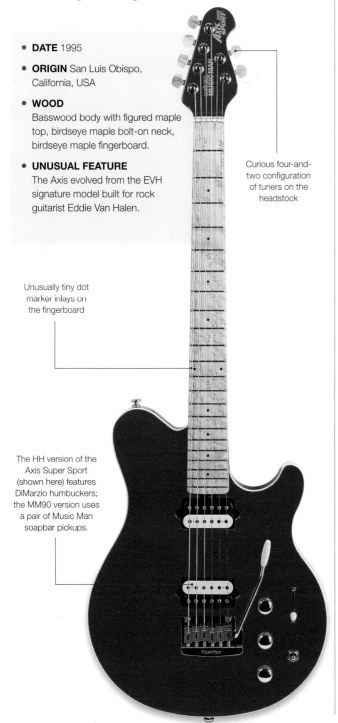

Leo Fender: the late years

When Leo Fender sold the company he founded in 1965, he was 56 years old and believed he didn't have long to live. So important was his name in the world of the electric guitar that CBS forced him into a non-competition deal that meant he was not allowed to set up a new guitar company for ten years after the sale date.

In 1975, he became president of Music Man. Its business structure, however, was complex. Former Fender employee Forest White owned Music Man, while Fender owned his own business, CLF Research, which produced the guitars for Music Man. In 1979, a bitter rift emerged between the two parties over financial arrangements, and CLF refused to build any more Music Man guitars. White brought in a young luthier named Grover Jackson in an attempt to keep Music Man going, but ultimately he was forced to sell the company. Fender, meanwhile, at the age of 70, set up a successful new company – G&L – producing classic Fender-style instruments.

Although a wealthy man, Leo Fender led a famously frugal life, bringing his own egg-salad sandwiches into work each day. He died on March 21, 1991, in Fullerton, California, a result of complications caused by Parkinson's disease. He is remembered globally as one of the most important figures in the story of the electric guitar.

ABOVE: *Well into his eighth decade, Leo Fender continued to play an active role in the development of new products with G&L, the company he co-founded.*

Ibanez

After the Gibson 1977 lawsuit, taken out in an attempt to curb the Far Eastern copy industry, Ibanez began to concentrate on the production of original models, which featured modern design elements such as slim necks and radical body shapes. The 1980s saw the company produce a number of notable 'pointed' metal guitars, later producing high-end superstrats in conjunction with guitar wizard Steve Vai.

Axstar AX45, 1984

With body styling that resembles an American B. C. Rich model, the Ibanez Axstar series was in many ways a typical mid-1980s rock guitar. It was initially available in three different models (AX40, 45 and 48), each with different pickup configurations. The AX45 here has a humbucking bridge pickup and two single coils, whereas the AX40 has two humbuckers and the AX48 two humbuckers and a single-coil. In 1986, the neck design of the Axstar was overhauled, and a series of Steinberger-styled headless models was introduced.

Rosewood fingerboard with small dot marker inlays

- **DATE** 1984

- **ORIGIN** Matsumoto, Japan

- **WOOD**
  American basswood body, maple bolt-on neck, rosewood fingerboard.

- **UNUSUAL FEATURE**
  The Axstar has a distinctly B. C. Rich-style body.

The original Axstars featured passive pickups; the 1986 models incorporated active circuitry.

Jem 77 BFP, 1987

In 1986, Steve Vai, one of the most technical of rock guitarists, took up an offer to design his own production instrument for Ibanez. The resulting guitar was the Jem, perhaps the ultimate superstrat, designed for the most versatile range of rock sounds and high-speed single-note soloing. It was available in a series of garish colours and patterns. The pickups are by DiMarzio: front and back are PAF Pro Humbuckers with a single-coil centre. The wiring is also interesting, featuring a five-way selector switch that combines the middle pickup with a humbucker coil in positions 2 and 4.

Floyd Rose-style locking tremolo system

- **DATE** 1987

- **ORIGIN** Matsumoto, Japan

- **WOOD**
  American basswood body, maple bolt-on neck, maple fingerboard.

- **UNUSUAL FEATURE**
  The decoration is elaborate, with intricate tree-of-life fingerboard inlays.

A unique feature of the Jem series is the monkey-grip carrying handle.

The blue floral pattern (BFP) from which this Jem takes its name was printed on cloth that was attached to the body and given a heavy nitrocellulose finish.

RG550, 1987

The briefest glimpse of the RG550's profile shows a clear link to the Jem series from which it was derived. The RG series, including its high-end Prestige option, was introduced in 1987 and features a characteristic slimline neck and high-output pickups that add up to make it an ideal rock guitar. A common problem with these original models, however, was severe neck warping that was caused by its thin profile. In 2007, Ibanez launched the RG550XX 20th Anniversary model, which addressed this issue.

- **DATE** 1987

- **ORIGIN** Matsumoto, Japan

- **WOOD**
  Basswood body, maple bolt-on neck, maple fingerboard.

- **UNUSUAL FEATURE**
  The slim neck made stability an issue on early RG550s. The neck design on later models made it a powerful rock tool.

To improve stability on the 2007 20th Anniversary model, the neck was built as a five-piece laminate, with three strips of hard rock maple and two thin strips of walnut, each layer having the grain arranged at a perpendicular angle.

The neck is supported by twin titanium rods on either side of the truss rod.

The RG saw the first appearance of the characteristic Ibanez pointed cutaway horns.

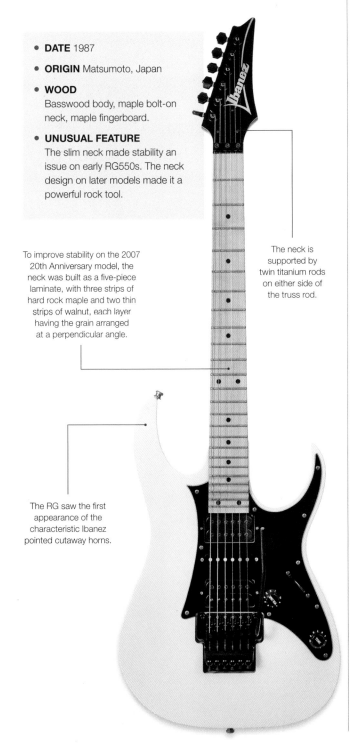

The evolution of Ibanez

ABOVE: *The Ibanez Iceman is broadly based on a Gibson Firebird, but with unique oriental styling. In 1977, Paul Stanley of Kiss was able to develop his own signature Iceman – the PS10.*

The first Ibanez electric guitars were built in 1957, and throughout the 1960s they were a mix of curious oriental styles and copies of established American and European classics – among them imitations of Burns and Hagströms. Towards the end of that decade, the demand for cheap, low-end electric guitars began to wane, and many Japanese manufacturers decided to move their businesses into other areas. Those that remained, however, began to concentrate more on producing quality instruments.

During the 1970s, Ibanez continued to produce copies, in particular high-quality versions of Gibson originals. In 1977, this resulted, perhaps bizarrely, in legal action by Gibson against Ibanez for copying headstock designs. An out-of-court settlement was agreed, and Ibanez thereafter concentrated on original designs.

In the 1980s, Ibanez raised its profile with a number of hi-spec ranges aimed at the rock market that were endorsed by celebrity players. The company now has one of the broadest ranges of production guitars of any manufacturer.

Beyond six strings

The guitar has not always been a six-string instrument. Those that pre-dated the modern classical guitar, emerging during the Renaissance and Baroque periods, were fitted with varying numbers of courses (pairs of strings, and sometimes three or more), and it wasn't until the end of the 18th century that six became the norm. However, there are still those for whom six strings just isn't enough.

Chapman Stick, 1974

Not a conventional guitar as such, the Stick is not even played in the same way. Developed in the late 1960s by US jazz guitarist Emmett Chapman, the Stick is a tapping instrument: sounds are produced by pressing the strings down against the frets rather than plucking them with a pick or fingers. The instrument is held in a near-vertical position, the right hand tapping the top five strings, and the left hand tapping the five bass strings. The skilled player can conjure up complex combinations of bass, rhythm and lead lines.

- **DATE** 1974
- **ORIGIN** Los Angeles, California, USA
- **WOOD**
  Ironwood (later models have used ebony, maple, wenge, padauk, bamboo and synthetic resins).
- **UNUSUAL FEATURE**
  Playing the Stick requires a completely different technique from a standard guitar.

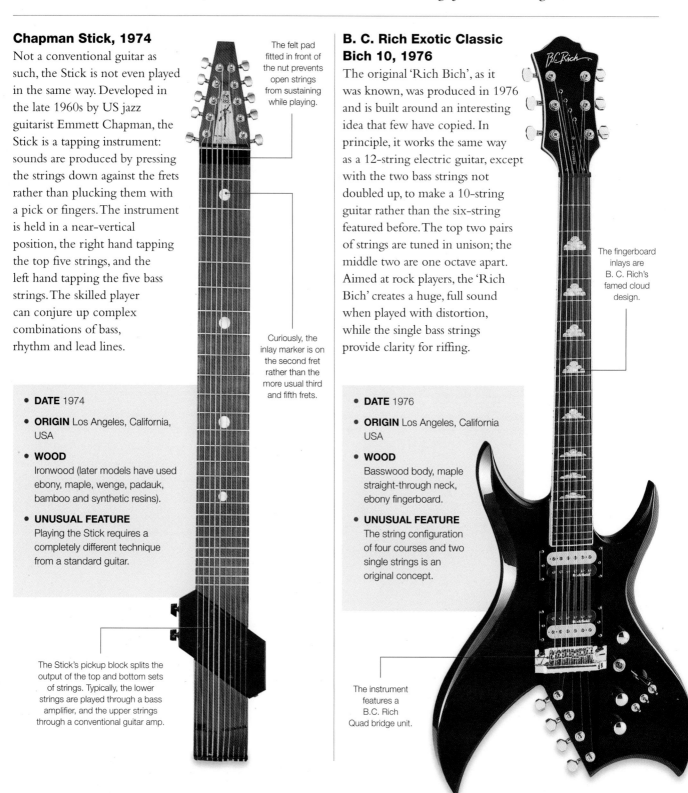

The felt pad fitted in front of the nut prevents open strings from sustaining while playing.

Curiously, the inlay marker is on the second fret rather than the more usual third and fifth frets.

The Stick's pickup block splits the output of the top and bottom sets of strings. Typically, the lower strings are played through a bass amplifier, and the upper strings through a conventional guitar amp.

B. C. Rich Exotic Classic Bich 10, 1976

The original 'Rich Bich', as it was known, was produced in 1976 and is built around an interesting idea that few have copied. In principle, it works the same way as a 12-string electric guitar, except with the two bass strings not doubled up, to make a 10-string guitar rather than the six-string featured before. The top two pairs of strings are tuned in unison; the middle two are one octave apart. Aimed at rock players, the 'Rich Bich' creates a huge, full sound when played with distortion, while the single bass strings provide clarity for riffing.

- **DATE** 1976
- **ORIGIN** Los Angeles, California USA
- **WOOD**
  Basswood body, maple straight-through neck, ebony fingerboard.
- **UNUSUAL FEATURE**
  The string configuration of four courses and two single strings is an original concept.

The fingerboard inlays are B. C. Rich's famed cloud design.

The instrument features a B.C. Rich Quad bridge unit.

Ibanez Universe, 1990

In 1987, rock virtuoso Steve Vai's collaboration with Ibanez produced the Jem superstrat. Three years later, driven by Vai's interest in evolving the electric guitar, Ibanez launched a seven-string version, the Universe. The seventh string, as is common on such guitars, is generally tuned a perfect fourth lower than bottom E – to a B – taking it into the sonic realm of baritone guitar. This kind of seven-string instrument has found a very definite niche among the more progressively minded speed-metal player.

- **DATE** 1990
- **ORIGIN** Matsumoto, Japan
- **WOOD**
  American basswood body, maple bolt-on neck, maple fingerboard.
- **UNUSUAL FEATURE**
  The first seven-string superstrat.

Apart from the additional string and lack of grip hole, the Universe is identical in specification to the six-string Ibanez Jem.

With its two-octave fingerboard, the seven-string Universe, when tuned conventionally (B, E, A, D, G, B, E) has an extraordinary note range of four octaves and five semitones.

DiMarzio Blaze II pickups are fitted.

The bridge unit is an Ibanez Lo-Pro Edge 7.

Steve Vai

From a technical perspective, there are few rock guitarists in the same league as Steve Vai (b. 1960). Born in Long Island, New York, Vai began playing guitar at the age of 13. Famously subjecting himself to lengthy and disciplined practice routines, he later studied at the Berklee College of Music. At the age of 19, he sent a transcription of Frank Zappa's fiendish "The Black Page" to the composer along with a tape of his playing, and within a year he was playing in Zappa's band. During the 1980s, Vai sought more rock-oriented engagements, joining Alcatrazz and ex-Van Halen David Lee Roth's solo outfit.

It was his award-winning 1990 solo album *Passion and Warfare* that established Vai's reputation for seemingly impossible pyrotechnics, in particular the track "For the Love of God". The six-minute instrumental is a tour de force, combining every contemporary rock technique, including vibrato effects, double-handed tapping, harmonics and volume swells. In 2008, readers of *Guitar World* magazine voted it among the top 30 guitar solos of all time.

ABOVE: *While regarded by many modern players as the ultimate rock guitar virtuoso, Steve Vai has also been criticized by some who see his complex playing as over-indulgent showboating. In 2004, he published his 30-Hour Path to Virtuoso Enlightenment, a brutal regimen conceived to be worked through over the course of three ten-hour sessions.*

Diffusion ranges

During the 1960s, the production of Japanese imitations made little difference to the likes of Gibson and Fender – they were of such poor quality that they posed no real threat. Furthermore, most teenage beginners couldn't afford the real thing, so playing a copy was the only real option – and, indeed, made the real thing all the more desirable – until, that is, the copies started matching the originals in quality.

Squier Stratocaster, 1982

By the early 1980s, Fender copies by Japanese makers Tokai and Greco were widely perceived as matching the originals. Fender's clever reaction was not to take legal action but rather set up Fender Japan. Using a dormant brand acquired in the 1960s, the first Japanese-built Fender Squier Stratocasters shipped in 1982. Cheaper than US Fenders but of a similar quality, the Squier brand was an immediate success, marginalizing the market for copies, and remains a significant factor in the Fender Corporation's global success.
The guitar shown here is a 2002 20th Anniversary model, part of a matched pair decorated with graffiti.

In 2011, a Squier Stratocaster was launched that was capable of doubling up as a controller for the Rock Band 3 video game.

- **DATE** 1982 (this model, 2002)
- **ORIGIN** Japan, Mexico, South Korea, China, Taiwan, Indonesia (this model), India
- **WOOD** Agathis body, maple bolt-on neck, maple fingerboard.
- **UNUSUAL FEATURE** This guitar is one of a matched pair.

Fender's Squier range tends to use woods that are readily available in the country of manufacture – such as agates and basswood.

Epiphone Les Paul, 1989

Once one of the great guitar marques, when Epiphone was bought out by Gibson in 1957, it began to release diffusion versions of Gibson models. Until Epiphone production moved to Japan in 1970, there was little qualitative difference, both brands being built at the Kalamazoo plant, often by the same personnel. During the 1980s, production switched to Korea and then, in 2002, to China. Like Fender's Squier range, the mass production of the Epiphone brand has for some time been central to Gibson's global business success.

- **DATE** 1989
- **ORIGIN** Sameck, South Korea
- **WOOD** Mahogany body with maple top, maple bolt-on neck, rosewood fingerboard.
- **UNUSUAL FEATURE** Extremely high-quality Les Paul copy.

The neck of the Epiphone Les Paul is bolted on rather than set like Gibson models.

A thin layer of maple is fitted to a solid mahogany body, in the manner of Gibson-branded Les Paul models.

Epiphone G-310 Emily the Strange, 2009

A popular counterculture cartoon figure, Emily the Strange is a dark-haired teenage girl with a gothic outlook on life. She first appeared advertising a brand of skateboard and surfwear, later spawning a series of comic books and a feature film. The G-310 is a basic Epiphone SG, graffitied with one of Emily's catchphrases. In truth, this a more-than-reasonable instrument that isn't appreciably inferior to its Gibson counterpart, and it is available at less than a third of the price.

- **DATE** 2009

- **ORIGIN** Qingdao, China

- **WOOD**
  Basswood body,
  maple bolt-on neck,
  rosewood neck.

- **UNUSUAL FEATURE**
  The Emily cartoon decoration aims the model squarely at the young-adult market.

The neck is a bolt-on, unlike Gibson SGs, which are set.

The body artwork of the Emily SG is continued on the headstock.

The G-310 was a surprise hit for Epiphone; aimed initially at teenage girls – with Emily the 'anti-cool' 13-year-old pictured on the body – it was more often seen played by young emo males.

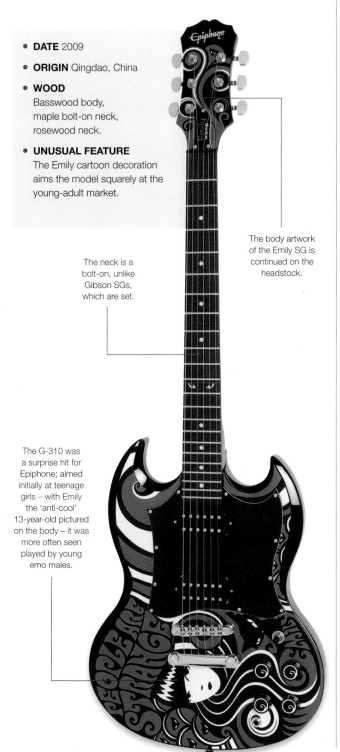

Guitar production tiers

The tiered production system championed so successfully by Gibson and Fender is a strange phenomenon, and one that is, in part, predicated on snobbery.

When Fender Japan first appeared in the early 1980s, it was to provide classic Fender designs at a lower price than the US-built models, steering customers away from the copies being produced in the region. By contracting some of those factories that had been manufacturing inferior imitations, Fender also managed to stem some of the supply. The high quality of these early Japanese Fenders resulted in a consensus at the time that there was little difference in practice between the Squiers and the original US models. This factor in itself helped to make the Squier brand become such an enormous success.

As manufacturing costs rose in Japan, further cut-price tiers of production were added: Mexico, South Korea, Indonesia and, more recently, China. In the modern era, Fender's specialized high-end guitars are produced at the Corona plant in California, whereas the majority of the company's standard models are built at Ensenada, Mexico, and the Squiers are built in Asia. The story is similarly true with the Gibson and Epiphone brands. In truth, all of the guitars produced are fine, serviceable instruments, but – rightly or wrongly – those produced in Mexico and Asia lack the cachet of those built in the USA.

ABOVE: *The 1990s 'riot grrrl' scene saw the first widespread uptake of the electric guitar among teenage females. As a consequence, new companies such as Daisy Rock emerged to produce instruments specifically for this market. In 2006, Fender joined forces with the Japanese Sanrio Corporation to produce a Squier model named after the Hello Kitty cartoon character.*

Europe in the 1980s

The 1980s saw the mass production of European instruments gradually dwindling, caught between the big names in the USA and the low labour costs in the Far East. Names such as Hofner have continued with success – and other famous brands such as Framus, Burns and Hagström have since re-emerged, third parties producing reissues of classic designs – although manufacture is usually in the Far East.

Musima Deluxe 25, c.1972

Guitars by Musima were produced in the former German Democratic Republic, now East Germany. The Deluxe 25 was clearly based around the Fender Jazzmaster/Jaguar design, and it remained in production into the 1980s. Higher in quality than other Eastern European guitars of the period, the Musima is of a similar standard and build to a cheap Japanese copy, with a plywood body, plastic neck binding and a thin single-coil sound that may appeal to those with retro tastes.

The fingerboard features plastic block marker inlays.

- **DATE** c.1972
- **ORIGIN** Markneukirchen, Germany (former German Democratic Republic)
- **WOOD**
  Plywood body, beech set neck, beech fingerboard (stained to look like rosewood).
- **UNUSUAL FEATURE**
  The four-position tone switch.

The instrument has a separate bridge and tailpiece – the Deluxe 25V also sports a vibrato unit.

Stratocaster-style output jack socket.

Defil Jola 2, c.1977

During the Cold War era, Poland was one of the more Westernized of the Iron Curtain states, and rock music and other cultural imports from the West were broadly tolerated. By the early 1980s, there was a thriving punk and metal scene, to some extent a response to the imposition of martial law, and sales of cheap electric guitars soared. The Defil factory was among the country's major manufacturers of the time. While instruments such as the Defil Jola 2 had a look that was contemporary for the mid-1970s, these were nonetheless primitive guitars that were, out of necessity, widely customized.

The headstock of the Defil Jola 2 features three-a-side tuners – unlike the Fender-style six-in-a-line used on its predecessor.

Unusual full-width fingerboard markers

- **DATE** c.1977
- **ORIGIN** Lubin, Poland
- **WOOD**
  Hardwood body, maple bolt-on neck, rosewood fingerboard.
- **UNUSUAL FEATURE**
  The Jola has sliding volume and tone controls instead of the usual rotary potentiometers.

The Jola 2 is, surprisingly, one of the few production guitars to use fader controls.

Hofner Pro Sound Graphic S5E, 1982

One of the most interesting European production guitars of the period, the S5E is notable for its electrics, the standard tone adjustment being replaced by a graphic equalizer – instead of a single rotary control, tone is adjusted by a series of five faders, each controlling a specific band of audio frequency. The guitar features three single-coil pickups which can be selected in combinations by using the five-positional indents on the rotary control.

- **DATE** 1982
- **ORIGIN** Bubenreuth, Germany
- **WOOD**
  Double-lined maple body, maple neck, rosewood fingerboard.
- **UNUSUAL FEATURE**
  The graphic-equalizer tone control allows for precise tonal choice.

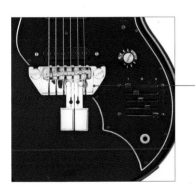

ABOVE: *This model is fitted with a string bender, rather like a Bigsby Palm Pedal, and has levers attached to the G and B strings, enabling them to be raised by a tone. This is a niche effect used generally by country players to recreate the effects of the levers on a pedal steel.*

The graphic equalizer is broken into five frequency bands from 200 to 3,200 Hz. Each band can be boosted or cut by up to 18 decibels.

Hohner Shark's Fin, 1987

The Hohner company was founded in 1857 in Trussingen, Germany, producing accordions and its world-famous harmonicas. Like many other musical instrument manufacturers, during the 1950s Hohner also started to produce electric guitars and basses. The 1980s saw the company's profile as a guitar producer peak, although by this time manufacture had shifted to Japan. The SE603 Shark Fin appeared in 1987 as part of Hohner's Arbor Series, and was a late arrival in an increasingly niche metal-guitar market. Taking its cues directly from the 'spiky' models produced by Jackson, the SE603 quite clearly takes its name from the six-in-line headstock.

- **DATE** 1987
- **ORIGIN** Japan
- **WOOD**
  Laminate hardwood body, bolt-on maple neck, rosewood fingerboard.
- **UNUSUAL FEATURE**
  The shark's-fin headstock shape is highly distinctive.

The fingerboard features dot marker inlays.

The body shape is stylistically similar to metal guitars made by superstrat-producing companies such as Jackson and Ibanez.

This model features two humbucking pickups.

The combined bridge and tailpiece also includes a non-locking vibrato unit.

Signature Stratocasters

The idea of a Fender signature model had been discussed in the early 1980s, both James Burton and Jeff Beck having been approached. However, it was the phenomenal success of the Eric Clapton signature Stratocaster released in 1988 that created a vogue for limited-edition models created with personalized variations specified by some of the world's greatest players.

Eric Clapton, 1988

Approached by Fender in 1985, Eric Clapton's response was to request an exact replica of his own long-term instrument, Blackie – the composite Stratocaster he had famously constructed using parts from three different mid-1950s models. Clapton also specified a neck in the style of his favourite Martin guitar and what he described as a 'compressed' pickup sound, which Fender achieved by using Gold Lace Sensor pickups and active circuitry with a mid-range boost.

- **DATE** 1988
- **ORIGIN** Corona, California, USA
- **WOOD**
  Alder body, maple bolt-on neck, maple fingerboard.
- **UNUSUAL FEATURE**
  To create the sound Clapton wanted, Fender fitted Gold Lace Sensor pickups and active circuitry.

From 2001, Fender Vintage Noiseless single-coil pickups were adopted.

Jeff Beck, 1991

Admired perhaps more by other musicians than the general public, Jeff Beck has operated in many styles – from his early blues and R&B work with the Yardbirds to his complex jazz-rock during the 1970s. The Jeff Beck signature model, issued in 1991, was a souped-up Strat Plus featuring a double bridge pickup, Schaller locking machine heads and an LSR roller nut. It also featured a narrow C-profiled neck with a rosewood fingerboard.

- **DATE** 1991
- **ORIGIN** Corona, California, USA
- **WOOD**
  Alder body, maple bolt-on neck, rosewood fingerboard.
- **UNUSUAL FEATURE**
  Before this model, humbucking pickups had rarely been seen on Stratocasters; one of the coils can be switched out to revert to a standard Strat bridge pickup sound.

The guitarist's signature appears at the top of the headstock.

The Clapton model has a maple fingerboard.

The Dually pickup is effectively two linked single-coils, one of which can be switched out using the push button between the two tone controls.

The Beck model does not use a standard Stratocaster bridge.

Richie Sambora, 1991

Bon Jovi was one of the biggest US bands of the 1980s, its classic rock sound based around the vocals of Jon Bon Jovi and the fretboard heroics of Richie Sambora. The guitarist had established his reputation using Jackson, Kramer and Charvel superstrats – a loose genre of high-performance, Stratocaster-inspired rock guitars. In 1991, Sambora was honoured with his own signtaure Strat, which featured a humbucking pickup on the bridge and a Floyd Rose locking tremolo unit.

- **DATE** 1991

- **ORIGIN** Corona, California, USA

- **WOOD**
  Alder body with ash veneer, maple bolt-on neck, maple fingerboard.

- **UNUSUAL FEATURE**
  The model has a mix of pickups: a DiMarzio PAF Pro bridge humbucker and a pair of Fender Texas Special single-coils.

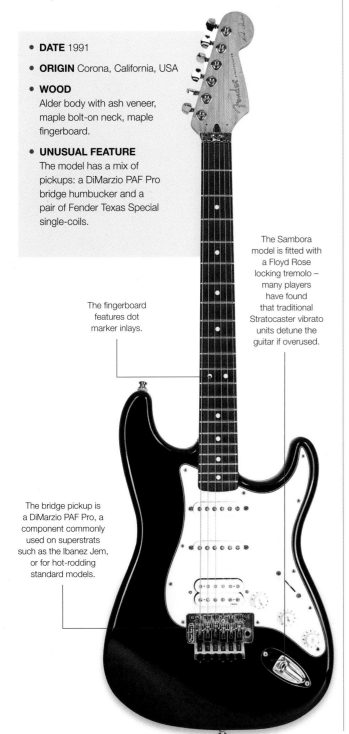

The Sambora model is fitted with a Floyd Rose locking tremolo – many players have found that traditional Stratocaster vibrato units detune the guitar if overused.

The fingerboard features dot marker inlays.

The bridge pickup is a DiMarzio PAF Pro, a component commonly used on superstrats such as the Ibanez Jem, or for hot-rodding standard models.

Stevie Ray Vaughan

ABOVE: *Stevie Ray Vaughan in concert, playing his customized Stratocaster, which he gave the name Number One.*

Born in Texas in 1954 – by coincidence, the same year as the guitar with which he would find fame first came off the production line – Stevie Ray Vaughan was inspired to take up the guitar by his elder brother, Jimmy, who later founded the Fabulous Thunderbirds. After most of the 1970s playing on the electric-blues scene in Austin, Texas, Vaughan achieved wider acclaim during the 1980s with his own band Double Trouble.

Vaughan came to public attention, however, as a rock session player, most notably on David Bowie's globally successful *Let's Dance* album. He was able to capitalize on this high-profile success, and during the second half of the 1980s, Stevie Ray Vaughan and Double Trouble were arguably the most popular live blues band in the world.

An exclusive Stratocaster user, his main instrument – which he called Number One – was a battered hybrid of a pair of 1962–63 models. Vaughan's unique customization was the addition of a left-handed vibrato unit, fitted initially so that he could imitate his hero Jimi Hendrix, who played a right-handed guitar left handed.

Having overcome sometimes debilitating alcohol and drug issues, Vaughan looked set for mainstream success, and he and Fender briefly discussed the idea of a signature model when, in 1990, he was killed in a helicopter crash. Two years later, he was paid the ultimate posthumous tribute, with an exact replica of Number One.

The birth of the superstrat

During the mid-1970s, specialist guitar workshops emerged in response to a demand for hot-rodding production-line electric guitars – frequently Fender Stratocasters. Some of this may have been down to the common perception that Fender's standards had slipped; another reason was the growing availability of third-party hardware alternatives. These souped-up instruments would soon become known as 'superstrats'.

Van Halen 'Frankenstrat', 1980

During the early 1970s, luthier Wayne Charvel opened a successful guitar-repair store in Asuza, California. In 1979, he sold the Charvel brand to one of his employees, Grover Jackson. The Charvel profile was already on the rise when a young guitarist named Eddie Van Halen burst on to the scene. Van Halen's 1978 debut album became an immediate rock classic, and the guitarist was depicted on the sleeve playing a custom-built Charvel, complete with his now-famous personalized striped decoration. Shown here is a commercially available exact replica of Eddie Van Halen's original 'Frankenstrat'.

- **DATE** 1980 (original model)

- **ORIGIN** Asuza, California, USA

- **WOOD**
  Ash body, maple bolt-on neck, maple fingerboard.

- **UNUSUAL FEATURE**
  This guitar was customized by Eddie Van Halen himself from a Charvel instrument.

This modern replica even incorporates Eddie Van Halen's unique rolled masking-tape pick holder.

The original pickup was a Gibson PAF humbucker removed from an ES-335. It was later replaced by a Seymour Duncan.

Jackson Randy Rhoads, 1981

In 1981, with Charvel's stock riding high, Randy Rhoads, the highly rated young guitarist with Ozzy Osbourne's band, approached the company to build his own instruments. One of the results was a Flying V shape with the upper half of the body extended to resemble a shark's fin. Grover Jackson was sufficiently impressed to contemplate putting the guitar into production, but believing the shape to be too outrageous for a Charvel, he rebranded it Jackson. When Rhoads was tragically killed in a plane crash, Jackson decided to name the guitar in tribute to him.

- **DATE** 1981

- **ORIGIN** Glendora, California, USA

- **WOOD**
  Maple body, maple straight-through neck, ebony fingerboard.

- **UNUSUAL FEATURE**
  The guitar takes the Gibson Flying V shape and alters it by having the upper fin elongated and lower fin shortened.

The design is a modern classic, still in production and widely used by metal players, among whom Rhoads' playing is still revered.

The Randy Rhoads design evolved from the guitarist's initial commission to produce a polka-dot Flying V-shaped instrument.

This version features a gold-plated scratchplate.

Jackson Soloist, 1984

Although only launched as a production model in 1984, custom versions of a Stratocaster-style body with a pointed Gibson Explorer-style headstock had been made at the Charvel workshop since the late 1970s. The Jackson Soloist became *the* basic superstrat template, with its body styling, Floyd Rose locking tremolo system – which enabled guitarists to perform dive-bomb pitch bends without putting the guitar out of tune – and the combination of single-coil and humbucking pickups.

- **DATE** 1984

- **ORIGIN** Glendora, California, USA

- **WOOD**
  Alder body with maple top, maple straight-through neck, ebony fingerboard. (Many different options were available.)

- **UNUSUAL FEATURE**
  This is unquestionably the most influential superstrat.

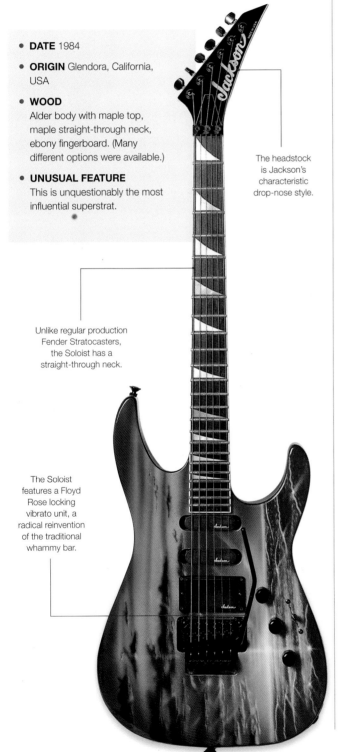

The headstock is Jackson's characteristic drop-nose style.

Unlike regular production Fender Stratocasters, the Soloist has a straight-through neck.

The Soloist features a Floyd Rose locking vibrato unit, a radical reinvention of the traditional whammy bar.

Eddie Van Halen

Born in the Netherlands in 1955, Eddie Van Halen's family emigrated to California when he was seven. A teenage guitar-obsessive, Van Halen admits to having spent hours on end copying solos by Eric Clapton and Jimmy Page – the two players he considers his major influences – note-for-note.

In 1976, Gene Simmons of Kiss saw Van Halen and his band live, and offered to record a demo tape. This resulted in a contract with Warner Bros. Released in 1978, Van Halen's eponymous first album was an enormous hit and is now recognized as one of the all-time-classic rock debuts.

The band's sixth album, *1984*, was a top-three hit and yielded the chart-topping single "Jump". During the same period, Van Halen's attention-grabbing, finger-tapping style led to a recording session invitation from producer Quincy Jones: the result was his sublime high-speed solo on Michael Jackson's global chart topper, "Beat It".

Since the turn of the millennium, the guitarist's ill health – including hip surgery to correct problems widely thought to have been caused by his stage acrobatics – placed the band on hold, and Van Halen dropped out of the public eye. In recent years, however, he has started touring again.

ABOVE: *Eddie Van Halen in 1978, with the first of his custom-built instruments – this one using parts procured from Wayne Charvel. Van Halen's characteristic decorative style has featured on all of his instruments.*

The growth of the superstrat

As far as the electric guitar was concerned, the 1980s really was the era of the superstrat. It was a time when no self-respecting rock guitarist would be seen playing a production instrument. When Fender, Gibson and other leading brands attempted to integrate some of the high-performance features found on their new competitors, it was usually with limited success.

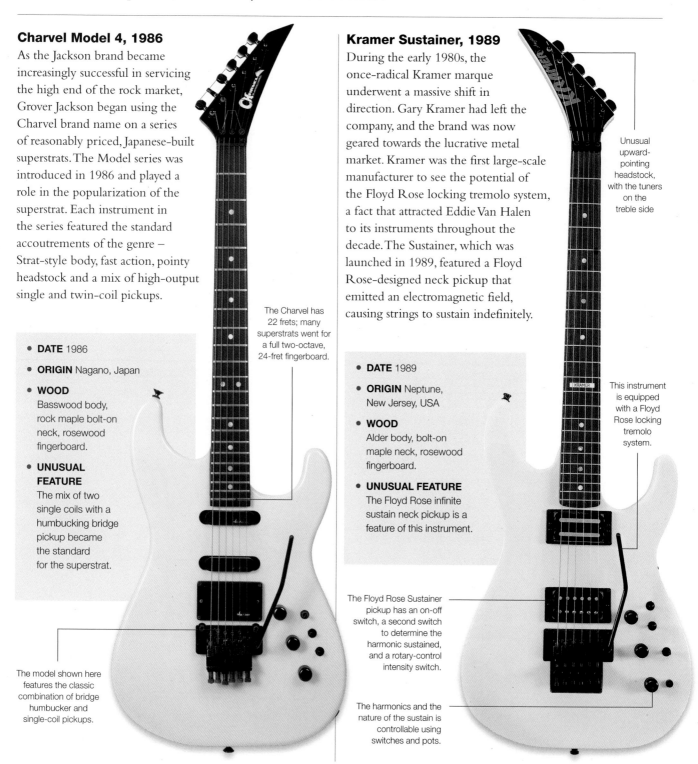

Charvel Model 4, 1986

As the Jackson brand became increasingly successful in servicing the high end of the rock market, Grover Jackson began using the Charvel brand name on a series of reasonably priced, Japanese-built superstrats. The Model series was introduced in 1986 and played a role in the popularization of the superstrat. Each instrument in the series featured the standard accoutrements of the genre – Strat-style body, fast action, pointy headstock and a mix of high-output single and twin-coil pickups.

- **DATE** 1986
- **ORIGIN** Nagano, Japan
- **WOOD**
  Basswood body, rock maple bolt-on neck, rosewood fingerboard.
- **UNUSUAL FEATURE**
  The mix of two single coils with a humbucking bridge pickup became the standard for the superstrat.

The Charvel has 22 frets; many superstrats went for a full two-octave, 24-fret fingerboard.

The model shown here features the classic combination of bridge humbucker and single-coil pickups.

Kramer Sustainer, 1989

During the early 1980s, the once-radical Kramer marque underwent a massive shift in direction. Gary Kramer had left the company, and the brand was now geared towards the lucrative metal market. Kramer was the first large-scale manufacturer to see the potential of the Floyd Rose locking tremolo system, a fact that attracted Eddie Van Halen to its instruments throughout the decade. The Sustainer, which was launched in 1989, featured a Floyd Rose-designed neck pickup that emitted an electromagnetic field, causing strings to sustain indefinitely.

- **DATE** 1989
- **ORIGIN** Neptune, New Jersey, USA
- **WOOD**
  Alder body, bolt-on maple neck, rosewood fingerboard.
- **UNUSUAL FEATURE**
  The Floyd Rose infinite sustain neck pickup is a feature of this instrument.

Unusual upward-pointing headstock, with the tuners on the treble side

This instrument is equipped with a Floyd Rose locking tremolo system.

The Floyd Rose Sustainer pickup has an on-off switch, a second switch to determine the harmonic sustained, and a rotary-control intensity switch.

The harmonics and the nature of the sustain is controllable using switches and pots.

Jackson Warrior Pro, 1990

Introduced in 1990, the Jackson Warrior Pro is one of the more dramatic of the shredder guitars. The body styling shows the influence of the Gibson Explorer, although with exaggerated pointed cutaways at both the neck and the rear. The Warrior features a straight-through maple neck with poplar wings and a two-octave, bound ebony fingerboard. The inlays are Jackson's characteristic pearl sharkfin design. At the time of its launch, it was the company's most expensive production model.

- **DATE** 1990

- **ORIGIN** Glendora, California, USA

- **WOOD**
  Poplar body, straight-through maple neck, ebony fingerboard.

- **UNUSUAL FEATURE**
  The body shape, with its multiple cutaways, is very distinctive.

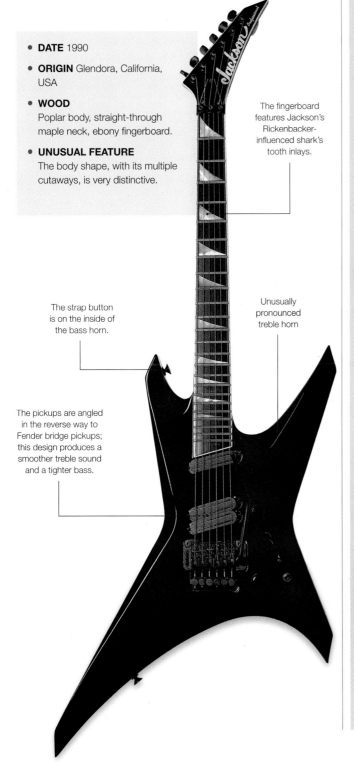

The fingerboard features Jackson's Rickenbacker-influenced shark's tooth inlays.

The strap button is on the inside of the bass horn.

Unusually pronounced treble horn

The pickups are angled in the reverse way to Fender bridge pickups; this design produces a smoother treble sound and a tighter bass.

Response to the superstrat

The emergence of the superstrat changed the electric-guitar market during the 1980s, and has had a lasting impact. The move towards these new instruments started in the 1970s, when players realized that they could, with relative ease, hot-rod their existing production models, commonly altering pickups and electrics for a wider variety of sounds, or opting for wholesale replacement of necks and bodies. Fender and Gibson, both of which were in something of a slump during the 1980s, responded with their own takes on the style, but enjoyed little success.

By the mid-1990s, the shredding superstrats had fallen out of vogue, and classic retro styles were back in. What remained, however, was a greater understanding of the potential options for any electric guitar. Fender subsequently issued Stratocasters – often signature models – that combined the instrument's iconic features with superstrat-style combinations of single and switchable humbucking pickups, locking vibrato units and scalloped fingerboards.

LEFT: *The 1991 M-III was Gibson's final attempt at producing a guitar capable of matching the tonal versatility of the superstrat. It featured three humbucking pickups, all of which could be switched into single-coil mode.*

Guitar synthesizers

From the early days of the electric guitar, inventors have sought to incorporate technological innovation into their instruments. In the early 1960s, one of the boldest attempts was to build a Vox Continental organ into a guitar; others took the simpler step of adding analogue effects. With the popularity of the affordable synthesizer in the 1970s came the inevitable hybrid: the guitar synth.

Roland GS-500, 1977

Founded in 1972, Roland quickly established itself as one of Japan's leading music-technology companies. The first Roland guitar synthesizer, the GS-500, appeared in 1977. It was an Ibanez Les Paul-style guitar that connected to an external synthesizer unit, a GR-500. A divided pickup tracks the actions on each individual string and transmits control voltages to the synth unit via a 24-way cable. The guitar also features a humbucker, allowing it to be used as a regular instrument.

- **DATE** 1977
- **ORIGIN** Osaka, Japan
- **WOOD**
  Mahogany body with two-piece maple top, mahogany set neck, rosewood fingerboard.
- **UNUSUAL FEATURE**
  This is a conventional guitar with an external synthesizer unit.

Synthaxe, 1986

It was former BBC Radiophonic Workshop composer Bill Aitken who came up with the idea of the Synthaxe. As ingenious as Roland's first guitar synthesizer hybrids had been, tracking of the notes – the accuracy with which the note played on the guitar was translated electronically – was still a problem. The Synthaxe addresses this by using two separate sets of strings, one for plucking and another for holding down the notes. Pitch data are generated electronically, the frets themselves forming part of the circuitry when they are pressed down.

- **DATE** 1986
- **ORIGIN** Whitney, UK
- **MATERIALS**
  Fibreglass covering metal chassis and neck.
- **UNUSUAL FEATURE**
  This instrument is a controller rather than a guitar in its own right.

The socket on the side of the GS-500 connects to the synthesizer unit, which is equipped with its own stand for on-stage accessibility.

The control panel features a combination of standard guitar controls and external controls for the GR-500 unit.

As the fingerboard is used to generate MIDI pitch data, the frets are spaced equally, making it feel unnatural to play for some guitarists.

The Synthaxe has no sound of its own; rather it sends data to an external, MIDI-equipped unit. It can thus be used to control synthesizers or other instruments, such as electronic drums.

The splitting of the two sets of strings makes the Synthaxe a curious playing experience for many guitarists.

Starr Labs Ztar Z6S-XPA, 2010

The guitar synthesizer never really achieved widespread popularity and is now something of a niche product. Roland has continued to develop the technology in a low-key fashion, leaving new companies such as Starr Labs to innovate. The Ztar comprises strings for plucking notes, but the fingerboard replaces strings and frets with pressure-sensitive switches. The flagship model, the Z6S-XPA, like other MIDI controllers, has no internal sounds of its own but is designed to work with Ableton Live, the popular computer audio recording and looping software.

- **DATE** 2010

- **ORIGIN** San Diego, California, USA

- **WOOD**
  Composite body, unspecified wooden neck with plastic switches.

- **UNUSUAL FEATURE**
  The fingerboard and frets have been replaced by 144 switches.

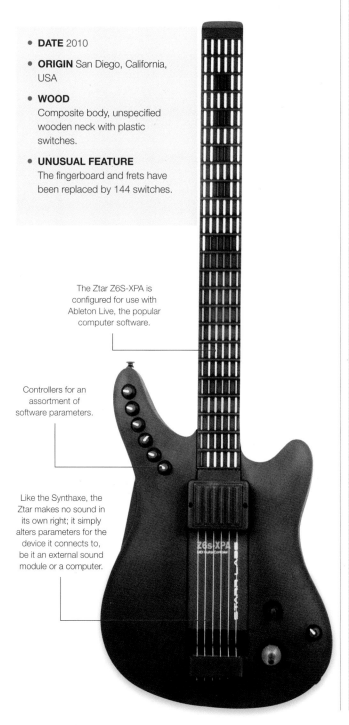

The Ztar Z6S-XPA is configured for use with Ableton Live, the popular computer software.

Controllers for an assortment of software parameters.

Like the Synthaxe, the Ztar makes no sound in its own right; it simply alters parameters for the device it connects to, be it an external sound module or a computer.

MIDI (Musical Instrument Digital Interface)

ABOVE: *Jazz guitarist Pat Metheny was an early user of guitar synthesizer technology. His favoured set-up was a Roland GR-303 linked via MIDI (Musical Instrument Digital Interface) to a Synclavier, an early digital sampling system.*

Developed in 1982, MIDI (Musical Instrument Digital Interface) is a standardized communications protocol that enables suitably equipped instruments – keyboard synthesizers, electronic drums, digital samplers or computers running certain kinds of software – to send data to one another.

For guitarists with MIDI-equipped instruments, this means that whenever a note is played, it is converted into MIDI note data, so it has a pitch value, a dynamic value and an instruction to switch the note on and off. The signal itself has no musical value – the same data could generate any number of different sounds, depending on how the sound modules at the end of the chain have been programmed.

Rather than buying a specific instrument or controller, some guitarists prefer to attach a MIDI pickup to a standard guitar. With the possibility of setting up a separate MIDI channel for each string, one guitar playing live can be used to trigger six separate sound modules.

The modern bass

Since the launch of the first solidbody bass guitar in 1951, as a breed, bass players have since shown themselves to be more open-minded and prepared to experiment than their guitar-toting cousins. New designs and construction materials have become widely accepted, and over the past two decades, use of five- and six-string basses has become increasingly common.

Wal Pro Fretless Bass, 1978

Founded in 1974 by Ian 'Wal' Waller and Pete Stevens, the British-made Wal bass became something of a professional's choice during the late 1970s. Initially custom made, instruments were built from exotic tonewoods and crafted to extremely high standards. Using active circuitry, Wal basses were known for their exceptional sound and playability. In 1978, Wal launched the Pro series, which had fretless five- and six-string models in the range. The unexpected death of founder Waller in 1988 dealt the brand a huge blow, but the company continued operating until 2007.

- **DATE** 1978
- **ORIGIN** High Wycombe, UK
- **WOOD**
  Ash body, laminate ash bolt-on neck, rosewood fingerboard.
- **UNUSUAL FEATURE**
  The Pro series came with four options:
  I – one passive pickup;
  II – two passive pickups;
  IE – one active pickup;
  Pro IIE – two active pickups.

Early Wal Pro necks were a ten-piece laminate construction. The centre was formed from hornbeam with two strips of mukalungu and maple alternating towards the edge of the neck.

The model here is a Pro II, and is equipped with a pair of passive pickups.

Steinberger L Series Bass, 1979

New York luthier Ned Steinberger produced one of the most striking and innovative bass guitars of the past four decades, the L Series. First built in 1979, they are noteworthy both in terms of appearance and construction. The most startling factor is the complete lack of a headstock; the strings are threaded from behind the nut and then tuned from behind the bridge. The Steinberger is built not from wood, but from a proprietary mix of graphite and carbon-fibre, which creates a punchy attack, an even tone and an impressive sustain.

- **DATE** 1979
- **ORIGIN** Newburgh, New York, USA
- **MATERIALS**
  Steinberger Blend, a graphite and carbon-fibre mixture, cast in two pieces.
- **UNUSUAL FEATURE**
  The lack of headstock was radical in its day.

The strings are threaded behind the nut.

Unusual among bass guitars, the Steinberger has a two-octave, 24-fret fingerboard.

The unique body shape enables unimpeded access to the entire fingerboard.

In spite of its small body size, the Steinberger headless bass is well known for producing an even, powerful sound.

Special strings are required, with the balls at both ends. The tuners are concealed behind the bridge.

Fodera Victor Wooten Monarch, 1983

Founded in Brooklyn, New York, the Fodera workshop produces high-specification handmade instruments for the professional end of the market – some of its guitars retail at more than $20,000 with no shortage of takers. The Monarch was Fodera's first model, built from 1983. A very early convert from that year was Victor Wooten, who purchased instrument number 037, which has remained his main instrument throughout his extraordinary career. This signature model is an exact replica of Wooten's favourite bass guitar.

- **DATE** 1983
- **ORIGIN** Brooklyn, New York, USA
- **WOOD**
  Mahogany body with flame maple top, three-piece maple set neck, Indian rosewood fingerboard.
- **UNUSUAL FEATURE**
  Instruments are built to order, so numerous personalized variations are possible.

Fodera instruments are immediately recognizable from the butterfly headstock inlay.

Fodera basses are characterized by a sharp, overhanging horn on the bass side.

The EMG pickups combine the split style of a Fender Precision with the single line of a Fender Jazz.

A single unit houses the tailpiece and adjustable bridge saddles.

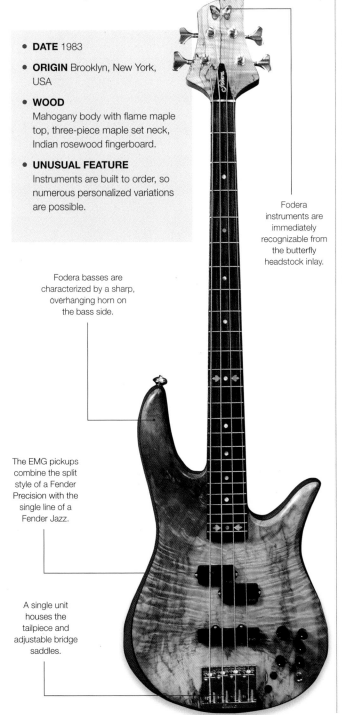

Warwick Corvette, 2008

Formed in 1982 in Markneukirchen, Germany, Warwick was originally a premium brand that produced a small range of models using the straight-through neck construction often found on high-end models. First built in 1995, the Corvette Standard is one of the company's best-known basses. It features MEC Dynamic Correction pickups – passive units with a powered pre-amp – that act as a kind of compressor, trimming the high frequencies and boosting the low. Corvette production has subsequently been moved to Korea.

- **DATE** 2008
- **ORIGIN** Markneukirchen, Germany (later models were built in Korea)
- **WOOD**
  Bubinga or swamp-ash body (custom models have been built using a wide variety of tonewoods), mahogany set neck, rosewood fingerboard.
- **UNUSUAL FEATURE**
  The MEC Dynamic Correction pickups help to boost the bass sounds.

The headstock features a three-and-two configuration with, unusually, the tuners angled towards the player.

The model shown here is a five-string bass – these have become increasingly common in recent times.

The circuitry in the powered pre-amp compresses the sound so that there is a good balance between the treble and bass frequencies.

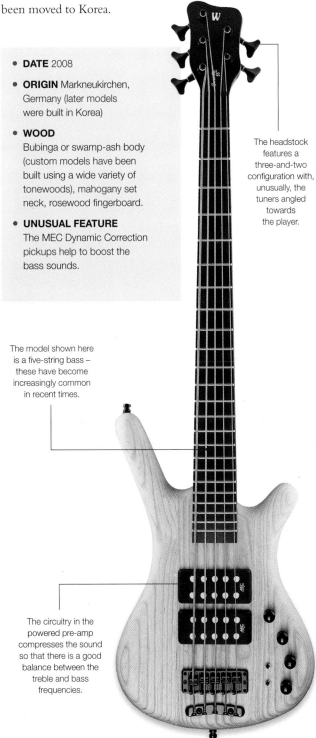

Curious Strats

During its 60 uninterrupted years of production, the Fender Stratocaster has appeared in numerous variations: different colour options and decorative finishes, and hardware and pickup configurations that are capable of dramatically altering the basic Stratocaster sound. Here is a selection of some of the more unusual offers that have been produced from the Fender Custom Shop.

Twin Neck Custom, 1989

During the first half of the 1970s, when the double-neck guitar was at the peak of its popularity, Fender was really not interested. The company didn't even produce a double-neck guitar until 1987, and the very first serial number produced by the Custom Shop (0001) was for a twin-six-string double-neck, one Stratocaster and one Telecaster. Two years later, the Custom Shop produced this more conventional model, with a Strat on the lower neck and an Electric XII, complete with hockey-stick headstock at the top.

- **DATE** 1989
- **ORIGIN** Fullerton, California, USA
- **WOOD**
  Ash body, maple bolt-on neck, rosewood fingerboards.
- **UNUSUAL FEATURE**
  This was the first Fender 12/6 double-neck.

The pickups are single-coil Lace Sensors.

The bridge of the 12-string contains individually adjustable saddles for each string.

Harley-Davidson, 1993

One of the most desirable of all Fender limited editions, this model was produced in 1993 to mark the 90th anniversary of the Harley-Davidson, America's most famous motorcycle manufacturer. Its spectacular metal finish features the company name etched on to the aluminium body. It was built at the Custom Shop's new premises in Scottsdale, Arizona, in a limited run of 109 instruments. Highly collectible, these models can now fetch in excess of $20,000 at auction.

- **DATE** 1993
- **ORIGIN** Scottsdale, Arizona, USA
- **WOOD**
  Aluminium body, maple bolt-on neck, rosewood fingerboard.
- **UNUSUAL FEATURE**
  The engraved aluminium body is highly distinctive.

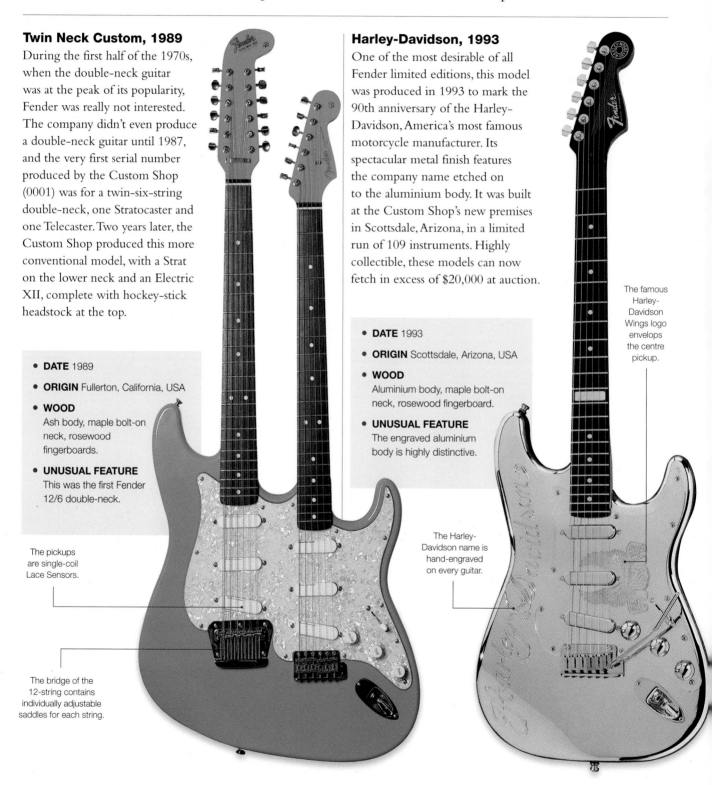

The famous Harley-Davidson Wings logo envelops the centre pickup.

The Harley-Davidson name is hand-engraved on every guitar.

Hendrix Monterey Pop Fesitval, 1997

On June 18, 1967, Jimi Hendrix reached the climax of his legendary Hendrix Monterey Pop Festival appearance by 'sacrificing' his hand-painted Fiesta Red Stratocaster – first by setting it alight and then smashing it against the floor. In 1997, Pamelina Hovnatanian – known professionally as guitar artist Pamelina H (who had attended the show as a child) – produced a hand-painted artwork that "evoked rather than reproduced" the original Hendrix design.

- **DATE** 1997
- **ORIGIN** Scottsdale, Arizona, USA
- **WOOD**
  Ash body with airbrushed finish, maple bolt-on neck, rosewood fingerboard.
- **UNUSUAL FEATURE**
  This is an authentic re-creation of a1965 Stratocaster.

The headstock is an authentic 1965 design, including the 'transition' logo – this was the period when Leo Fender sold his company to CBS.

The artwork on the body and scratchplate is hand-painted.

ABOVE: *Pamelina H's artwork includes a backstage pass graphic above the bridge unit. A matching laminated backstage pass was included with each guitar in the limited run of 210 instruments.*

Rather than an attempt to replicate Hendrix's own hand-painted Stratocaster, Pamelina H's artwork was 'inspired by' the original.

Catalina Island Blues Festival, 1999

The Fender Custom shop has become well known for producing one-off designs. Pamelina H, arguably the leading figure in the world of guitar art, produced this instrument for the 1999 Catalina Island Blues Festival. Taking a body intricately carved by George Amicay, Pamelina H created the spectacular mermaid artwork by using airbrushing techniques. The festival ran from 1997 to 2001, a different design being produced for each year.

- **DATE** 1999
- **ORIGIN** Corona, California, USA
- **WOOD**
  Ash body, maple bolt-on neck, rosewood fingerboard.
- **UNUSUAL FEATURE**
  George Amicay's carving and Pamelina H's airbrushed artwork are incredibly intricate.

Unusually, this guitar has no fingerboard inlays.

Also unusually for a Stratocaster, it is fitted with gold-plated lipstick-case pickups.

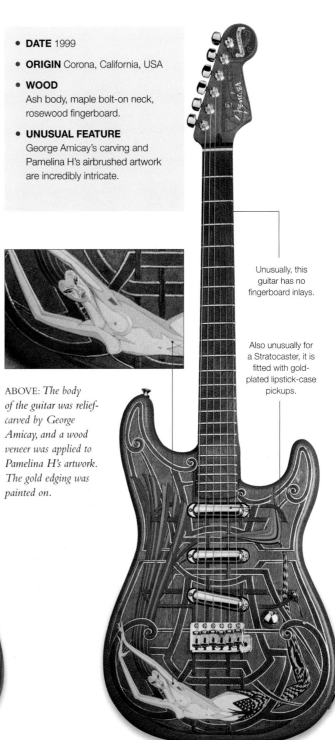

ABOVE: *The body of the guitar was relief-carved by George Amicay, and a wood veneer was applied to Pamelina H's artwork. The gold edging was painted on.*

Fender in the 1990s

During the 1990s, while Fender concentrated its business on classic designs from the 1950s, it did also launch a number of new models. There was nothing as outré as the Katana or Performer from the previous decade, however, as, even though these were new designs, they were firmly rooted in the Fender tradition, with an emphasis on Stratocaster and Jaguar shapes.

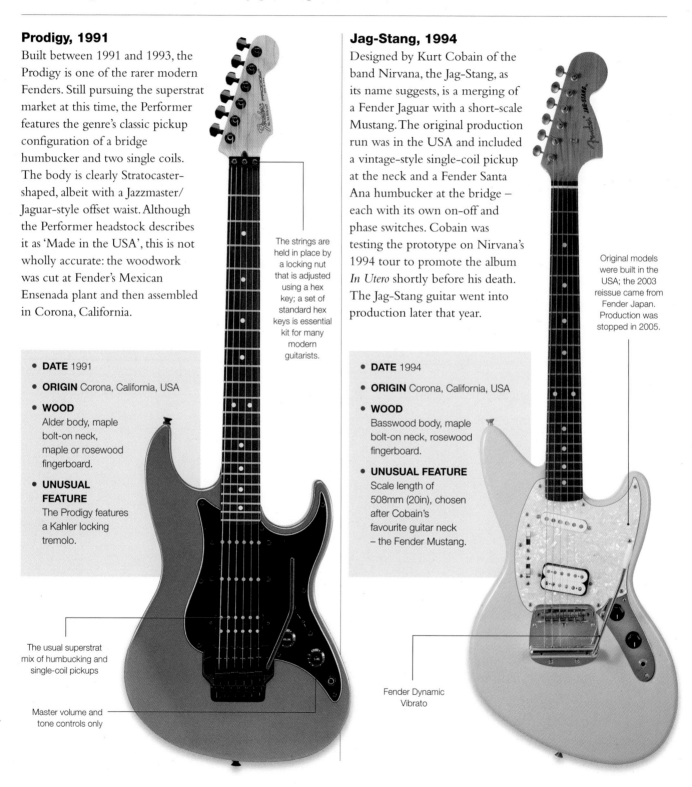

Prodigy, 1991

Built between 1991 and 1993, the Prodigy is one of the rarer modern Fenders. Still pursuing the superstrat market at this time, the Performer features the genre's classic pickup configuration of a bridge humbucker and two single coils. The body is clearly Stratocaster-shaped, albeit with a Jazzmaster/Jaguar-style offset waist. Although the Performer headstock describes it as 'Made in the USA', this is not wholly accurate: the woodwork was cut at Fender's Mexican Ensenada plant and then assembled in Corona, California.

The strings are held in place by a locking nut that is adjusted using a hex key; a set of standard hex keys is essential kit for many modern guitarists.

- **DATE** 1991

- **ORIGIN** Corona, California, USA

- **WOOD**
  Alder body, maple bolt-on neck, maple or rosewood fingerboard.

- **UNUSUAL FEATURE**
  The Prodigy features a Kahler locking tremolo.

The usual superstrat mix of humbucking and single-coil pickups

Master volume and tone controls only

Jag-Stang, 1994

Designed by Kurt Cobain of the band Nirvana, the Jag-Stang, as its name suggests, is a merging of a Fender Jaguar with a short-scale Mustang. The original production run was in the USA and included a vintage-style single-coil pickup at the neck and a Fender Santa Ana humbucker at the bridge – each with its own on-off and phase switches. Cobain was testing the prototype on Nirvana's 1994 tour to promote the album *In Utero* shortly before his death. The Jag-Stang guitar went into production later that year.

Original models were built in the USA; the 2003 reissue came from Fender Japan. Production was stopped in 2005.

- **DATE** 1994

- **ORIGIN** Corona, California, USA

- **WOOD**
  Basswood body, maple bolt-on neck, rosewood fingerboard.

- **UNUSUAL FEATURE**
  Scale length of 508mm (20in), chosen after Cobain's favourite guitar neck – the Fender Mustang.

Fender Dynamic Vibrato

Cyclone, 1997

Introduced in 1997, the Cyclone was styled on the Mustang student guitar of the 1960s, but with a significantly different specification. The body of the Cyclone is built from poplar, and is thicker than the body of a Mustang, which in recent guises had been built from basswood. Five years later, a number of cosmetic changes were introduced to the Cyclone II, including racing stripes. The new model also offered a wide variety of pickup options. The entire Cyclone range was discontinued by Fender in 2007.

- **DATE** 1997

- **ORIGIN** Ensenada, Mexico (a US-built version was offered briefly in 2002)

- **WOOD**
  Poplar body, maple bolt-on neck, rosewood fingerboard.

- **UNUSUAL FEATURE**
  The humbucker/single/single pickup configuration is rare on a Fender.

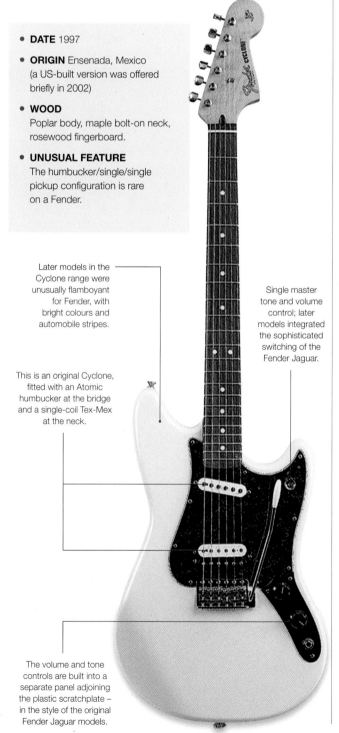

Later models in the Cyclone range were unusually flamboyant for Fender, with bright colours and automobile stripes.

This is an original Cyclone, fitted with an Atomic humbucker at the bridge and a single-coil Tex-Mex at the neck.

Single master tone and volume control; later models integrated the sophisticated switching of the Fender Jaguar.

The volume and tone controls are built into a separate panel adjoining the plastic scratchplate – in the style of the original Fender Jaguar models.

Toronado, 1998

Part of Fender's Deluxe series of Mexican-built instruments, like the Cyclone, the Toronado also has a 629mm (24¾ in) scale length – which is the same standard length as Gibson guitars and 19mm (¾ in) shorter than most other Fenders. The Toronado body is styled on the lines of the Jaguar and Jazzmaster, and is fitted with a pair of Fender Atomic humbucking pickups. In 2004, a Korean version – known as the Toronado HH – was introduced, featuring metallic colours as well as racing stripes.

- **DATE** 1998

- **ORIGIN** Ensenada, Mexico

- **WOOD**
  Alder body, maple bolt-on neck, rosewood fingerboard.

- **UNUSUAL FEATURE**
  The instrument has a 629mm (24¾in) scale length – shorter than a normal Fender.

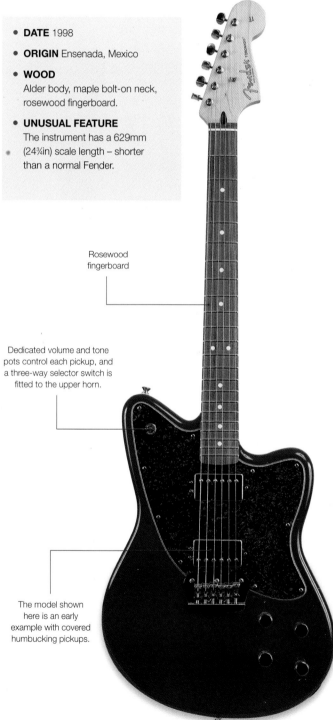

Rosewood fingerboard

Dedicated volume and tone pots control each pickup, and a three-way selector switch is fitted to the upper horn.

The model shown here is an early example with covered humbucking pickups.

The reissue vogue

By the 1990s, the vintage-guitar market was enjoying a period of rapid growth, with second-hand prices for vintage Fender and Gibson models – even those barely 20 years old – well beyond the pockets of most ordinary musicians. Taking advantage of this developing trend, both Fender and Gibson began programmes of reissuing authentic replicas of popular classics.

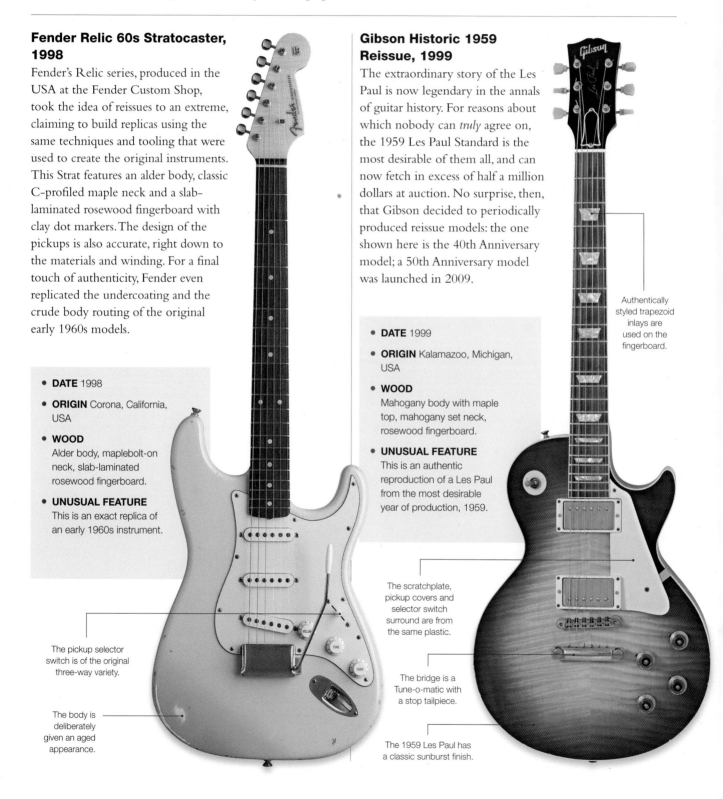

Fender Relic 60s Stratocaster, 1998

Fender's Relic series, produced in the USA at the Fender Custom Shop, took the idea of reissues to an extreme, claiming to build replicas using the same techniques and tooling that were used to create the original instruments. This Strat features an alder body, classic C-profiled maple neck and a slab-laminated rosewood fingerboard with clay dot markers. The design of the pickups is also accurate, right down to the materials and winding. For a final touch of authenticity, Fender even replicated the undercoating and the crude body routing of the original early 1960s models.

- **DATE** 1998
- **ORIGIN** Corona, California, USA
- **WOOD**
  Alder body, maplebolt-on neck, slab-laminated rosewood fingerboard.
- **UNUSUAL FEATURE**
  This is an exact replica of an early 1960s instrument.

The pickup selector switch is of the original three-way variety.

The body is deliberately given an aged appearance.

Gibson Historic 1959 Reissue, 1999

The extraordinary story of the Les Paul is now legendary in the annals of guitar history. For reasons about which nobody can *truly* agree on, the 1959 Les Paul Standard is the most desirable of them all, and can now fetch in excess of half a million dollars at auction. No surprise, then, that Gibson decided to periodically produced reissue models: the one shown here is the 40th Anniversary model; a 50th Anniversary model was launched in 2009.

- **DATE** 1999
- **ORIGIN** Kalamazoo, Michigan, USA
- **WOOD**
  Mahogany body with maple top, mahogany set neck, rosewood fingerboard.
- **UNUSUAL FEATURE**
  This is an authentic reproduction of a Les Paul from the most desirable year of production, 1959.

Authentically styled trapezoid inlays are used on the fingerboard.

The scratchplate, pickup covers and selector switch surround are from the same plastic.

The bridge is a Tune-o-matic with a stop tailpiece.

The 1959 Les Paul has a classic sunburst finish.

Fender Classic '72 Custom, 2004

The year 1972 was a key one for the Fender Telecaster, as three new models – the Thinline, Custom and Deluxe – were all introduced. In 2004, Fender launched the Classic '72 series, replicas of these three by now long-discontinued Telecaster models. The original Custom was produced until 1981, but it had retained a cult following in the years after its production ceased. The Classic reissue was at first built by Fender Japan, but production was later moved to the Ensenada plant in Mexico.

- **DATE** 2004

- **ORIGIN** Hamamatso, Japan and Ensenada, Mexico

- **WOOD**
  Alder body, maple bolt-on neck, maple or rosewood fingerboard.

- **UNUSUAL FEATURE**
  The pickups fitted to Japanese models create a different sound from the Mexican-built models.

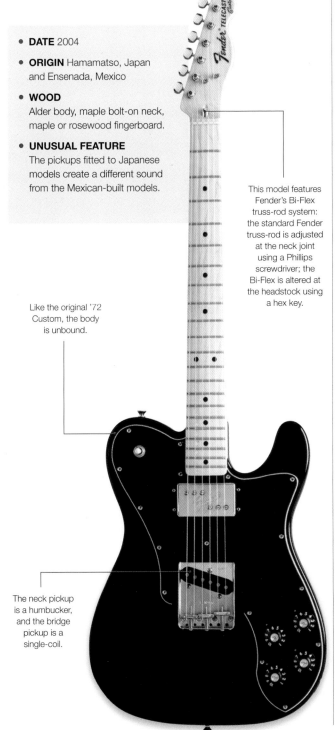

This model features Fender's Bi-Flex truss-rod system: the standard Fender truss-rod is adjusted at the neck joint using a Phillips screwdriver; the Bi-Flex is altered at the headstock using a hex key.

Like the original '72 Custom, the body is unbound.

The neck pickup is a humbucker, and the bridge pickup is a single-coil.

Gibson Les Paul 1958 Aged Reissue, 2008

The popularity (and rarity) of the 1958 and 1959 Les Paul models among young electric blues-rock players led Gibson to revive the design in 1968. Original models from 1958–59 are now so desirable that they pass hands for six-figure sums, and are rarely seen. In 2008, Gibson exhibited a new level of fetishism with an instantly collectible 200-run 50th Anniversary model that matched as closely possible the technical specifications of an original 1958, and was artificially aged to appear as if it had taken half a century of heavy use.

- **DATE** 2008

- **ORIGIN** Kalamazoo, Michigan, USA

- **WOOD**
  Mahogany body with maple top, mahogany set neck, rosewood fingerboard.

- **UNUSUAL FEATURE**
  The artificial ageing by Gibson luthier Tom Murphy helped to make this an instant classic for collectors.

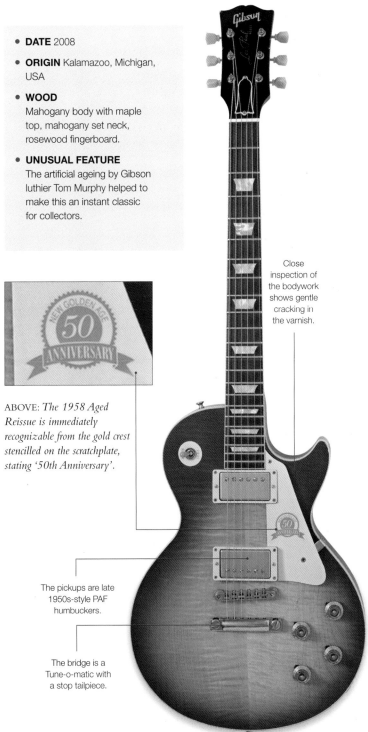

ABOVE: *The 1958 Aged Reissue is immediately recognizable from the gold crest stencilled on the scratchplate, stating '50th Anniversary'.*

Close inspection of the bodywork shows gentle cracking in the varnish.

The pickups are late 1950s-style PAF humbuckers.

The bridge is a Tune-o-matic with a stop tailpiece.

Washburn and Parker

Here we'll take a look at two small but nonetheless significant US guitar manufacturers. The Washburn brand name goes back to Chicago in the 1880s and makes much of its links to the early blues players, but the company as we know it today has only existed since 1974. Parker is an even newer name, noted especially for producing the Fly, one of the most important new guitars since the early 1990s.

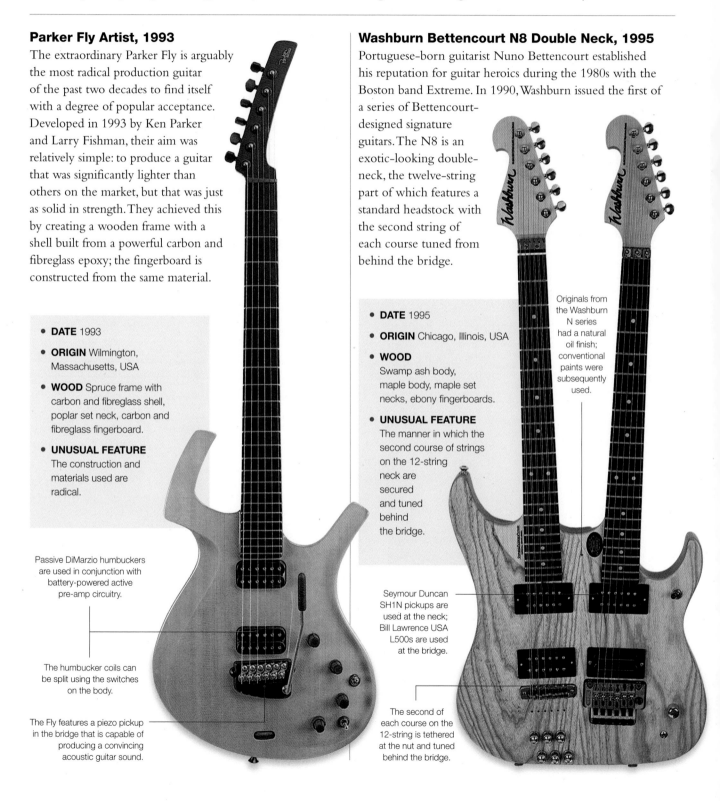

Parker Fly Artist, 1993

The extraordinary Parker Fly is arguably the most radical production guitar of the past two decades to find itself with a degree of popular acceptance. Developed in 1993 by Ken Parker and Larry Fishman, their aim was relatively simple: to produce a guitar that was significantly lighter than others on the market, but that was just as solid in strength. They achieved this by creating a wooden frame with a shell built from a powerful carbon and fibreglass epoxy; the fingerboard is constructed from the same material.

- **DATE** 1993
- **ORIGIN** Wilmington, Massachusetts, USA
- **WOOD** Spruce frame with carbon and fibreglass shell, poplar set neck, carbon and fibreglass fingerboard.
- **UNUSUAL FEATURE** The construction and materials used are radical.

Passive DiMarzio humbuckers are used in conjunction with battery-powered active pre-amp circuitry.

The humbucker coils can be split using the switches on the body.

The Fly features a piezo pickup in the bridge that is capable of producing a convincing acoustic guitar sound.

Washburn Bettencourt N8 Double Neck, 1995

Portuguese-born guitarist Nuno Bettencourt established his reputation for guitar heroics during the 1980s with the Boston band Extreme. In 1990, Washburn issued the first of a series of Bettencourt-designed signature guitars. The N8 is an exotic-looking double-neck, the twelve-string part of which features a standard headstock with the second string of each course tuned from behind the bridge.

- **DATE** 1995
- **ORIGIN** Chicago, Illinois, USA
- **WOOD** Swamp ash body, maple body, maple set necks, ebony fingerboards.
- **UNUSUAL FEATURE** The manner in which the second course of strings on the 12-string neck are secured and tuned behind the bridge.

Originals from the Washburn N series had a natural oil finish; conventional paints were subsequently used.

Seymour Duncan SH1N pickups are used at the neck; Bill Lawrence USA L500s are used at the bridge.

The second of each course on the 12-string is tethered at the nut and tuned behind the bridge.

Parker MIDIFly, 1998

Widely viewed as the best guitar MIDI controller around, the Parker MIDIFly has all the features of a standard Fly, although, unlike the early models, it was built with a solid mahogany body, as most standard Flys were by this time. The MIDIFly has both MIDI in and out sockets, connection to which is made via the MIDIAxe junction box, which then connects to an external sound module or suitably equipped computer for recording. There is also accompanying computer software for editing and configuring the MIDI interface.

- **DATE** 1998

- **ORIGIN** Wilmington, Massachusetts, USA

- **WOOD**
  Mahogany body, mahogany, carbon and fibreglass set neck, carbon-fibre fingerboard.

- **UNUSUAL FEATURE**
  Contains MIDI sockets alongside audio sockets.

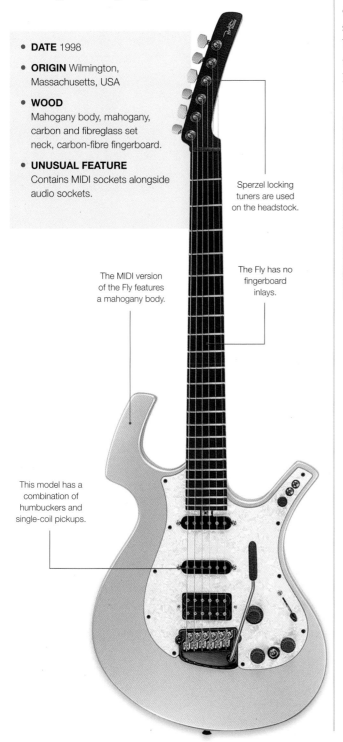

Sperzel locking tuners are used on the headstock.

The MIDI version of the Fly features a mahogany body.

The Fly has no fingerboard inlays.

This model has a combination of humbuckers and single-coil pickups.

Washburn Dimebag Darrell Stealth, 2000

When Washburn teamed up with 'Dimebag Darrell' Abbott in 2000, he was one of the most popular shredders of his time, having established his reputation with Pantera, one of America's top-selling metal bands. The Washburn Stealth was based on the Dean ML that Dimebag had popularized earlier in his career. The shape is Gibson-inspired – a Flying V crossed with the upper half of a Gibson Explorer, with all the extremities exaggerated. The Dimebag story ended in tragedy in 2004 when he was gunned down on stage by a paranoid schizophrenic who had become convinced that the guitarist was 'stealing' his thoughts.

- **DATE** 2000

- **ORIGIN** Chicago, Illinois, USA (budget models built in Korea)

- **WOOD**
  Mahogany body, mahogany set neck (Korean models bolt-on), ebony fingerboard.

- **UNUSUAL FEATURE**
  The V headstock is distinctive.

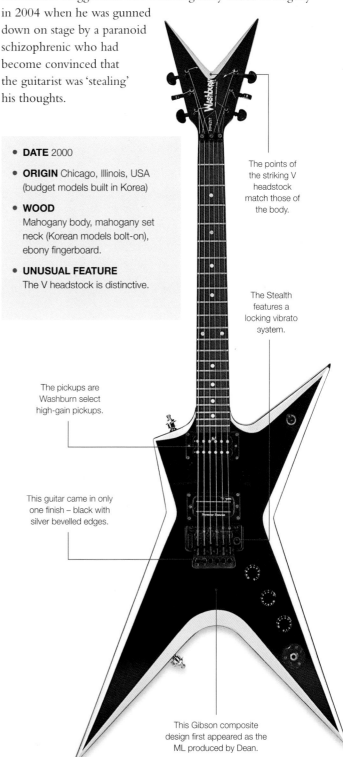

The points of the striking V headstock match those of the body.

The Stealth features a locking vibrato system.

The pickups are Washburn select high-gain pickups.

This guitar came in only one finish – black with silver bevelled edges.

This Gibson composite design first appeared as the ML produced by Dean.

Les Paul special models

Like most of the long-established guitar brands, a good deal of Gibson's business comes from limited-edition reissues of classic models. Sometimes these are attempts to replicate a popular original model from a specific period; on other occasions they are linked to a specific musician or a related brand. Here is a small selection of modern Les Paul special editions.

Gibson Les Paul 60 Corvette, 1995

"The Chevrolet Corvette and the Gibson Les Paul exemplify the innovative vision of two great American companies in the early 1950s" – so ran the press release for an intriguing pair of guitars. The 60 Corvette is, as the name suggests, a Les Paul Standard styled in the manner of a 1960 Corvette. Available in a variety of authentic Chevy paint jobs, the curved white panel follows the same contour as that found on the sides of the car, and includes the three chrome fins. The Corvette logo appears on the fingerboard as an inlay. Later that year, the Gibson Custom Shop produced a similar tribute – this time, 1963 Corvette Stingray styling was applied to an SG.

- **DATE** 1995

- **ORIGIN** Kalamazoo, Michigan, USA

- **WOOD**
  Mahogany body with maple top, maple set neck, rosewood fingerboard.

- **UNUSUAL FEATURE**
  The guitar was issued with authentic 1960s Corvette colours and styling features.

Standard marker inlays are replaced by the word 'Corvette' between the 2nd and 13th frets.

The curved white central panel is modelled on the detailing of the original car.

Gibson Duane Allman, 2003

Although he died in 1971, in his short life Duane Allman left a legacy of fine recordings of Southern rock. A noted Les Paul player, Gibson honoured him in 2003 by releasing a replica of his 1958 Standard that now resides in the Rock and Roll Hall of Fame. The run was limited to 55 guitars, apparently since Gibson struggled to find the wood that emulated the gull-wing flame pattern of Allman's guitar. Like the original instrument, the reverse of the body has the word 'DUANE' constructed from hammered-in fretwire.

- **DATE** 2003

- **ORIGIN** Kalamazoo, Michigan, USA

- **WOOD**
  Mahogany body with maple top, mahogany set neck, rosewood fingerboard.

- **UNUSUAL FEATURE**
  As with the original, Duane Allman's name appears on the back which is made of hammered-in fretwire.

The reverse of the headstock has the letters 'DALLMAN' stamped in, directly above the number in the run – from 1 to 55.

The fingerboard features classic Gibson trapezoid inlays.

This model has PAF humbuckers.

Epiphone Zakk Wylde Les Paul Custom Buzzsaw, 2004

Metal guitarist Zakk Wylde has been honoured with a number of Epiphone and Gibson signature guitars. He is particularly well known for two of his decorative patterns: the black-and-white Bullseye and the orange-and-black Buzzsaw shown here. The Buzzsaw is a Les Paul variation built in the Far East, kitted out with heavy-duty EMG humbuckers. Wylde's signature Epiphones are very popular with fledgeling rock players.

- **DATE** 2004

- **ORIGIN** Qingdao, China

- **WOOD**
  Mahogany body, maple set neck, rosewood fingerboard.

- **UNUSUAL FEATURE**
  The orange-and-black Buzzsaw pattern is a Zakk Wylde signature design.

The fingerboard has block marker inlays.

Unusual even for a modern Les Paul, the Zakk Wylde Epiphone is fitted with EMG active humbucking pickups powered by a 9-volt battery.

Both black-and-white Bullseye and orange-and-black Buzzsaw variations are immediately recognizable as Zakk Wylde signature models.

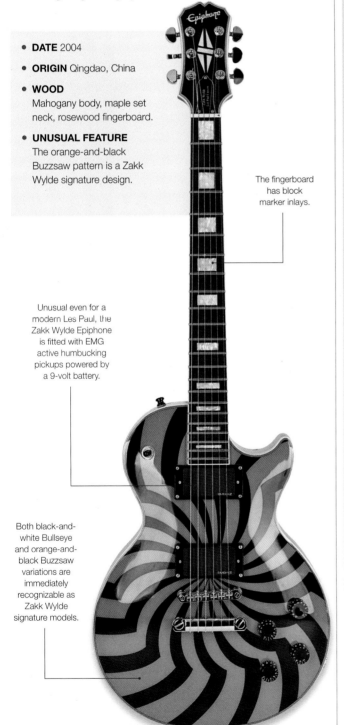

Zakk Wylde

ABOVE: *Zakk Wylde in action with Black Label Society during the band's 2011 UK tour. As always, Wylde is seen playing his signature black-and-white Bullseye Gibson Les Paul.*

Born in Bayonne, New Jersey in 1967, Zakk Wylde came to prominence in the late 1980s. Having sent a tape to Ozzy Osbourne, he joined the former Black Sabbath singer's band in 1989, and has been Osbourne's principal sideman for much of the time since. (Randy Rhoads, Osbourne's former guitarist, who had been tragically killed in a plane crash in 1982, remains Wylde's most significant influence, both as a player and performer.)

Wylde also tours and records with his own band, Black Label Society. With varying line-ups, it has been a staple of the global rock-festival circuit, and Wylde is now established as one of the finest classic-rock players of the modern era – a fact acknowledged in 2006 by his induction into the Hollywood Rock Walk of Fame.

Wylde is also well known for his endorsement of a variety of signature Gibson and Epiphone Les Paul models, all of which feature his characteristic black-and-white/black-and-orange Bullseye and Buzzsaw designs.

Boutique brands

What exactly is a boutique guitar? Typically, it is an instrument produced in very small numbers to an extremely high standard and sold to the kind of musician for whom retail price is a far lower priority than quality. Characteristically, such guitar manufacturers are also likely to offer a wide range of options, enabling the player to own a high-end, personalized instrument.

Campbell American Transitone, 2006

Founded in New England in 2002, Campbell American is one of the leaders in a growing US boutique market. Taking on a number of workers from the Guild factory in nearby Rhode Island when it was closed, Campbell American produces a small range of highly original custom instruments. Its most popular model is the curiously shaped single-cutaway Transitone. The appeal of a company such as this is the degree of personalization possible – the Transitone is available in a wide variety of materials and with options for at least four different brands of pickup to be fitted.

The Transitone is available with a variety of pickup options, including Seymour Duncan JB or Jazz, DiMarzio Bluesbucker, Lollar and TV Jones. This model features Seymour Duncan Charlie Christian Repro pickups.

- **DATE** 2006
- **ORIGIN** Westwood, Massachusetts, USA
- **WOOD** American linden body (maple, ash, mahogany or sapele can also be specified), maple neck, rosewood fingerboard (other options available).
- **UNUSUAL FEATURE** Retro body style.

Duesenberg Mike Campbell, 2008

Any small guitar company seeking endorsement by a name player will be forced to investigate less publicly celebrated figures: the German Duesenberg brand linked up with Mike Campbell, well respected for his work as Tom Petty's long-standing sideman. Duesenberg guitars are not wholly German-built, but parts are built to order in Korea and Germany and assembled at the company's workshop in Hanover. Campbell's signature model is a hollowbody archtop with a Duesenberg Grand Vintage humbucker at the bridge and Domino single-coil at the neck.

Rosewood fingerboard with dot marker inlays.

- **DATE** 2008
- **ORIGIN** Hanover, Germany
- **WOOD** Maple back and sides, hand-carved spruce top, maple set neck, rosewood fingerboard.
- **UNUSUAL FEATURE** German silver scratchplate.

The bodywork of the Duesenberg is finished to look like a Shelby Ford Mustang, complete with racing stripes.

Rob Williams Deluxe, 2008

British luthier Rob Williams builds instruments, as he says, "the old-fashioned way, by hand, by one bloke". His background has taken in repair work in the USA for Fender and Gibson, and later for Patrick Eggle guitars in the UK. At the top of Williams' CD range, the Set Neck Deluxe, befitting its moniker, is crafted from a variety of exotic woods – the model shown here is topped with flamed koa – and features two handwound humbucking pickups. For a final touch of extraordinary luxury, the embedded output-socket surround is carved from rosewood.

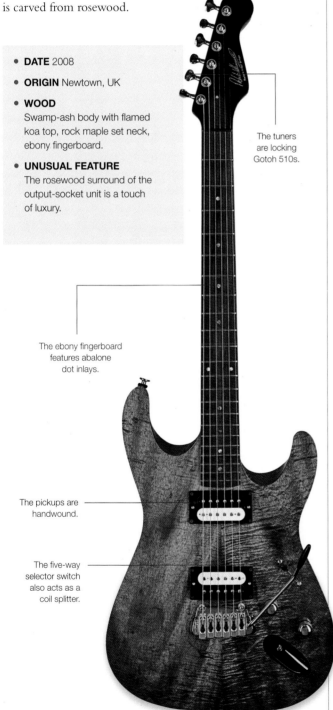

- **DATE** 2008
- **ORIGIN** Newtown, UK
- **WOOD**
  Swamp-ash body with flamed koa top, rock maple set neck, ebony fingerboard.
- **UNUSUAL FEATURE**
  The rosewood surround of the output-socket unit is a touch of luxury.

The tuners are locking Gotoh 510s.

The ebony fingerboard features abalone dot inlays.

The pickups are handwound.

The five-way selector switch also acts as a coil splitter.

Grosh HollowTron, 2009

Don Grosh trained as a carpenter and cut his teeth as a luthier building guitars at Valley Arts (now Gibson-owned) for California's top session players. In 1993, Grosh set up his own custom shop producing a small number of designs, generally based on 1950s instruments. The Gretsch-inspired HollowTron is a hollowbody set-necked instrument with cat's-eye f-holes, Bigsby vibrato unit and a pair of TV Jones Classic Filter'Tron pickups.

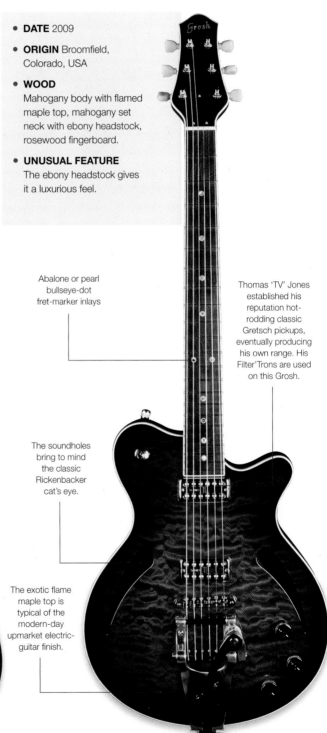

- **DATE** 2009
- **ORIGIN** Broomfield, Colorado, USA
- **WOOD**
  Mahogany body with flamed maple top, mahogany set neck with ebony headstock, rosewood fingerboard.
- **UNUSUAL FEATURE**
  The ebony headstock gives it a luxurious feel.

Abalone or pearl bullseye-dot fret-marker inlays

Thomas 'TV' Jones established his reputation hot-rodding classic Gretsch pickups, eventually producing his own range. His Filter'Trons are used on this Grosh.

The soundholes bring to mind the classic Rickenbacker cat's eye.

The exotic flame maple top is typical of the modern-day upmarket electric-guitar finish.

Paul Reed Smith

Arguably the most important new large-scale guitar manufacturer since the early 1980s, Paul Reed Smith's guitars were born of a desire to bring together the best aspects of the Gibson and Fender traditions. While they are expensive guitars, their attractive appearance and tonal versatility has made them massively popular among professional players in every musical genre.

Paul Reed Smith
First Guitar, 1975

Uniquely for such a successful luthier, all of Paul Reed Smith's early one-off guitars – some built when he was a teenager – have been well documented. The model shown here is based on a single-cutaway Les Paul Junior and was built while he was a student at St Mary's College of Maryland. The guitar, which now stands proudly in the entrance hall of the PRS factory, earned its owner – who was a mathematics major – four college credits for completing an instrument "of professional quality".

Smith settled early on the Gibson Les Paul Junior as his basic template; the classic PRS design would be based on the twin-cutaway version.

- **DATE** 1975
- **ORIGIN** St Mary's City, Maryland, USA
- **WOOD** Mahogany body, mahogany set neck, rosewood fingerboard.
- **UNUSUAL FEATURE** This instrument has a Gibson Les Paul Junior single-cutaway-style body.

This first Paul Reed Smith has two single-coil P-90-style pickups.

Paul Reed Smith
First 'Dragon', 1979

By 1979, Smith was establishing himself as a custom luthier of note, having sold guitars to the likes of Peter Frampton and Roy Buchanan. His model was still the Gibson Les Paul Junior, but now in its twin-cutaway form – and this has remained Smith's default body shape. This 1979 model is notable for the first appearance of the dragon motif. As a 16-year-old, Smith had dreamt of a guitar with intricate dragon inlays. Two decades later, this would form the basis for one of the most collectible modern guitar series.

The Americana inlays on the fingerboard show a bald eagle in different states of flight.

Smith took the Les Paul Junior shape and introduced a German carve – where the carving on the body dips below the height of the edge before rising towards the middle.

- **DATE** 1979
- **ORIGIN** Annapolis, Maryland, USA
- **WOOD** Mahogany body, mahogany set neck, rosewood fingerboard.
- **UNUSUAL FEATURE** This guitar features ornate dragon inlays on the bodywork – a taster for the later PRS Dragon series.

The control panel of this guitar is very simple, featuring one rotary potentiometer and two mini-switches controlling the humbucker on the bridge.

Paul Reed Smith Carlos Santana, 1980

As a young guitarist, one of Smith's heroes was Carlos Santana, and as a young luthier, his ambition was to build a guitar for his idol. In 1980, Smith met Santana before a show and showed him his new model. The guitarist was sufficiently impressed to use it at that night's concert. Afterwards they discussed alterations, and Smith left with a commission for a new instrument that would become Santana's preferred instrument for most of the 1980s.

- **DATE** 1980

- **ORIGIN** Annapolis, Maryland, USA

- **WOOD**
  Mahogany body with figured maple top, mahogany set neck, rosewood fingerboard.

- **UNUSUAL FEATURE**
  The guitar has a vibrato arm designed especially for this instrument.

ABOVE: *Santana had not liked the pickups on the guitar Smith had shown him. A pair of humbuckers were designed to order from Seymour Duncan.*

Smith retained the single pot/double switch controls of his Dragon. When the Santana model went into production 15 years later, a more conventional master volume and tone control was incorporated, as shown here.

The bass horn is less pronounced than on later models.

PRS Custom 22, 1985

1985 was the year when Paul Reed Smith 'Fine Handcrafted Guitars' moved to a factory facility and became PRS. The first models to come off the production line were the Custom range. Constructed on the lines of the Les Paul Junior, like Smith's earlier guitars, the Custom features a one-piece mahogany body capped with a distinctive maple top and bound at the edges. The pickups are humbuckers, but through the use of a five-way rotary switch they can also create Fender-style single-coil tones.

- **DATE** 1985

- **ORIGIN** Annapolis, Maryland, USA

- **WOOD**
  Mahogany body with carved figured maple top, mahogany set neck, rosewood fingerboard.

- **UNUSUAL FEATURE**
  This Custom features the intricate fingerboard inlays that characterize PRS guitars.

By this time, the now-familiar asymmetric PRS headstock design, with Paul Reed Smith's signature, had become standard.

The Custom 22 is named after its 22-fret fingerboard; PRS also made a two-octave, 24-fret model.

Over the years, PRS has continued to refine the Custom's electrics – the five-way switching system and pickup options, in particular.

The growth of PRS

In 1985, Paul Reed Smith made the transition from custom luthier to guitar producer. At first, overambitious and innovative ideas such as PRS amplifiers and a range of acoustic and bass guitars were quickly abandoned. It soon became clear that, while PRS guitars were very expensive, there was a definite market for such a versatile high-end instrument.

PRS Artist, 1991

By 1990, PRS was producing around 400 guitars each month, and that year the company grossed over $4 million. However, there were many traditional Gibson players who loved PRS guitars but bemoaned the lack of the 'fat' Les Paul sound. Smith began working with different construction techniques and making modifications to the dimensions to produce a better-quality acoustic sound. The results of these experiments were first seen in the flagship Artist range.

Inlay and purfling include an abalone-inlaid signature headstock logo.

- **DATE** 1991

- **ORIGIN** Annapolis, Maryland, USA

- **WOOD**
  Mahogany body with carved figured maple top, mahogany set neck, rosewood fingerboard.

- **UNUSUAL FEATURE**
  The wood quality is exceptionally fine.

The woods used in the upmarket Artist series were chosen from stock, and were deemed to be too good for standard production PRS guitars.

PRS McCarty, 1994

During the 1980s, Paul Reed Smith had befriended Ted McCarty, the man who had presided over Gibson in the 1950s. Smith acknowledged that he had learnt a lot from the man who had introduced the original Les Pauls. In 1992, Smith was approached by session guitarist Dave Grissom to produce a guitar that sounded like the original Les Paul used by Duane Allman. Based broadly on the Dragon design, with a thinner neck and PAF-style pickups, Smith named the resulting instrument the McCarty.

The McCarty model included some features that PRS players might have considered retro, such as non-locking tuners and the three-way toggle selector.

- **DATE** 1994

- **ORIGIN** Annapolis, Maryland, USA

- **WOOD**
  Mahogany body with East Coast maple top, mahogany set neck, rosewood fingerboard.

- **UNUSUAL FEATURE**
  The McCarty has a pair of brass-covered humbuckers styled on the Gibson PAF.

The body uses Michigan maple – the same wood used for the tops of 1950s Gibson Les Pauls.

Unusual stoptail bridge unit

PRS Dragon, 2002

One of the hallmarks of the PRS brand has been the number of limited-edition models produced, the most noted of which is the Dragon series. Inspired by Smith's teenage dream of a guitar with a dragon inlaid down the neck, the first PRS Dragon appeared in 1992. Each one in a run of 50 guitars featured a beautiful dragon mosaic made from 201 pieces of abalone, turquoise and mother-of-pearl. These first models have been known to fetch in excess of $40,000 at auction. The Dragon 2002 was the first single-cutaway guitar in the series. Announced at the 2002 NAMM trade show and offered for $30,000, orders for all 100 of the limited run had been taken by the end of the day.

- **DATE** 2002
- **ORIGIN** Annapolis, Maryland, USA
- **WOOD**
  Mahogany body, flame maple top, set Brazilian rosewood neck and fingerboard.
- **UNUSUAL FEATURE**
  It is one of the earliest PRS models with a single cutaway.

Until 2000, all PRS guitars had been built around the same basic body shape; the single cutaway design so strongly resembles a Gibson Les Paul that it was the subject of legal action by Gibson.

The design by Jeff Easley was created using over 300 pieces of shell and stone.

The bridge is a single-unit PRS stoptail.

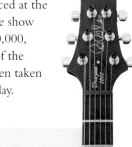

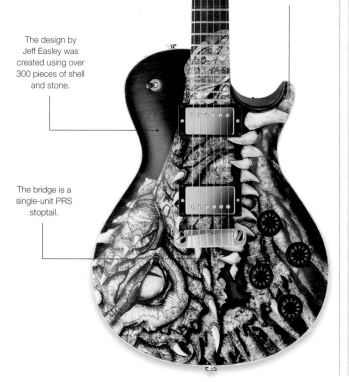

ABOVE: *Carlos Santana playing a PRS guitar in concert in London at the end of 2010.*

Born in Mexico in 1947, as a teenager Carlos Santana moved with his family to San Francisco. The Santana Blues Band was formed in 1967 and soon gained a reputation for its Latin-infused rhythms and Santana's searing, feedback-driven lead playing. In 1969, the band, by then known just as Santana, was one of the surprise hits of the legendary Woodstock Festival. This success led to the band's eponymous debut album hitting the top five.

The band's 1970 follow-up, *Abraxas*, was a global success from which such hit singles as "Black Magic Woman" and the sublime guitar instrumental "Samba Pa Ti" were taken. By now, Carlos Santana was one of the most influential guitarists in the rock world.

By the 1990s, however, Carlos Santana found himself struggling. His music was out of fashion, and he was without a record deal. His fortunes changed spectacularly with the 1999 *Supernatural* album, which saw the guitarist paired with a series of younger vocalists. The track "Smooth", with its irresistible cha-cha rhythm and Santana's neat fills, became a global hit, and the album went on to sell 15 million copies in the USA alone – by some distance Santana's biggest commercial success in his whole career.

Do-it-yourself guitars

With such a wide variety of production electric guitars available, it may be surprising to find some musicians still unsatisfied with what's on offer. Of course, there have always been a certain players with very specific requirements, or others who simply want to create something personal or innovative, or an instrument that sets them apart from everybody else.

Brian May Red Special, 1963

Perhaps the most famous of homebuilt guitars, the Red Special was made in 1963 by 16-year-old Brian May and his aviation-engineer father, Harold. A highly unorthodox instrument, it was built using wood from a reclaimed 18th-century mantel, and the body was chambered and covered with mahogany to give a solidbody appearance. The pickups were customized Burns Tri-Sonics, but were, rather unusually, wired in series rather than parallel. Abandoning his postgraduate studies – a PhD in astrophysics – May formed Queen and would use the Red Special on all of the band's biggest hits.

Versions of the Red Special were issued by Burns and Guild, but they are now produced by May's own company.

- **DATE** 1963
- **ORIGIN** London, UK
- **WOOD**
  Oak and blockboard body, covered front and back with mahogany, oak straight-through neck, painted oak fingerboard.
- **UNUSUAL FEATURE**
  The woods used are uncommon in guitar making.

Each of the three pickups has two control switches. One is a simple on-off switch, while the other controls phase polarity.

The body was finished with wood stain and Rustin's plastic coating – a varnish popular with British furniture makers.

Township Oil Can Guitar, 2000

Out of necessity – either through lack of availability or affordability – some musicians have built their own guitars. The oil can guitar is thought to be based on the four-string ramkiekie, an instrument said to have been developed by the Khoi people of South Africa after they came into contact with early European settlers. Township Guitars, based in Cape Town, exports high-quality oil can guitars across the globe. The distinctive metallic tone is vaguely reminiscent of a metal-bodied resonator, but when combined with the single-coil pickup creates a sound unlike any production-line instrument.

- **DATE** 2000
- **ORIGIN** Cape Town, South Africa
- **WOOD**
  Reclaimed Castrol oil can body, maple bolt-on neck and support, rosewood.
- **UNUSUAL FEATURE**
  The reclaimed materials used in the construction of this instrument give it a unique look and sound.

Soundholes are punched into the surface of the oil can.

This guitar features the original type of oil can body, but Township Guitars has also produced instruments from reclaimed olive oil cans.

John Entwistle Fender 'Frankenstein', 1967

In 2003, a year after his death, 350 personal items belonging to The Who's John Entwistle were auctioned at Sotheby's. On offer was Entwistle's 'Frankenstein' – a Fender he built himself from the remains of five smashed basses, and which he used exclusively from 1967 on some of the band's benchmark albums, including *Tommy* and *Quadrophenia*. As Entwistle himself admitted, demanding craftsmanship was not required: "Two hours with a Phillips screwdriver and a soldering iron, and I was ranting around my hotel room screaming, 'It's alive, it's alive!'" The 'Frankenstein' had been expected to raise around $7,000 at the auction; bidding ended at $100,000!

- **DATE** 1967

- **ORIGIN** Fullerton, California, USA

- **WOOD**
  Ash body, maple bolt-on neck, maple fingerboard.

- **UNUSUAL FEATURE**
  The guitar is a composite of four Fender Precisions and one Fender Jazz.

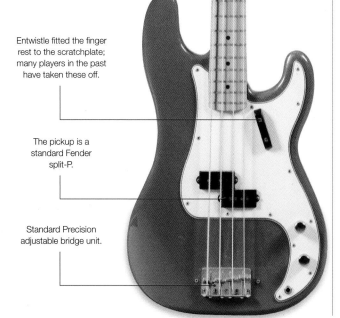

String guides are fitted to the headstock on the D and A strings.

Although built from five smashed basses, Entwistle's 'Frankenstein' appears to be a regular Fender Precision.

Entwistle fitted the finger rest to the scratchplate; many players in the past have taken these off.

The pickup is a standard Fender split-P.

Standard Precision adjustable bridge unit.

The do-it-yourself tradition

The electric luthier combines traditional, centuries-old craftsmanship with a touch of the experimental scientist. Despite this, the electric guitar is a relatively simple piece of technology that anyone who has rudimentary carpentry abilities and an understanding of basic electronics could easily make for themselves.

In the West, the unskilled, home-made tradition goes back to the diddley bow, which was taken over to the southern states of the USA by enslaved West Africans during the 18th century. This instrument was little more than a wire screwed at either end to a board, and was played by plucking with one hand and altering the pitch by sliding a bottle up and down. Later, during the American Civil War, cigar-box guitars became popular among troops away from home.

Numerous websites exist with detailed instructions on how to build instruments such as these, which, with care, can produce extremely usable results. Making an instrument from scratch can also provide the guitarist with a greater understanding of the factors that make their instruments work – indeed, many successful luthiers have been inspired by experimenting in this way.

ABOVE: *Blues artist Steven Wold – better known as Seasick Steve – was well into his 60s before he made his mark as a musician. Much of his work sees him backing himself with a home-built guitar and a stomp box. He is shown here playing a cigar-box electric guitar.*

Gibson Robots

Throughout this directory we've seen a great number of attempts to enhance the functionality of the guitar, from organ guitars in the 1960s, guitar synthesizers in the 1970s and, since then, a variety of approaches to MIDI control. The first decade of the new millennium saw Gibson come up with perhaps the most radical development in guitar technology – the Robot guitar.

Les Paul Robot, 2007

Gibson's first Robot guitar addresses an area of concern for every string player – tuning. German guitarist Chris Adams spent a decade developing his own Powertune system. With a small computer built into the underside of the stop bar, the system automatically checks the intonation for each string and sends messages to each of the six tuners, adjusting them where necessary. In 2007, Adams licensed the Powertune system, enabling Gibson to install it into the Les Paul Robot model.

- **DATE** 2007
- **ORIGIN** Kalamazoo, Michigan, USA
- **WOOD**
  Mahogany body with maple top, mahogany set neck, ebony fingerboard.
- **UNUSUAL FEATURE**
  The automated computerized tuning system was a first.

ABOVE: *The Powertune system not only enables guitarists to stay in tune, but also to change tuning by rotating the Master Control Knob.*

Dark Fire, 2008

A year after the first appearance of the Robot, Gibson came up with a new Les Paul, the Dark Fire. Not only did it feature Powertune, but it was also integrated with Chameleon Tone Technology – a system of on-board modelling electronics that provides eight different guitar tones, from acoustic to metal. These can be reprogrammed using computer editing software. The Dark Fire comes with the Robot Interface Pack (RIP), which enables the guitar to be plugged directly into a computer.

- **DATE** 2008
- **ORIGIN** Kalamazoo, Michigan, USA
- **WOOD**
  Mahogany body with maple top, mahogany set neck, ebony fingerboard.
- **UNUSUAL FEATURE**
  In addition to the Powertune automated-tuning system, the Dark Fire features Chameleon Tone Technology.

The neck pickup is a P-90H soapbar, a modern version of the classic single-coil P-90, reworked to reduce the notorious problem of 60-cycle hum.

The Master Control Knob (MCK) is the means by which the Dark Fire's on-board robot features are manipulated.

Firebird X, 2011

The Robot series seems to have polarized the opinion of hardcore Gibson fans: some traditionalists certainly seem to view them as an aberration. Gibson has carried on undeterred, however, and in 2011 produced the Firebird X, the most heavily armed of the series. The three additional toggle pots on the body mark it out as a very unusual beast, enabling software effects such as compression, distortion and echo to be switched in. There is also a piezo switch that produces a convincing acoustic sound.

- **DATE** 2011
- **ORIGIN** Kalamazoo, Michigan, USA
- **WOOD** Mahogany with maple top, mahogany set neck, ebony fngerboard.
- **UNUSUAL FEATURE** On-board features include the Pure-Analog updatable audio-engine circuitry.

ABOVE: *The Firebird X features some of the most extraordinary technology ever seen on a guitar. Among the controls are a pair of toggle pots, which appear to be standard pickup-selector-type switches, but have a rotatable toggle shaft that enables sounds and effects to be morphed rather than crudely switched in.*

The coils in the three mini-humbuckers can be switched on or off, to reverse polarity, or switched between series and parallel wiring.

The bridge piezo pickup includes hex outputs so that each string can provide a separate output for computer or live-performance set-ups.

ABOVE: *Steve Stevens is best known for his work with Michael Jackson and Billy Idol. Having pioneered the use of Roland guitar synthesizers in the 1980s, he is shown here in 2008 with a Gibson Dark Fire.*

As far as guitars with in-built computing power go, the Firebird X is currently the final word. While a retail price of around $5,000 may seem high, there are surely plenty of limited-edition Gibson classics that cost more. Like any computer system, however, such instruments will stand or fall by the quality of upgrades to their operating systems, software and processing power. Where does this lead? As digital sampling becomes ever more subtle and sophisticated, will we see guitars with terabytes of in-built data that, at the flick of a switch, can produce convincing violin or cello tones? Since the mid-1980s, MIDI-equipped guitars have been able to control other devices to the same end, but the appeal would be in its self-containment. After all, the Firebird X isn't doing too much that can't be done through external figural processing.

For some, however, robot guitars are controversial instruments, striking at the heart of the very simplicity that gives the electric guitar much of its appeal. It remains to be seen whether 50 years from now these instruments will be viewed as having ushered in a new breed of 21st-century musical instrument, or whether they will appear as a brief blip, viewed much as we look on, say, the Vox organ guitar of the early 1960s, the makers of which doubtless sincerely believed at the time that they were writing the script for the future of the electric guitar.

Index

LEFT: *The 1972 Telecaster Deluxe was the first guitar to be fitted with Fender Wide Range pickups.*